SOUTHERN LEHIGH
HIGH SCHOOL LIBRARY

THE LETTERS *of a* COMBAT RIFLEMAN

by

Charles Davis

Best regards,
Charles Davis
Dec. '04

All Rights Reserved
Copyright © 2001 by Charles Davis
No part of this book may be reproduced or transmitted
in any form or by any means, electronic or mechanical,
including photocopying, recording, or by any information
storage and retrieval system without permission in
writing from the publisher.

ISBN # 0-8059-5047-8
Printed in the United States of America

This book is dedicated to my daughter, Alice Jane, killed by a drunk driver while I was in training in Georgia; but never forgotten.

To my son C. William Davis and his wife Jacqueline, our four grandchildren: Jessica Davis; Billy Jean Kelly, her husband Sean, and their son Travis River Kelly; Anthony Davis; and Wesley Davis.

To all my comrades in arms who served with me in the 415th Infantry especially Max Delrogh and Carl Zurcher.

And last but not least, to my wife Jean who waited for me and who saved all the letters I had written her.

CODE

A.S.T.P.	Army Student Training Program - students taken out of college to furnish infantry replacements
BAR	Browning Automatic rifle
C P	Command Post
B bar	chocolate bar
D P	displaced person
E T O	European Theater of Operations
F. O.	Forward observer (artillery)
G.I.	government issue
GI's	dysentery
HE	high explosive
line of departure	point from which an attack is started
louy	lieutenant
night problem	military maneuvers at night
O D	olive drab
P.N.G.	Pennsylvania National Guard
P X	Post exchange
repeldepel	replacement redeployment depot
S P	self propelled gun
S.S.	*Stars & Stripes* newspaper
T D	tank destroyer
T OT	time on target fire (artillery)
W P	white phosphorous

CHAPTER I
Rifleman Replacement

There's a lot been written and said about war, such s "war is hell," "war is confusion," "the Army that makes the least mistakes is the one that wins," and many many more such phrases. Well, I went through the battles in Germany and I found that all of the above are true. And to this you might add, too, that war is a great adventure for a rifleman—if you survive. By a great adventure I don't mean something that is good or nice to experience. It is not something you would want to experience over again. Sherman's definition is the best. And none of us want to go to hell twice.

I went into combat as a rifleman replacement, joining the 104th Oregon Timberwolf Division at Zundert, Holland. This American division was attached to a British corps of the first Canadian Army. Zundert was the town where our division headquarters was located. They selected me from among 400 replacements to fill a secretary's job. For reasons all my own I turned the job down. I was sure the war was going to be over in a few days and besides I hated office work. It wasn't that I wanted to be a hero, I told them my number was 475, and to a soldier that means Rifleman.

I was a rifleman from way back and that was what I was best fitted for and that is what I wanted to be. Well, my friends told me I was crazy and I agreed with them. The guy that got the job in place of me was probably the happiest man in the world. For the next one hundred eighty-five days, I was one of the unhappiest men in the world. That is how long the war lasted after I made up my mind to fight with the rifle instead of the typewriter.

The captain in charge at Division Headquarters seemed to be pretty mad about the whole affair. The first sergeant, whom I was to meet later in

Germany, didn't make me feel happier. He made us police up the cigarette butts and match sticks from the soccer field where we slept the one night we stayed in Zundert.

When we moved out every man knew the outfit he was headed for, except me. The captain, about as efficient and as interested in his work as the other ninety percent of the officers in the army in this war, ordered me to get on a truck, any truck.

I climbed aboard the nearest one, knowing I was headed for the north, from whence came the thunder and lightning the night before. Our convoy moved up to the Service Company of our regiment, located in some green pastures, approximately four miles behind the fighting.

We were close now but this was still definitely rear echelon stuff. Most of the fellows attached to Service Company acted pretty nice to us replacements. I soon found out why. This division had just entered combat about a week ago. The first battalion of our assigned regiment had been practically wiped out trying to cross a canal. The old-timers, or I should say the one-week veterans, naturally didn't know a lot more than what we replacements did, especially in a rear echelon outfit like service company. Later on I was to notice how some fellows tried to "put on the dog" when new men came up. But most of us were always glad to see replacements or reinforcements as they were to be called later.

We unloaded from the trucks and they called the roll and that left me standing all alone. The officer in charge asked me what I was doing there. I explained the situation and he replied, "You'll have to stay here with Service Company until we get orders on you."

That was a good break for me. When I got to the end of the chow line that night I thought I had been served by the best kitchen in the whole U.S. Army. That mess gear piled high with steak and vegetables, smothered with sliced peaches and juice was a terrific contrast to the meals I had been eating in Belgium. In the third Replacement near Leige we had to sleep and eat in a forest. Repeldepel was the slang expression for replacement redeployment depot. The chow line in the Belgian woods extended for several hundred yards. They fed one thousand men at each kitchen. It rained every day we were in Belgium and the mud was above our ankles in the area where the chow lines formed. German buzz bombs just cleared the treetops, and at night we used to listen to and time the procession of big British bombers as they flew toward the German Reich.

This transfer to the green fields of Holland was like moving from the slums to the suburbs. Only now, instead of buzz bombs and big bombers we had five-inch artillery shells and fighter planes barreling overhead.

For the first time, I saw war. The five inchers were British guns and they were set up in the fields all around us. The glass windows of the farm houses round about rattled and crashed from the concussions. In the distance the Spitfires dived below the horizon. From the slit trenches dug about the field, it looked as if the rear echelon boys were ready to take a dive, too, if necessary.

For the next few days I sweated out the shortest, sweetest little chow line in the European Theatre of Operations. The meals were excellent. We had boiled ham, pork chops, steak, and roast beef, not to mention the vegetables, fresh bread, and desserts. I had to sweat it out because I thought the first Sergeant would suggest that I eat with one of the line company kitchens, located in the next field. They were serving C rations to the replacements still waiting around to go up on the line and join their companies.

The second day I watched some of the first battalion boys getting ready to leave. They were going to go up with the kitchen trucks in the evening. As they hustled around and loaded their cartridge belts with the .30 caliber stuff, I had a strange feeling come over me. I think I've read stuff like it before. Here I was in a pasture in Holland with a lot of men I had known for only a month or two. I was going to die, I was sure. It seemed such a futile, silly way to die for one's country. The rest of the world seemed so distant and I had a feeling that I was just another dumb, bewildered piece of cannon fodder caught and tricked into fighting a war that nobody was interested in anymore.

I knew the war was going to end in a few days, maybe tomorrow. And I was going to be killed just as it ended.

The other boys were serious, too, but they didn't show any emotion. I liked the way they suddenly became interested in their rifles and how they were so eager to get enough ammunition to fill their belts. That's something that always interested me and now it made me feel good to know that at least they were interested, too. It was true that only two percent of the men that entered the army knew anything about a rifle. And due to the method used by the army in promoting rifle marksmanship, less than two percent of the men ever took any interest at all in their weapons. Many times I heard men say they were going to buy an army rifle after the war just so they could stand it in a corner and go and spit on it every day. The army method of training made a man hate his weapon instead of admire it for the precision piece of mechanism that it was. Until the day they actually entered combat, ninety-nine percent of the American infantrymen hated their weapons. In that field in Holland I was witnessing a great and sudden change, a change from hate to love. That heavy piece of steel and wood that had dug into their shoulders and irritated them was now their best friend in the world. These M-1s were to become so loved and admired in the days to come that the boys were going to elevate them to a class with their wives and sweethearts.

The trouble now was that these rifles were not going to respond to this sudden, new found love. Like a woman, a rifle must be handled so that you get the full benefit out of it. These men had no more understanding of the rifles they were now fondling than they had of their girlfriends back in America. Sure, they knew most of the nomenclature —the names and functions of the parts. They knew how to prime them and how to pull the trigger.

But that was about the limit of their knowledge. If they only knew how to make them work for them their troubles would be over. Well, at least the war would be over a lot sooner and that would mean a lot of lives saved.

The boys hustled around that pile of bandoliers like chickens around a pan of feed. A lot of them weren't boys anymore, of course, because they were scraping the bottom of the barrel when we were inducted. I was one of the very few in this group of four hundred replacements that came under the twenty to thirty age group. And I was almost thirty. About ninety percent were either in their teens or their thirties. Many were fathers, including myself.

I managed to stay on with Service Company for a few days and now when I look back on it, that rear echelon business was not bad. We never experienced any gun fire and we knew very little of what was going on up in the lines. The kitchen crews generally brought back tales of valor and bloodshed. Quite a lot of equipment was coming back, too, some of it with the spilt blood on it. I got rid of a lot of my stuff and picked up an old pack for my new one. The old style pack had seen some combat, it was plain, and I often wondered just what happened to that boy named Green. Despite the blood stains his name was plainly visible in indelible pencil. But the initials escape me now.

The armor-artificer was busy during these days. He had to work mostly on Browning Automatic Rifles, He showed me the first P-38 I ever saw. This automatic pistol was to become very popular and famous with our outfit and every American combat soldier in Europe always took for granted you were talking about it and not the fighter plane whenever you mentioned P-38.

The first sergeant was an amiable fellow and never once challenged me as I prayed my way through his chow line. Sometimes, even when he was serving the potatoes or spinach, he piled it on my plate just as he did on the veterans' plates. It seemed to me that the top kick must have been a real human being. In fact I think he must have even persuaded some nice girl to marry him and give him a couple of kids. I used to watch and laugh as he tried to chase those little Dutch kids out of the field. He would no sooner have them rounded up and out one gate than another dozen would come begging and scavenging from a different direction. When a first sergeant doesn't even scare little children, you may know he has a kindly face. And this one even had a kind heart. In final desperation he grabbed his carbine and threatened to shoot the children, but even this didn't help and so finally there was nothing else to do but post a guard.

On November 4, 1944, I wrote in my diary, "More good chow today. Bacon, and plenty of it for breakfast. Pork chops for dinner. Some of the boys went up. I said good-bye to my buddies. They were all as normal as usual. Most of all they were interested in their weapons and ammunition."

In a letter to my wife and son, dated October 26, 1944, I said, "Still did not get a letter. I am hoping I get some Christmas packages. Our weekly ration isn't very much. It seems we are always hungry."

THE LETTERS OF A COMBAT RIFLEMAN

That was our main thought during these days—how to satisfy our hunger. The other main problems that confronted us were how to keep dry and where to find a place to sleep and keep warm.

Many times during those days in France I spoke about the weather both in my letters and in my diary. In the same letter I wrote, "Right now everything is quiet and the sun is out and it feels warm if you sit in a sheltered spot. It is almost like Pennsylvania. It reminds me of many a November afternoon when I was hunting."

On October 15, near LeMans, France, I wrote in my diary, "Life is tough. Plenty of rain and mud. Plenty of C rations. But who wants C rations!" Then on October 17, "Some sun and boy, it feels wonderful! It is hard to get the exact time. Everyone's watch seems to be different. Of course we don't worry because all we do here is just try to keep body and soul together. Chow time is the only important time. With no mail, that is the only thing we think about—food, and wood for a fire."

On October 19, we were, "Welcomed again this morning with some rain. It has rained everyday since we landed in France. Food is ever on our minds here and we do not go hungry. The chestnuts are good either boiled or roasted. There seem to be apples everywhere."

The next day I wrote, "Last night there was a new moon in the autumn sky. The red and gold landscape with dark shadows against a backdrop of the setting sun might have been a Pennsylvania scene. I pray the war will soon be over."

On November 5, I wrote, "Someone mentioned it was Sunday. I forgot what day of the week it was, sitting in this field in Holland."

Every day is alike in combat. We began to realize that when we hit the beach in Normandy, coming through as replacements. That was back in the early part of October.

"Rain, mud, and short rations here on the beach," was how I recorded it.

We had been living in pup tents ever since that day. That is except when we could get into a house somewhere. And the crowd I was with were pritty good at locating desirable living quarters. In England we stole coal for our fire. In France we stole wood and took over a deserted farm building where we lived until some officers caught us. In Belgium it was tough. If you got caught cutting down a tree that was greater than ten inches in diameter you were fined Fifty Dollars. Everything under ten inches in diameter had been cut before we arrived at that terrible spot.

There was only one thing left to do. We quickly made friends with the natives. Within a week, we had eight or nine different homes where we could stay for the night. Some of these places were as far away as Namur, forty-five kilometers distance.

October 30, my diary says, "Stayed overnight in Huy. It was really wonderful to sleep in a real bed. We got the people up about midnight to ask them for a place to stay. As usual, they were very, very nice. We would have been satisfied with the barn but they insisted we sleep in their son's bed. Their son is a prisoner in Germany. He was a Belgian aviator. They had a very lovely home. The lady of the house made breakfast for us and then we took off for camp."

Two nights later we slept in the home of Cherenne Marcel, in the small village of Modave. Marcel was the champion accordion player of Belgium in 1938. He played for us after supper and we couldn't help but think of him as a great success in America. Marcel autographed my diary and wrote, Champion Belge. 26, Juin 1938." That was a happy year for this young Belgian and now he had promise again for many more.

We called that woods in Belgium our camp, but it was only a place to check our baggage. We had to report back at least every other day to get a good meal and to find out the latest rumors about our moving. Also the acting first sergeant always posted an AWOL list every morning on the tree outside his tent and we had to get back to cross our names off before it got on the books.

I pitched a shelter tent in that field in Holland with a young lad named M'Donald. For some reason or other he wanted to move. That was the last thing in the world that I wanted to do. In the last two months I had lived in five different countries and about ten different camps. So there I was with only half a tent. M'Donald walked off with his half. My diary tells about the solution to this problem.

"Visited a farmhouse nearby and shaved and washed up. Invited to come back for some beer." Then on November 6, "Last night Sid, Willy, and I went to visit the Dutch family. We talked and had some beer. As I didn't have a tent up and it was raining, I slept in their barn, which is attached to the house as are most barns in Belgium and Holland."

That same day I wrote, "Our division is pulling out of the line and that means I will not fight here. Suppose we will head for Germany, who knows. But it will probably be a couple of more weeks before we can get back to fighting. In the meantime rumor says the war will be over by the eleventh. We all hope so.

The eleventh, of course, was Armistice Day and as all army rumors have a lot to do with wishful thinking, the rumor was that the war would end on Armistice Day. Little did we know of the one hundred eighty-five days to come. And little did I realize the speed with which we would be transplanted from one active front to another.

On the night of November 6, I went up by truck to join my outfit just as they were pulling out of the line, finished with their baptism of fire in Holland. I was assigned to "L" company, better known as Love company, a rifle outfit in the Third battalion, 415th Infantry. At battalion headquarters about sixty of us replacements stood in a dark street waiting—and wondering where we were going to sleep that night. We had been pushed around form Kilmer to Oudenbosch. It was always, "hurry up and wait" as we called it. We had hurried up and waited so long that what little morale we ever had was completely lost by now.

An officer emerged from one of the houses along the narrow street and said. "You'll have to wait here for a while."

That was like throwing a hand grenade into the middle of our group. There was a lot of shuffling and mumbling and one fellow shouted, "What the hell is the score!"

The answer we got from the officer was the tip off to the kind of outfit we were now entering.

"Who said that?" he shouted, rushing up to the edge of our group and staring into our midst. "You're in an outfit now that won't stand for that kind of stuff. You're going to have to change your ways," he threatened.

I can't remember the direct quotes but this officer ranted on for another ten minutes while we stood bowed and silent in that dark cold street. We were cold and hungry and sleepy and homeless and on top of that we were being treated like ignorant, worthless, undisciplined beggars. We were a rough bunch, I must admit. And no doubt we were undisciplined, too. But we were Americans and we were men. And we came up there to help in the fight, some of us of our own free will. We expected better treatment than that. Undisciplined as we were, it was the most outstanding group of replacements that ever joined that regiment.

The dogmatic, arrogant, imperious, autocratic, opinionated, and obstinate manner of the officers of this division appeared to be the standard of all officers in the army during World War II. We were to find this out more and more during the coming months. Officer replacements coming up were just as bad. In fact, even the other officers would ridicule them, even though they had no room to talk.

From now on until the war was over and then even until the division was deactivated, we were to hear of the wonderful training discipline of this division when they left the States. I can only guess at the results in Holland but from what I heard, everything was complete confusion. It was the excellent support of the British armor and artillery that enabled them to advance. Of course, if you compare the record of new divisions going into the line, the 104th Timberwolves rate as some of the best. But I can't see why a new outfit must take a terrible beating before it is able to put up a good fight. With expert training a new division should be able to go into battle and make a good showing without being all shot to pieces and requiring thousands of replacements.

There were about eight of us replacements that went up to Love company. It was only a short walk to a group of farm buildings along the road. I slept in the hay mow and that was one of the best beds I had in a long time. The next morning I found out that I was also in one of the best companies in the regiment in regards to the chow situation. We had hot cakes and bacon and good hot coffee. For the first time I met Max, the supply sergeant whom

I was to become well acquainted with later. Max was bustling around company headquarters like an old fat hen around two dozen chicks. He was fat and short and he looked rather young. My first reaction was to dislike him because he refused to give me a cigar. I realized now that he was saving them for the officers. He handed the enlisted men plenty of cigarettes and Hershey chocolates. The Hershey bars were the type that will not freeze in the Arctic or melt in the tropics. I wonder what effect the stomach made on this chocolate. Most of the GIs liked them but I had already reached the point where I had to be near starving before I would eat them.

It was here in this barn that I saw for the first time the waste as a result of combat. There were all kinds of rations, cigarettes and equipment lying around and apparently abandoned. I had never seen anything like this in the repeldepels and not realizing the changed values of things at the front, I started to stuff my old style combat pack with everything I could pick up, including matches, cigarettes, C rations, K rations, etc. I hated C and K rations but I had to eat once in a while and we never knew when we would get hot chow again. Also, these items were always good for bartering with the natives. Well, as it ended up, I had to throw half of the stuff away again. It was impossible to get it all in one small combat pack.

About an hour after breakfast, the acting first sergeant assembled us new men in back of the barn and proceeded to ask us questions about our knowledge of infantry weapons. I remember Sergeant William Noble saying, "We need some men in the machine gun section and the mortar sections." The weapons platoon had been hit hard. I had told him that I could operate any infantry weapon and so I said "Well, if you need men in those sections, I'll be willing to take either the machine guns or mortars."

He didn't seem to like this and then he said he would take the list in to the company commander and let him make the placements. We assembled again in a short while and Sergeant Noble read out the assignments and at the same time told the men the names of the platoon leaders and platoon sergeants. I was assigned as a basic, to company headquarters. From there they could put me in any platoon, as needed.

At the time, I did not realize what a break this was. To a man in a rifle platoon, company headquarters is definitely rear echelon stuff. And to a certain degree this is true, but measured in feet or yards, company headquarters of a line (rifle) company may only be the width of a city street from the positions of the forward most riflemen. In company headquarters I was to find it much safer. In company headquarters you never have to pull outpost duty or seldom if ever go on patrols. As part of the rifle company, however, we did push out with the platoons when they went forward in the attack. Then there were three distinct groups in the headquarters of a rifle company. In the first group we have the company commander, four runners, (one for each platoon), radio man, communications sergeant, and the company commander's bodyguard who acts also as an assistant runner, radio and communications man. This is known as the command group and they push out with the platoons in the attack. The second group is under command of the executive officer or first sergeant and they generally follow up in the rear of the company or move up later after the new positions have been taken and consolidated. The third group includes the supply sergeant, and his assistant or assistants, armor-artificer and the kitchen. The company clerk stays back at division headquarters and still gets the combat infantry badge.

I didn't know it at the time but I was to get another break at the beginning by being placed in the second group, the one that moved up later. Of course, in a short time I was to find myself in the command group and later a squad leader in one of the platoons. But this gradual movement into the most forward and dangerous job was to be a blessing for me. Now when I look back perhaps it is the reason that I did not crack during those one hundred eighty-five days of front-line duty. It seems that every man has a limit to the amount of punishment he can withstand. A soldier can keep going for a long time, especially if he is broken in gradually. But if the sudden dealing in death comes instantly upon a man or if he is forced to stand up under fire for days and weeks on end and things are really hot, it is sometimes more than the average man can take.

I've seen new men thrown directly into the hottest outpost duties crack in a few days but when they got back to company headquarters where they were not under quite as much pressure, they gradually came around and were as good a bunch of soldiers as the rest.

Two of those seventeen weeks of training in the States could be used a lot better by putting the men into outfits in quiet sectors. These could be special units with fifty percent of the personnel permanent and the other fifty percent constantly changing. They could also be broken in gradually by requiring them to serve with company headquarters for at least two weeks and then moving them into the platoons.

But regardless of how a man is broken in or how good he is he is still liable to combat fatigue if he is under constant and intense shellfire for long periods of time. And any amount of time from three days plus can be considered a long period. Therefore, jobs should rotate in rifle companies. Every man is supposed to be able to do the other man's job anyway, so this rotation plan would be one method of insuring the carrying out of this know-all idea and at the same time give a man a chance to get back into company headquarters where he would not be under such great pressure. This plan would produce great leaders, too, because by the time a man got a squad or platoon he would be a well-rounded soldier. Of course, a good percentage would never get a chance to complete the cycle. Anyway, it would make for a good understanding, and above all else we need understanding.

Next the acting first sergeant introduced us to the company commander. Noble was acting top kick because the man who had held the job from the time they formed back in the States had been killed. There were a few other causalities and quite a few of these had trench foot.

Captain Hallahan was just about what I expected a line company commander would be like. He appeared to be young and lean and nervous. He reminded me of myself but he was lots bigger. Later he told me he was in northern New York state in 1940, as a horse holder in the cavalry, during the First Army maneuvers that year. I was holding down the same job but in a different outfit at the very same time. The difference was that I left the national guard while her remained.

"I want to welcome you fellows into Love company," the captain said in a low voice. He was not a good speaker, but I knew he was sincere. I figured that the place for the good public speakers was back in the States and it didn't make any difference to me if the CO was not a good talker. All I wanted was a man who knew his stuff and who would be fair to his men. Captain Hallahan fulfilled this order and as I was soon to find out, he was also a very brave man. I don't recall that any man ever made an unkind remark about Captain Hallahan.

Of course he gave us some tips. "I want to stress especially, recognition. Be sure who you are shooting at," he continued, stressing this point. "I've been shot at half a dozen times by our men. And I'll be moving among you, plenty, especially at night.

And always dig in whenever you have the opportunity, even if you are going to move in a short while."

Next the captain stressed staying awake when so ordered. "If there is a one hundred percent alert that means that everybody stays awake. We'll see that you get sleep whenever it is possible. But if you are told to stay awake, you must stay awake until you get other orders."

This sounded tough and I didn't like it but I realized that what he was saying was true. I was in it for keeps now and if I should fall asleep on my post I knew what the consequences would be. Sleep was always an important thing in my life and now I was being told that I could sleep only when allowed to do so by an order from my leaders. Little did I know that for the next six months I was to be awakened at least once very night. Some nights it was going to be no sleep a all. If I would have known the horrors and hardships ahead, I think I would have cracked right there in that Dutch barnyard.

The meeting with Captain Hallahan ended quickly. All I knew was that I was in company headquarters and that we were headed for Germany.

It wasn't long before a column of trucks lined up in the road running by our group of farm buildings. Now I pulled my first detail. The individual duffel bags were piled in a shed and we had to sort them according to platoons. At the same time the bags that belonged to the dead and wounded men were sorted in a separate pile. I was trying to keep a count of those that were dead and wounded and as far as I can remember the total was about sixteen.

The Letters of a Combat Rifleman

I was a bit bewildered as to which truck to get on and I could hardly believe that I was lucky enough to get a seat. Now I noticed for the first time the advantage of being in company headquarters. Ours was a small group and we had plenty of room in the truck. Plenty, that is, considering the way they packed replacements in trucks. You can comfortably seat fourteen men in an army truck and they used to put twenty-nine replacements in one truck and that included their full amount of baggage, too. This figure was topped by stacking sixty-five prisoners of war in he same size truck.

I found myself sitting next to a boy named Helmut. He had a crooked nose and wore glasses. Helmut couldn't have been more than nineteen years old and so I understood his eating habits. His favorite dish was C rations and even though it was still early morning, he was already opening a C ration as we waited for the trucks to pull out. Helmut didn't make a very good first impression on me by gorging those C rations. I couldn't understand where such a little fellow put so much food. We became life long friends when I contributed two cans of meat and beans to his growing pains. Frankly, I was delighted to think that someone would accept them as a gift.

CHAPTER II
The Siegfried Line

The trip by truck to Germany was a long cold ride. The wind was blowing hard and whipped bits of hail against our backs. It was dark as we passed through Aachen, Germany. This was the town we had read and heard so much about. The First Division had a tough time taking it.

Just a few miles farther on we pulled off the main road and entered a narrow, rough road cutting through a pine forest. Under November 7, in my diary, I wrote, "Bivouacked in one of the black forests of Germany where I suppose many a ghost of the Wehrmacht tread. A German helmet lay nearby."

Well, I couldn't see that helmet until the next day. That forest was pitch black and when we unloaded from those trucks I couldn't see anything but the tops of the trees. We were ordered to pair off and settle down for the night. To take a step off the side of the road was like walking off a cliff. There was a steep bank and broken branches, tree roots, and of course, the trees themselves. Being new in the outfit, I couldn't find a partner by voice alone so I went to work feeling around with my hands for the best spot to lie down.

It was another night of misery. Perhaps a man can get used to sleeping on the ground like that because I sometimes think now that I did get used to it myself, a little bit. Of course, I never got very much sleep because I could never get warm, but I never took sick.

The next day was a busy one. We made fires to keep warm while we cleaned our rifles and checked our equipment. I turned in the things I didn't want, piling them in my duffel bag. I had plenty of clothes on, including a pair of fatigue clothes over my woolen uniform. Sergeant Noble made me take these off because he said I looked too much like a German. Some of their camouflaged overalls looked like the fatigue clothes from a distance. To make up for this loss, I put on another woolen shirt. To compliment the two woolen shirts, I had a pair of long handles, two pairs of socks, shoes, leggings, woolen trousers, field jacket and a sleeveless wool sweater that my wife had knit for me several years before. During the next six months this outfit was to be shed only about a half dozen times. Little did I realize that morning that I would be wearing the exact same clothes, day and night for the next five weeks.

And those next five weeks were to be plenty rough. They were to be the toughest days of all.

Up until this point I had received no ammunition except a clip I had managed to grab back in Holland while with Service Company.

"Go over to the trucks and see a fellow named Eddie and get some ammo," said Sergeant Noble. I found Eddie but he had no ammo. That's organization and training for you! This division was supposed to be well trained and here I was going into the front lines with only one clip of ammunition!

In my diary on November 8, I wrote, "We are now in Germany and we are going into the front lines. Relieve an outfit at the front just at dark. I still have no ammunition except for a clip I borrowed from one of the fellows. We had promises of a nice setup and we took our bedding rolls along as well as combat packs. I had mess gear, rations, writing paper, raincoat, socks and toilet articles in my pack. It was cold so we had on overcoats and gloves."

It was plenty cold that night and then as if to make it like the movies and maneuvers, it started to rain. I don't remember what my feelings were as we walked up the road after getting off the trucks behind a hill. I wasn't happy, of course, but I wasn't afraid. The war would be over soon, I thought, and I would be a combat veteran and on my way back home to my family. That hill up into Munsterbusch, a suburb of Stolberg, was a long, hard climb. We struggled with our bedding roll and rifles and got wet on the inside from sweat and on the outside from the rain. It was dark as we entered the edge of the town and halted. This same street was to be the background for a famous full-page picture in Life magazine showing some first aid men carrying a wounded man out on a stretcher. As we moved in, it was dark and wet and I ducked in the shadow of a doorway to escape the rain, hoping at the same time not to set off a booby trap. I was still very booby trap conscious from the training camps.

In order to get past the first street corner we had to squeeze by a knocked-out American tank. This was the town where the First Division was stopped. From the looks of things, they were stopped dead. This was the first of several knocked out American tanks that I was to see in and about Munsterbusch.

We got settled for the night and the next day I wrote in my diary. "Here we sit on the front lines. At the moment I am in a heated building. Last night I slept here on a mattress. This can't last long.

"It really is a strange set-up for the front lines. Some of our OP's (out posts or observation posts) are only one hundred to two hundred yards from the Jerries. Where I am we have some light and heat and good bunks. Some of the outfits are already complaining which prompted the CO to say, 'Next they'll be sending up for bed sheets and pillow cases.'"

Well, it may not seem so strange but after going through those terrible repeldepels, this front line service in heated buildings, seemed like home—almost. For the most part, we lived in the cellars and almost every room had a stove. There were plenty of briquettes (molded coal) to keep the fires going on night and day. I often wondered about those fires attracting the attention of the enemy, but this risk was one that we always were willing to take. The first thing we always did after taking a town was to light a fire and heat water. That was the general policy of our outfit from Stolberg to the Mulde River. Of course, as we ran into civilians, the matter of a smoking chimney had no significance.

The setup here at Munsterbusch is very important as this is where we ran into the stiffest resistance the Germans ever put up in front of the Timberwolf Division. In our sector we were on higher ground than the Germans. In our area and to our front we had open fields, city streets and patches of woods. A railroad ran parallel to our front, about one hundred yards in front of our forward positions. Other important features were a shoe factory and a slag pile.

As far as I know, all three rifle companies in our battalion were on the line. Item and King companies were on our right. The second battalion was on our left.

Far to our right was Hill 287, overlooking Stolberg and dominating the whole scene. Hill 287 was a bristling hedgehog of defense, honeycombed with all sorts of buildings and no doubt pill boxes as this was a part of the vaunted Siegfried Line. Opposite Hill 287 was our 414th Infantry regiment.

Love company, which was almost at full strength, had to cover plenty of territory. The first platoon was far out on the left flank, located in a small group of buildings and a concrete pill box. They also had an outpost to their left front. This outpost was in a steel and concrete bunker. The second and third platoons were relatively close together in a row of houses, the third platoon on the right.

Across the street and to the rear of the second platoon, our weapons platoon had their mortars set up in back of their buildings. Mike company gave us support with heavy machine guns and 81 mm mortars and a section of anti-tankers manned a 57 mm gun right up on the line with our riflemen. Sitting back up on the hill about three hundred yards, the tank destroyer outfit attached to us dug in their truck-drawn guns right in plain view of the enemy. They drew plenty of fire and suffered several casualties. I don't remember seeing any artillery FO (forward observer) during our stay in Munsterbusch but we had an FO from Cannon company and he gave us excellent support. His OP was located in a soap factory, just across the street from company headquarters.

Company headquarters was about two blocks to the rear of our platoons and was located in the rectory of a Catholic church. It was a big and well-built house but was pretty well blasted with shell fire. The First Division boys had cleared the dining room on the first floor, and this is where we ate our meals, served hot, twice a day. The CP: (command post) was in the cellar which contained about five separate rooms and a narrow hallway. Somehow or other we all were able to find a spot to lie down.

Lighting was our greatest problem during our first days here in Munsterbusch. Living almost entirely in the cellar, we had to have artificial light day and night. I was lucky enough to have a flashlight that I had managed to buy in Zambre, Belgium. It helped me to get around the sleeping forms on the floor. Our other sources of light were one Coleman gasoline lantern for the CP, and candles, if we could get them. To guide us about the house at night we hung compasses at all doors and stairways. Their luminous dials were the only use we were to get from them during six months of combat.

On November 10, I wrote in my diary, "We are still here in the same place but I don't think it will last long because it is too good. There is talk all the time of better heat, light, and communications. While talking about the lighting last night I had to laugh when the CO said, 'All I am is a plumber's helper. I can do anything in the line of plumbing.'"

We didn't need any plumbing. Our latrine was a straddle ditch in the front yard (away from the Jerries) and our water supply came up in Jerry cans with the kitchen jeep.

The weather was our big worry as it was very cold and always wet. My diary says, "I don't know how anyone can stand it in a fox hole. Yesterday it snowed some and last night again it rained hard."

Cold chills ran up and down my spine that second night as reports came in over the telephone. The First division outfit had warned us not to send out any patrols. It was suicide, they said, because every one that they had sent out was shot up and captured. Just remember, the First division was our best and most experienced division. The Timberwolves were still green troops and so we didn't contemplate sending out patrols. But the Jerries must have known that the First had pulled out. The wires between our platoons and the outposts were cut! One of the best men in the First platoon was missing. Instead of us shooting up the German patrols, they were coming in and shooting up our outposts and cutting our communications.

There were only about five men in the bunker which the First platoon used as an outpost and in order to prevent surprise, two or three men were stationed outside. It was one of these boys that the Jerries got that night. It is still a mystery as to how they could come upon anyone standing still and capture him. The surrounding area was filled with gullies and muddy fields and anyone walking around here in he dark would certainly make plenty of noise. It is most likely that the wind and the rain drowned out any noise and the Germans knew exactly the spots where it would be natural to stand to protect the bunker. The grave of the missing body was found about a week later. No doubt he was not completely surprised and had put up a good fight before he was captured.

We were green troops fighting against the best soldiers in the world, Even our First Division was afraid to send out patrols. The German intelligence section knew that the First had been replaced by the 104th. And now they were coming in to get us. When darkness came each evening our heartbeats and fears were doubled.

At this time I don't believe we were using any radios. Our communications were all by runner and wire. There were no bell systems on the phones. A man had to sit there and listen. It was a twenty-four-hour-a-day job. There were wires going out to all the platoons and one wire back to battalion headquarters. The platoons ran out wires to their outposts.

It got dark early at that time of the year. This meant long hours of vigil every night. Besides the Outposts, every building that contained a unit had to have a door guard or perhaps two door guards. It was here in Munsterbusch that we suffered our first case of the jitters. It is strange how catching they are. The officers always appeared more afraid than the enlisted men. Perhaps it was because they didn't have to stand guard. If they could have gotten away with it they would have had a man standing at every opening. When the officers wanted to sleep they could lie down any hour of the day or night and go to sleep. They always had a bottle of whisky or Scotch to warm or comfort them, a light to read or write by and a bed to sleep in. There was no one tugging at their shoulder two or three times a night telling them it was their time to go out on guard or outpost. So it didn't hurt them at all to double the guards and outposts.

The OP maintained by the First platoon was increased to a full squad, which of course meant about ten men instead of twelve, as the squads were never at full strength. Four men were posted outside the bunker so that the Jerries couldn't come up and put a charge against the door. These four men all carried Thompson submachine guns if they were available. The water was almost knee deep on the floor of the bunker but there were bunks to lie down on.

It is still a mystery to me why we had to maintain this outpost. The bunker was about three hundred yards to the left from of the First platoon. There was no advantage to either side in holding it.

But we were just making more mistakes than the Jerries were. It was a case of deploy and destroy. We were doing the deploying and the Germans were doing the destroying. We had a big formidable force, but we were scattered over such an area that we were like weaklings. A few German soldiers were keeping hundreds of us awake and on edge. We had colds. Our feet were always wet. We had the GI's (dysentery).

The Letters of a Combat Rifleman

On November 13, I wrote in my diary, "Snow on the ground this morning. The weather sure is cold. An hour on guard and my toes are nearly frozen." Later the same day, "Some shells landed very close just now. The Jerries have been throwing some rockets over, we hear." The shells apparently were aimed at the tank destroyer outfit dug into our left front about three hundred yards away.

"A man has been shot in the First platoon," was an announcement we were to hear many times during the next few nights in Munsterbusch.

I held my breath each time and waited for the details. The man on the phone would continue, "He shot himself in the foot with a BAR." Well, that was always a relief. At least the Germans weren't coming in after us. Of course, these shootings were always "accidents." It was just coincidental that the man always happened to shoot himself—and always in the hand or foot. But perhaps I would have shot myself, too, if I had been faced with that outpost duty. and it kept coming up more and more often, too, because they kept increasing the number of men. It was a twenty-four hour job, too, because they couldn't come in from an OP during the daylight hours. They went out and relieved the old detail just as soon as it got dark and then they had to stay there until the next evening. You just didn't eat for twenty-four hours unless it was cold K rations. Ugh! The thought makes me sick.

There were plenty of men getting sick. Dysentery, or the GIs as we called it, was the main problem. Unless it was a severe case, you just went on sweating it out. Trench foot still took a few men but not like up in Holland. The Germans got a few but self-inflicted wounds were accounting for a big percentage of our casualties.

It was soon announced that we were waiting for clear weather so that we could make a big push. They said we would have the support of fifteen hundred planes. What a publicity outfit the air corps had, even in the front lines. They made it sound like every regiment was going to have twenty-five hundred planes roaring to their support.

The weather continued on as usual with the rain alternating with snow. We went outdoors as little as possible. Our first looting took place right in the priest's home. There were some beautiful unused Christmas cards in a desk on the second floor and I mailed quite a few to my friends back home. There was one of a house in the country that I liked best. And I sent that to my wife and son. It was a picture of the home I dreamed of in America.

The long hours of guard duty at night gave me a splendid opportunity to dream. I thought over the past and planned the future. My little daughter, who had been killed in Georgia while I was in training, wanted a house just like the one on the Christmas card. I thought of my dear little Alice Jane and of my wife and son more than anything else. Of course, I thought of other things such as what would I do if the enemy suddenly appeared, where was the best place to stand to keep warm and dry and still keep good watch, etc.

These long, cold, silent hours gave me time to pray. Every night I said my prayers as I stood guard. I never thought much about getting wounded. If I got hit, I figured I was going to be killed. And if I got killed, I prayed that I would go to heaven with my guardian angel, Jane. This thought comforted me more than anything else during my days of combat. I figured that if I were killed, it would be because the Lord wanted me to be with my daughter. If I survived, the Lord wanted me to go back home to my wife and son.

On Sunday, November 12, 1944, I made an important entry in my diary: "My soldier dreams came true today, or rather yesterday, when I became a sniper. I got a Springfield O3A4 snipers rifle with a Weaver scope. It has a beautiful barrel, highly polished, but I am afraid it has a couple of small pit marks. Paradoxically, I had a hard time trying to find a place to zero it in. We finally went up to an OP and fired at some signs in the direction of Jerryland. It was very difficult to observe the strike of the bullet but I did the best I could to zero it in at about two hundred yards. It is a very good scope and really brings the target up very good.

The rifle was a Springfield, and I believe it was made by Remington. The scope was a 330 model with Redfield Junior mount. It was sitting in the kitchen along with some other equipment the supply sergeant had stored there. I can't remember now who I asked concerning swapping my M-1 for the Springfield. I believe it was Eddie, the assistant supply sergeant. Eddie said, "Sure you can have it but you had better ask Danowski, first." Thomas Danowski was the executive officer, a man I was to enjoy working with during the months to come. This first lieutenant from Long Island, who was to turn out to be the best officer fighting man I ever knew, made a first-class first impression on me. Danowski said I could have the '03 and on top of that he helped me find the spot to sight it in. I knew no one in the company and it wasn't easy to persuade a squad or outpost to let you shoot from their building. There was always a great fear of drawing return fire. This fear seemed to dominate this American army all during the war. Of course, there were exceptions. And under the leadership of Danowski, our company was to prove to be one of the exceptions. No one could object when the first lieutenant okayed the firing.

The M-1 I turned in was a fine weapon, too. It was issued to me in England and I had sighted it in there on a one thousand inch range. This was not a new rifle and therefore worked much smoother than most of the rifles that the other replacements had issued to them. We were delayed quite a while in England for some reason or other and instead of going on the range once as was the usual custom, most of the men in our group had been able to fire three or four times. I squeezed into several other groups as they were on their way to the range and so had fired my rifle at least one hundred times. Some of the replacements ducked these practice sessions and actually sailed for France without knowing the zero of their rifle. Even in Belgium, they were still trying to locate the men who had not zeroed their rifles and there

The Letters of a Combat Rifleman

were still men who didn't want to bother with going to the range. I got into one of these rifle zeroing groups in Belgium, but when I heard that they had to walk eight miles to the range I just faded back into the woods. The army never made rifle practice easy. The ranges were always built about ten miles from camp. There never was any transportation available to take the men to the ranges.

Danowski soon came up with another idea that was to be the forerunner of many Danowski-Davis firepower setups. He suggested setting up a .50 caliber machine gun in the soap factory across the street from company headquarters. Mainly though, he wanted it for defense and we mounted it with the idea that it would be used only in case of a German attack. However, we set it up on the third floor of the building on top of some huge bags of powdered soap which in reality was an offensive position, not defensive. That, and several other incidents were to prove to me that the 104th Division was not well trained as was always claimed by its leaders. Terry Allen, division commander said when he landed in New York, "The division had six months and fifteen days continuous combat from October 23 until the end of the war. Whatever success the division has had is entirely due to discipline, unselfish teamwork, a high state of training, physical fitness and a most intensive belief in themselves as individuals and pride in their unit." The "high state of training" theme was played up in every publicity release and bulletin. Machine guns in defense were to be used in a low position so as to obtain the maximum of grazing fire, (fire the height of a man) was what I had learned in the national guard, years before. That .50 caliber would have been shooting over the heads of the enemy attacking force. The heavy machine guns attached to our company from Mike company were similarly mounted. Some riflemen you couldn't drag out of cellars while it seemed that most machine gunners were second story men. Instead of keeping together in a closely knit, powerful force, we deployed all over the landscape. Instead of dominating the enemy with fire power, we ducked and withheld our firepower.

The most often heard phrase during our seventeen weeks basic training was "cover and concealment." They kept telling us to dig in, seek cover, make sure you are concealed. They trained us as defenders when all or most of the time we were on the offensive. You can't seek cover and concealment and stop and dig foxholes and at the same time advance. We spent days learning how to dig foxholes. It was all time wasted. They had to be perfect in shape and dimensions.. A hole in the ground is a comparatively safe place regardless of shape or size. In six months of fighting in the front lines, which is at least twice as long as the average rifleman lasts, I dug exactly three foxholes. None of these were anywhere near perfect. In every case I firmly believe that I would have come through safely if I hadn't dug a hole. In one situation I believe my life was saved due to the fact that I didn't dig a foxhole but just lay flat on my stomach instead.

We did fear an attack by the Germans at this time. If we had any intelligence service at all we would have known that the main German force had moved out the day that we relieved the First. The German civilians were to tell us this when we finally got into Stolberg. It was only a tiny withholding force that was left behind to hold the last remaining pillboxes of the Siegfried Line.

Every night we became more frightened. About nine o'clock we would begin to hear a different outpost that had been cut off the line.. Sergeant Donaldson, our communications sergeant had the job of fixing these wires, usually cut by the Germans. The Jerries would follow the lines to the outpost after they had cut them and then they generally tried to kill or capture the occupants and were sometimes successful. It was a nerve-racking job going out to fix the wire, too, because you could never tell whether or not the Jerries would be waiting for you, knowing that you would be there to make repairs. Donaldson was to get it soon.

More notes from my diary, November 15, "Last night we doubled our guard because some of the boys were jittery. About 4 A.M. they fired at some noise they heard. Despite the fact they were within ten feet of me I did not hear the sound of the firing."

When I got the opportunity I sure did sleep! I was never troubled with insomnia while in the front lines. Eddie and a fellow who was to later become our mail clerk were the frightened men,.

The following morning I was on guard with Val, the big American Indian who had joined company headquarters with me. The diary says, "The noise and movement in the night was a large white rabbit! I saw it this morning about 5:30."

"The sun is out today," I wrote on November 16. "That can change a lot of things. Just this minute we had a shell land very, very closer. The closest yet."

The sun did change a lot of things, too, for there are blank pages in my diary for the next four days. And then November 21, "We have passed some very rough and exciting and also sickening days. Now its different. At the moment we are sitting here in my apartment in Stolberg, listening to Dinah Shore. The captain is inspecting his wounds and washing his feet. He just said, 'What would I do if the Krauts counterattacked now!' But the M.P.s entered here today so we must be pretty far back now."

"It's the Hit Parade now. The three top tunes are, (1) I'll Be Seeing You, (2) Swinging On A Star, (reminds me of Jane because we all went to see the show in which Bing Crosby sang that song while I was a Camp Wheeler, Ga.) (3) Time Waits For No One. We had a snack of sardines, tuna fish, bread, butter, jam, and coffee. To bed at 2400."

Dinah Shore is a great gal and a wonderful singer, but she could not wipe out the terrifying thought of the fighting we'd just gone through. The captain had been hit two or three times in the legs. None of these wounds ever stopped him.

CHAPTER III
===

Four Tough Days

The first day of the offensive, the First platoon succeeded in moving forward about five hundred yards to the shoe factory. Nothing seemed to be coordinated, so that the support that we had was more or less wasted. In the first place it seems that the company had orders to move out whenever they were ready. This meant, of course, that the Germans could concentrate their fire on each outfit as they pushed forward, since it is probable that no two companies moved at the same time. We didn't get going until late in the morning.

The supporting units were all there including the air corps. But they must have had those twenty-five hundred planes spread out between Holland and Italy. The artillery had their cub spotters in the air, too. Cannon company of our regiment gave some good support and the anti tank and tank destroyer outfits came through with direct fire. We also got some terrific direct fire support from a special purpose .155 mm gun, mounted on a tracked carriage. Everybody in the company was talking about this monster. But we didn't see it in operation. Just at dusk it would pull down the street on our right flank and make a right turn over into King company's area. It was said that nobody could be within one hundred yards of the muzzle, the blast was so terrific. It could fire only a few rounds and then it had to pull back again because the Jerries threw everything in the book whenever they saw or heard this special-purpose gun.

But as darkness came that night, the great night-fighting Timberwolves began to shake in their tracks—and walk backwards. As the shadows began to fall, the Jerries began to creep and flit toward the buildings occupied by the Third platooners. Grenades flew all over the place. Some of the boys got back and some didn't. The lieutenant leading the First platoon was killed by a mortar shell. For some strange reason, some of the leaders in the Third platoon got back before the majority of men. Perhaps they could crawl faster. It was a route. All available men in company headquarters were rushed outside our row of buildings (we had moved up to the row of houses forming the front line, late in the afternoon) to head off a German counterattack. I had a spot in the middle of a street that ran perpendicular to the line. We all took the prone position just in case of mortar fire, which had been coming in all day long. Despite this day-long heavy German fire we never heard of any Jerry positions being spotted or knocked out in front of us. Our cub observation planes had circled continuously, moving out well over the German lines and at a low height, too. But it never kept the enemy from using his weapons, and with telling effect.

I was cold and discouraged as I lay there on that hard macadamized road. I was mad, too, at the way things were bungled. The news from King company on our right was very discouraging. They were thrown back, too. There were no companies in reserve to rush up and help hold the ground that was taken. Company commanders lacked the experience and initiative to move what reserves they did have, if they had any, up to help hold the new line.

Things quieted down and we finally got back into a building. I thought I couldn't stand the cold much longer and I could hear other men complaining. Company headquarters was in the same house as Third platoon headquarters and things were really crowded. There wasn't anymore room to lie down and it was almost impossible even to walk around in the cellar. Sergeant Donaldson came staggering in wounded in the rear. He added to the confusion and fright. They should never let a wounded man talk. Donaldson rambled on about the Germans coming in closer and closer. He was scared and he made us scared.

There was no system for guarding the building. I was on the front door and stood an hour and a half longer than what I should because the first sergeant wouldn't send a man up to relieve me. Our new first sergeant was an old army man named White, the same guy that made us pick up cigarette butts back in Holland. White was destined to turn out to be the worst coward I met in the front lines.

One man approached while I was on guard, and he wouldn't halt or give the password. He must have been a Third platooner just getting back. Apparently, he was a bit dazed and it was a wonder he wasn't shot. I don't know why I didn't fire.

The next day is not very clear in my memory. The offensive was pushed, but without success. I had my first close call, saw for the first time an enemy soldier under arms and stumbled over my first dead American.

Williams, a young, tall boy from Washington state, and myself were ordered to get some K rations from a house about half a block away. They were to be distributed for lunch. The kitchen jeep was still getting up before and after the hours of daylight in order to give us two hot meals a day. The shellfire had been rather intensive all day and it wasn't even safe to go up into the hallway, let alone go outdoors. Consequently, Williams and I waited for a lull and then made a dash. We were running on the pavement and the shell burst in the middle of the street right beside us. Williams looked at me in amazement when we reached safety. Neither of us had been touched! But a Tech-sergeant, standing beside his tank, half a block away, was killed! They pulled him into a house and covered his body with a rug. He was the fellow I tripped over, later.

The wire to battalion was constantly being cut by this shellfire and that kept us busy in headquarters. Finally they decided to lay a new wire and Williams and I volunteered. Off we went on the run with the spool between us. As soon as we crossed the street we were under enemy observation. The shells came in thick and fast but we timed them right and got back to battalion with the new wire. It was during one of these wire repairing trips that I came in contact with the new communications sergeant. A fellow named Orval Reed from Deer River, Michigan. "Sugar," as he was known, was to become one of my best friends and turn out to be one of the best soldiers in the company.

Casualties were cutting down our ranks plenty fast. Captain Hallahan had been hit three times in the legs but was still getting around. But with our thinning ranks and sick and wounded men we started to attack again the third day. During the morning the antitankers with their 57 mm gun mounted in an opening in the row of buildings were firing direct at the pillboxes and houses immediately in front of them. The AP shells generally bounced right off the pillboxes and some of the houses must have been built over pillboxes because AP shells were seen bouncing off a few of them.

I borrowed a pair of six-by-thirty field glasses and searched for targets. This was the first time I actually used my Springfield. There were no definite targets, but I fired at all the openings that looked in any way suspicious. It was at this time that I saw my first German soldier. He was standing in the sun against the corner of a building. The range was a good mile and so I didn't attempt to hit him. Still much farther in the distance were two enemy soldiers sitting beside a combination house and pillbox along what looked like a cement highway running parallel to our front about a mile and a half away. This was a position where a good spotting scope would have been very handy. I was to find out later that rifle companies never received spotting scopes. Our regimental observers had good Bausch and Lomb scopes and artillery outfits had them. However, I do not recall ever seeing a forward observer from the artillery outfits ever using a spotting scope. They always had field glasses, which can not compare with a spotting scope.

When the boys moved out that third day, a tank went forward with them. It took an hour to locate the men from battalion who were supposed to go forward and remove the mines. They refused to go. That was just the beginning of the trouble we were to have with supporting units during our days of combat.

The tank went as far as it could without running over the mines. A young boy named Gasch from our Weapons platoon, volunteered to man one of the machine guns on he tank, filling in for the dead T/4. That was the beginning of many similar instances of riflemen taking over other jobs.

Our own mortar section was laying down fire almost all morning, but I did not recall that there was any preliminary fire from any weapons at all as the men moved forward. I gave some overhead rifle fire, but what could one rifleman do! It was only the Third platoon that moved and they consisted of about eighteen men.

The tank stopped just short of the railroad tracks and began to fire at the group of houses that the Third platoon had occupied two days before. The riflemen continued on but had difficulty getting through the rolls of concertina wire that ran along the railroad. Then they were in an open field about one hundred yards long. This field was full of mines and naturally the Germans had guns set up so that they could cover it with plenty of fire. The tank fired a few rounds and then proceeded to back up, even though it was not being fired upon. This did away with the only overhead fire that the riflemen had and then the machine guns and rifles opened up on them and they hit the ground and that was just what the Germans wanted. The mortar fire cut them to pieces.

There were several acts of heroism during this action. A boy named White (not the first sergeant) who just recently came in as a sergeant replacement, was the leader during the attack. "Red" (for his bright red hair) White was a squad leader and he set the precedent of squad leaders leading the fight. He reached the forward most position despite the fact that he was hit in the neck and head. The platoon leader, a lieutenant replacement who had just joined the company, too, had his carbine shattered and he was badly wounded. A man named Shaeffer, father of three children, had been killed. As usual, the individuals that escaped the other attacks returned safely to the company. These few men were to finish the war without ever being hit. They were to rise in rank, too, one receiving a battlefield commission. To this day they think their actions went unnoticed.

Another boy named MacDonald fractured his hand on the railroad but that didn't stop him from going out twice to aid the wounded. Later he was seriously wounded.

Finally it was determined there were still several wounded men lying in that open field or along the railroad. It would take a lot of aid men to get them out. Luckily there were quite a few aid men from battalion and regiment with us. We did get the men out of the cellar but that was as far as they would go. They refused to go forward and pick up the wounded. They argued that the Jerries had fired on a stretcher team the day before in the

First platoon area. In all probability this was a mistake. We made plenty of mistakes too. We never purposely fired on German aid men.

This is where First Lieutenant Thompson, a new replacement, introduced himself. I'll never forget his entry into combat—as compared with our group of replacements. Lieutenant Thompson, from Pittsburgh, Pa., ordered two men to be sent to battalion headquarters, the day he arrived, to carry his baggage and equipment up to the front lines. It so happened that "Sugar" Reed and myself were the appointed porters. When we reached battalion there was only one piece of baggage. Young "Sugar" grabbed that. It's a wonder he didn't put his shoes out in the hall every night for someone to clean!

But Lieutenant Thompson was an example of the typical army officer. Even in the front lines it was already noticeable that officers received special privileges and considerations, ate better, slept better and drank better. They were above the enlisted men, superior. In other words, so called supermen, something like the idea of Nazis being the super race that was destined to lead and rule the world.

This caste system was a counterpart to the Nazi idea. Just the thing we were fighting! Here were a few men dictating the lives of hundreds and thousands. The few lived on the best of the land. The thousands lived like dogs and worked like slaves. Yes, the work in the front lines was done by the enlisted men. It was enlisted men who maintained the outposts and listening posts, that formed and led most of the patrols, that maintained communications and pulled all the guard duty. There were exceptions of course. And it was only a few enlisted men that really carried on the fight for all other officers and enlisted men.

Lieutenant Thompson, however, was no coward. He yelled at the medics and he swore at the Jerries. The aid men said they had orders from their officers not to go out to pick up wounded men. That counteracted any order that our officers might give. Anyway our officers never thought of ordering the medics forward.

Finally it was decided that we would take the medic's helmets and form a party of riflemen to go out, posing as aid men. Lieutenant Thompson was a volunteer. He dropped his pistol but insisted on taking two hand grenades in his pockets.

"No, you can't take those grenades," said Lieutenant Danowski.

"The hell with it. I'm going to get even with those Jerries," replied Thompson.

"Well, you're not going out if you don't put those grenades down," ordered Danowski. Reluctantly, Thompson laid down the grenades. The whole act was rather foolish and uncalled for. I don't think, however, that he wanted to appear as a hero. In the front lines there are very few men that don't get excited once in awhile.

I set my rifle up against the building, dropped my cartridge belt and took the two grenades out of my jacket lapels. That medic must have felt like a sad sack when I stepped in front of him and took his helmet off his head, handing him my own. One aid man finally volunteered and the fourth man on the stretcher was Lieutenant Thomas Danwoski. Father Quinn, our chaplain, unfurled his flag and we marched off down the road into no-man's-land.

Everything seemed quiet. We took the same route of approach as the riflemen and tank. Just our side of the railroad were three rows of mines across the road. It would have been impossible for the tank to pass this spot without first removing the mines. However, to give overhead fire the tank was in a better position in back of the mines because the ground sloped down sharply at the railroad and then gradually until it hit the first group of buildings. When we hit the barbed wire we started to look for wounded men. We were in sight of the Jerries now but everything remained quiet. First we began to see a lot of equipment. Gas masks, packs, cartridge belts, bandoliers and rifles were strewn over the ground. I never saw such a disheartening sight in all my life. Why did men throw away even their rifles? That question had bothered me ever since I heard that men had come staggering back to our lines without their rifles. The lieutenant's carbine was there on the ground, shattered at the receiver. It was useless. As we walked on further I began to realize why men come back without even their rifles. The only cover in that open field full of concealed mines was a narrow ditch about eighteen inches deep. It was full of mud and water. The shoulders of a big man would just about squeeze into it.

The grotesque form of a shattered American soldier's body filled the ditch about twenty yards from the railroad. Nobody recognized him and Thompson kneeled down and searched for his dog tags but couldn't find them. Papers or letters finally identified the dead man as Elmer Shaffer, a replacement, father of three children. Why did the army put him in the infantry?

There were a few shell holes but we didn't see another man. After a few minutes we started back.

"Hey," someone yelled. We all looked around and saw a man waving to us from a shell hole about thirty yards farther than we had searched. As we approached this man we could see the Jerries standing by a machine gun mounted in a basement window of the nearest house, about fifty yards away. They knew how to mount a machine gun!

It was a good thing they could not hear us talking. The man who called to us was a boy named Schwartz, and he was not wounded. We told him to pretend he was wounded and we would take him out. Next to Schwartz was a man suffering from shock. He was wet and cold and trembling from head to foot. In each hand he clutched a fragmentation grenade. His grip was like steel and it was difficult to get the grenades from him. Out in front of Schwartz was a helmetless redheaded youth, twice wounded but still full of fight. Howard J. "Red" White was hit in the neck and head.

We threw the stretcher away and supported the men as they walked toward our lines. I had "Red" White.

"Watch those mines," I said to Red as we stepped over one, partially covered with dead grass.

"That's all right," answered Red, "I've been walking on them all afternoon."

I was afraid to look back but I finally ventured a glance over my shoulder, just before we started to climb up over the railroad embankment. The Jerries were still watching. There was not a shot fired. We made it back to our lines without any trouble.

Our shot-up Third platoon now numbered about nine men. This included the three or four men who always managed to get back first. After this third attack there were about ninety men in Love company. A rifle company should contain two hundred. A rifle platoon calls for forty men.

I stood in the doorway of our house and watched an overloaded ambulance pull back up the street toward the rear. There was another vehicle parked there close to our door. Arms and legs protruded from the canvas covering. One fellow identified the body of the first platoon leader by the gold watch still on his wrist.

It wasn't with revenge in my heart that I took off down the street with my '03 and binoculars. It was with the spirit of a hunter who is long over due on bringing home a trophy. The trophy I wanted was the end of this rotten war. It could be ended only by unconditional victory. This victory could be brought about only by pressing the attack, dominating the enemy. I wanted to constantly attack because I wanted the end of the war.

Turning in at a doorway I stumbled over a carpet covered form. It was the dead tanker. He would have to wait for the next load. The house was a shambles. It was difficult to move about the rooms because of broken ceilings and debris. I finally located a top floor room where I could see the window of the house that contained the German machine gun. The window of the room I occupied was greatly enlarged by gun fire.

I took a sitting position on the table in the middle of the room and opened fire. The distance was so great I couldn't tell, even with the binoculars, whether or not the machine gun was still there. And I didn't know if my shots were hitting the right spot. But my shooting served notice to the Jerries that we were still around and that we were not entirely dominated. We wanted victory because we wanted the end of the war. We would win because we had a better cause.

The next day the Third platoon was ordered to form a patrol to go forward and see if any Germans were still occupying the positions in front of us. Motor transports were heard during the night and it was rumored that the Jerries had pulled out. The whole platoon formed the patrol. The rest of the company lined up in single file and went through the First platoon area, meeting up with the Third platoon in Stolberg.

It was late in the afternoon when we reached our new positions. There had not been one shot fired during the movement. Wire was laid to the platoons and outposts established for the night. It was dark before I finally located our company headquarters and then I climbed through a window amid a crashing of glass and chinaware. It was an awful sensation to be grouping about in the dark in a strange house and trying not to make any noise. Someone should invent glasses for infantrymen which would enable them to see in the dark.

About 11 P.M. I was chosen to accompany a battalion officer back to his headquarters and then lead up a wire team from battalion. Lieutenant Buckley was the man. He looked more like a teenage kid. And as I was to find out later, he often acted like one.

The battle to pierce the remaining positions of the Siegfried Line was over. Stolberg had been taken. The First battalion was moving on Eschweiler, population about fifty thousand.

On November 22, I wrote in my diary. "What we need in this town now is an M.P. to direct traffic. The boys are having a lot of fun going around on bicycles and motor cycles, wearing top hats.

"It was rough out today with plenty of rain that seemed to want to turn to snow. Feet were feeling the results of the cold and dampness.

"Another red letter day for mail when I received seven letters! Jean and Bill are well, thank God. Herc (my younger brother) wrote and his family is okay, too.

"No snack tonight but we just had some hot coffee that really hit the spot.

"Went out once today for a bicycle ride around the town. The bikes here have small generators on them for their blackout lights. Some of the bikes are very nice jobs.

"Rumors are in the air tonight," I continued to write. "Tomorrow is Thanksgiving Day and perhaps we will eat on the run!"

The day before I had participated in my first patrol. Lieutenant Danowski took Lloyd Williams and me on a circle route to our front, passing through a railroad station, some woods, and a railroad yard. Williams, headquarters bazooka man, fired his rocked launcher several times. I took a few practice shots at the railway signal lights. The Springfield '03 seemed to be shooting a little to the left and low.

During the day company headquarters maintained an observation post high up in a chemical factory. From this position I could see trolley sheds on the outskirts of Eschweiler. We watched the first battalion boys advance toward these sheds and could see the Jerries running around in confusion. Roy Clemens of Illinois who went through the repeldepels with me later told me about this incident. Roy took his first prisoners at this spot.

It was at this O.P. that I first fired the now famous grease gun or M-3 submachine gun. It impressed me as easy to operate but of a slow rate of fire.

While here in Stolberg we met our first German civilians, too. They were mostly women and children. And believe it or not, they were living almost next door to us for two days before we knew they were there. We were still inexperienced combat men!

The Letters of a Combat Rifleman

Captain Hallahan and quite a few of the rest of us were visibly moved by the sight of the hungry children eating our K rations.

To our amazement the German civilians told us that the main body of German troops had moved out of Stolberg ten days ago! This did not impress me until I remembered that it was exactly ten days ago that we had relieved the First division!

Let us at this point go over the attack on Stolberg and review and comment on certain other phases of the war.

Quite a bit had been written about he postponement of the invasion of Europe. This comment, criticism, etc., has been all from the viewpoint of generals, admirals, historians, politicians, and typewriter strategists.

From a combat infantryman's point of view it would have been suicide to invade the continent in 1942 or '43.

Here we went into Munsterbusch, a suburb of Stolberg, with our positions already prepared and waiting. Our communications were all established. Everything that the First division knew about the enemy was handed over to us.

We waited for fair weather and then we attacked. In the attack we employed twenty-five hundred planes. We did not see one single solitary German plane! We had plenty of armor. We had self-propelled special purpose .155 guns. We had plenty of direct fire guns, not to mention the artillery and small arms.

We were never under direct fire and we were never bombed or strafed! We attacked for three days and couldn't move the enemy. Our company strength went from one hundred ninety men to ninety. We finally walked into Stolberg after the enemy had withdrawn. In official statements they claimed that the Timberwolf Division had one of the lowest casualty rates of any division in combat. What would have happened to an inexperienced army landing on the beach of France in 1942 or '43? They would have been annihilated!

CHAPTER IV
Things to be Thankful For

Thanksgiving Day, November 23, 1944. My diary says. "We have many things to be thankful for. Thank God we are alive and well." We moved to the next town today (Eschweiler). It has quite a large population and there are still a few civilians around. Had a wonderful Thanksgiving dinner in our new home. It is quite a place. Some wealthy Nazi must have lived in the second floor apartment. I have my own bed with silk covered mattress! It is like heaven. Got myself a bicycle, too.

The cellar proved to be the most interesting place in this building. It has several rooms and each contained a variety of items stored away for safety. It was during the inspection of these rooms that Tom Jennings and I came across a gold nugget in the form of a sealed bottle of D O M Benedictine. We had never tasted such a smooth, warming drink I all our lives. It was just what we needed to spark our Thanksgiving Day dinner. . And it did! We kept it secret and we sure did enjoy that secret!

Tom was from Philly and that made us almost neighbors. The bottle of D O M made us lifelong friends. Despite the fact that Tom was thirty-nine years old he never complained about the physical hardships. And the many laughs that he set in motion helped to carry Love company headquarters through many a trying experience. Tom had a family back in Philly and he loved to talk about his two boys. He should have been home taking care of them instead of sweating out death in the front lines. Why did they ever put old Tom in the infantry.

It was while we were in Eschweiler that we started to "write up" awards for bravery. Hoover was one boy and the captain was included, too. There were several others. In a letter to my wife, I wrote, "But, honey, they just asked me to do some typing so now I'm stuck for the rest of the day. It burns me up because they have a company clerk. Where he is I'll never be able to tell you."

I was picked to make up these citations and like every one else in the company I didn't even know where to start. And like all citations that were ever sent in by Love company, and probably every rifle company, they bounced back. Silver stars were reduced to Bronze stars and Bronze stars were sent back for more details and additional exploits. It seemed that a rifleman had to be a one man army to get any kind of award.

And why does the army saddle riflemen with clerical work and censoring of letters? Every company in combat should have a high ranking noncom to act as historian, photographer, and censor. His sole duty should be to censor all outgoing mail and keep a record of all actions and campaigns; take a picture of each individual in the company at least every thirty days; send reports to the families of men killed and wounded and write up all citations. If one of your close relatives were killed by an automobile wouldn't you want to know all the details? How would you feel if the police told you it was secret information? What would you say if everyone you talked to and wrote to said that they were sorry but they could not tell you anything?

Mothers and fathers and other loved ones have sought in vain to get the detail of the death of their sons and brothers and husbands. The most they usually received was a brief telegram from the War Department.

A Pennsylvania Gold Star mother wrote to me in California after the war. She said, "I see you must be of the 104th div. My son Ivan C. Kunes of the 104th Inf. Div. (The Timberwolves) was killed in action in Germany, Dec. 11, 1944.

"Did you know him and do you know anything about his death? If you should happen to know anything will you please write and tell me everything. I've tried and tried to get more information about him.

"If you'd care to tell me about yourself, I'd be very glad to hear it.

"And if you want to know more about my son, Ivan, I'll write and tell you.

"We miss him so much. Thank you."

It took a lot of investigation to get even a few details about this boy's death. The officers in his company in the 414th Infantry didn't even want to tell me! I wrote to the mother giving the few details that I had dug up and she answered me:

"Rec'd. letter today. Sgt. Hanson wrote me a nice letter but the way he wrote he wasn't with Ivan but told me what another boy told him. I wish that this boy would write to me. Do you know whether the boy that was hit and was going to give Ivan first aid, Lived? I would like to get in touch with him or some one that was right with him. That would be Ivan, thinking of some one else's safety before himself. It just seems it was to be so but it's hard to take. We are proud of him, but we miss him so much and he had so much to come home to.

"I am sending in today for the Timberwolf book. St. Hanson told me it would cost $3.50. We want it very much.

"Thanks for writing. I will give your letters to Ivan C. Kunes' wife to keep for their son."

Those letters speak the feelings of all Gold Star mothers and also the other close relatives.

"Sunday, November 26, we have to leave this swell place this morning. We move up again."

The movement from Eschweiler to Weissweiler was made on foot. Many tanks lined the road as we moved forward and it was a slow, halting march. It was just as we entered Weisweiler that I saw my first dead enemy soldier. He was lying beside the road with a hole like a .50 caliber bullet through the center of his head. It wasn't any more pleasant than the sight of my dead comrade in the ditch. I cannot say what kept me from fainting as I witnessed these and many more sights in the months to come. During the later years of my training with the national guard the mention of the word blood in connection with first aid classes made me feel faint and sick at the stomach.

There was one advantage we had in fighting in cold weather—we couldn't help seeing the dead but at least we didn't have to smell them. The weather was so cold that two Jerries who had been killed down the road another one hundred yards were almost standing in an upright position. In fact, their arms were still upraised and their hands were still clutching a communications wire that they had been trying to fasten to a telephone pole.

My diary continues, "We are now in the next town. Didn't have to go far. Saw plenty coming up. It was rather terrible. The boys here say they had to fight for every room. One exposed part of the road was littered with everything, including a fighter plane, a jeep and an ambulance (German).

"We are staying on one of the main streets and it is not so nice here. We have a good cellar and a stove. however.

"The Germans say, according to *Stars & Stripes* 'The decisive battle of the west is being fought in the Aachen sector. The allies have assembled the greatest concentration of men and material there ever employed at a single point during the entire course of the war, the Russian front included.'" (*Stars & Stripes*, Nov. 24, 1944)

Those masses of vehicles on the roads verified this German news item and it made us feel good. I wasn't any longer thinking that the war was going to end in a few days. It just seemed like a job had to be finished and it may take another day or it may be a year. In my prayers every night I asked the Lord for a miracle. I asked Him to end the war tomorrow. I didn't know it then, but I was to live long enough to have that prayer answered some day.

We had to stand and wait on the outskirts of Weisweiler. There were a few brick houses about and it wasn't long before I got into the doorway of one. There was continuous mortar and artillery fire hitting a very steep hill just in front of us. We were standing in the field at the base of this hill wondering what to do and what the score was before we had sense enough to get into the buildings.

The houses were crowded with riflemen of the 414th Infantry and we got the story from them about the room to room fighting. I was conscious then of my clean, smooth shaven face. The 414th boys looked like bums. I realized that within a day or two I would look exactly like them, that is, if I were still alive.

I was afraid of that mortar fire. The weather was biting cold and I began to shiver. The dread of more terror and hardship ahead didn't keep me from shaking.

Tom Jennings was standing nearby and that reminded me of the canteen (German boy scout type) full of Scotch that I had in my pocket. Captain Hallahan was one officer that was free with his whisky ration. He left a quarter-filled bottle sitting on the table when we left Eschweiler and so I filled the canteen. That Black and White was even better than the D O M Benedictine because we needed it a hundred time more than we ever needed the D O M.

Finally we pushed into the center of the town where we bunched together on the main street. A few light American tanks were still smoldering. The occupants must have all been killed. Apparently they had been knocked out by bazookas as one big Jerry rocket launcher lay on the side of the road nearby. To drive any type of tank down the main street of a town is suicide unless there is plenty of protection from riflemen.

On November 27, I wrote, "Last night the moon was very bright. The clearest night yet. Today it is cloudy again. There is plenty of activity around this spot and our outfit has an assignment. Just now I am relaxing beside the kitchen stove, smoking a German cigar. They make good cigars."

The activity consisted mostly of intermittent shelling. One boy, a runner in company headquarters got hit in the back. It was a very tiny hole but he never returned to the company. Several others were hit.

My feet were giving me trouble. It was a slight case of trench foot. Several of my toes were swollen and split open. It was this day that I decided to go back to the aid station, about five blocks away. To avoid being hit I always picked out the next spot I was going to run to and then made a dash. Near the center of town was a GI standing in a doorway just across the street from an aid collecting station. I was waiting for the next shell to land before I started my run to join the GI. It came in and landed in the middle of the street. I reached the doorway just in time to see the GI walk across the street, holding his left eye in his hand. The aid men told me to come back the next day but once I reached my company I never worried about more treatments for my sore feet.

Five men, including Lieutenant Danowski had left us in Eshweiler for a trip to Paris. They returned to the company after we had reached

Weisweiler. We laughed when they told us that the French women welcomed them as "great warriors coming from combat." The zing, zing of the shells landing in the streets of Weisweiler was a long cry from the "zig-zig" of the Paris dames.

November 28, Tuesday. "Passed a rather quiet day. This evening the boys are talking about pass words. We are wondering who thinks them up. The other night it was 'Velvet—Pipe.' Of course, Jennings came out with 'Granger—Rough Cut' but they didn't waste any ammo. It was 'Sleepy—Night' one time and a patrol approached a certain guard and the leader called, 'Sleepy?' The guard answered, 'No, I feel okay.' A classic one was 'Wild—Virgin!'"

Wednesday. November 29, "Washed my feet today and best of all got clean 'long handles,' the first change in about five weeks. Received three letters from my sweet wife and managed to write to her. It is near noon and I haven't heard any rumors. It looks like we got in a good PX ration of Harvester cigars and Suchard chocolate."

That was the last entry in my diary. We shoved out of Weisweiler that night and the chain of events of the next week or more were to be marked with violent clashes with the enemy and the weather.

I had very seldom been selected for any good job or opportunity in my life. But in combat it seemed that I was always being chosen. Lloyd Williams was asked by the company commander to pick a man to work with him. Lloyd selected me.

It must have been about 10 P.M. when eight of us Love company men piled on the CO's jeep and headed into the darkness toward the next town. The party included the company commander, his driver, Gene Bailey, Williams, myself and several leaders and noncoms. One shell on top of that jeep would have struck a terrific blow to dear old Love company.

Things were quiet, however, and although I was shaking from fear and from the cold, the .50 caliber machine gun I was hanging onto gave me the hold and confidence I needed to keep from falling off the jeep. Eight men with full equipment makes quite a load for a jeep.

This wasn't the last ride I was to take off with Gene Bailey. During the months to come we were to work together on many projects. The termination of our companionship was to come suddenly and tragically.

The road eastward out of Weisweiler led under the famous Autobahn or German military highway. We were to see and use this four-lane super highway quite a bit in the weeks ahead. We went under the Autobahn because there were no roads that crossed it. You entered and left on a cloverleaf. Due to our air supremacy and highly mechanized transport this super highway was to be of greater benefit to us than to the builders.

About a mile away we rolled into Frenz, a very small town on the edge of the River Inde. Just down the river about one mile and on the same side was another small town, Lamersdorf. We drove to the edge of Frenz, nearest

The Letters of a Combat Rifleman

Lamersdorf where there was a battalion headquarters of the 413th Infantry. I don't mind saying that I was almost frightened out of my skin during the next few hours.

The battalion CP was located in a big combination farm house and barn. Several of the farm animals had been killed and in the intermittent moonlight they cast grotesque outlines against the flaming sky. The only building nearer to Lamersdorf than the CP was afire from roof to cellar. To add to this the Jerries were sending over screaming Mimis.

We began to get the lowdown from the 413th boys. They had been attacking Lamersdorf all day without success. It was just at dusk that a replacement lieutenant led about fifteen men into the edge of Lamersdorf and then the town was quickly cleared. A network of trenches between the two towns was the main stumbling block. This trench system was now the route into Lamersdorf and it was filled with dead bodies. From the talk around the CP it seemed that these dead men formed a bridge into Lamersdorf, there were so many of them. Several Sherman tanks were knocked out, adding to the toll of death and destruction.

Naturally everything being confused I soon found myself alone. Of course, this took time. First our command group pulled out and left Bailey and me with the 413th headquarters. Then the 413th headquarters pulled out. I don't know what the setup was supposed to be, but I thought that I should have gone foreword with the rest and then returned to the edge of Frenz with Williams so that we could lead the company down into Lamersdorf. The details are a bit confused now, but it seems that Bailey started to walk to Lamersdorf in order to find out if the CO wanted the jeep moved forward. Then along came our company in single file. I pointed them in the general direction that I had seen the other men take and they started out without a guide. In the meantime there was a lot of shelling going on and I was beginning to be afraid that the jeep would get hit. I got in to drive it under the archway but I couldn't find the switch or starter. I was mainly afraid of pulling the wrong lever and throwing on the headlights, not knowing of course that this was impossible as the controls were safeguarded against such a mistake.

I was becoming more frightened every minute. It took plenty of courage to walk out to the jeep. And then I was afraid to go back in the building again. Finally I placed myself behind a pile of bags containing feed or grain and stood watching out the window toward Lamersdorf.

Our wonderful medics were the next men to appear., They had a jeep, too. It seems there were quite a few wounded men in Lamersdorf and they were wondering if it were possible to drive down there and get them. There had been jeeps down into Lamersdorf and back and I told them this fact. However, that didn't convince them and so they set out on foot.

Now came the pint-sized 413th. Headquarters men had told me that our company was as big as their battalion! And now I could see it. The battalion from the 413th didn't take any longer to file past me than Love company did. No wonder a company was relieving a battalion. Those boys were exhausted, too. One officer said. "We'll get a jeep to carry those machine guns." Just at that moment there was a man walking by carrying an M-20 machine gun. He dropped it in our jeep. I ran over and told him that it was Love company's jeep and not his but he just kept walking ahead. Well, it turned out that Love company had one more light machine gun.

Finally Bailey appeared. He came quickly and quietly and for a while I thought he was a German. It didn't take us long to get back to Weisweiler and hit the sack. Eddie, who was now acting supply sergeant, and his artificer, Fellmier were still waiting up even though it was about 3 A.M. Max was back in the hospital, having been injured in a jeep accident.

The next day it was my problem to get up to the company. Our battalion headquarters was already in Frenz. Eddie and I drove to Frenz, but we couldn't find our company runner there and the wire to our company was knocked out. I got quite a kick out of the battalion wire men complaining about Love company wiremen. It seems that the battalion men didn't want to go out of Frenz to fix the wire. As a matter of fact they didn't even want to leave the cellar. Of course you couldn't blame them what with a shell coming in every few minutes. But someone had to win the war and as usual the poor line company riflemen had to shoulder the main load.

Eddie got orders to bring in hot chow as soon as it got dark. I was to go up with them. We drove back to Eschweiler to give the mess sergeant the order and to pick up some supplies. I had my complete outfit with me having expected to go forward from Frenz. This included two fragmentation grenades with the levers through the button holes of my combat jacket pocket lapels. This must have made quite a few of the rear echelon boys nervous. One of them finally said, "Hey, boy, that's no way to carry grenades. You better take them off of there." I just smiled and didn't say a word. During my time in the front lines that is the way we carried grenades. I never saw or heard of any accidents even though in some cases the levers were broken off. As long as that pin and the top part of the lever remained in place, it was impossible for the grenade to explode. And those pins were in so tight that sometimes the ring would stretch and break before the pin would come out.

It was a rut-filled muddy road that we took into Lamersdorf that night. The jeep and trailer just about made it. The noise of the motor and mud seemed to be shouting to the Germans that here was a good target. I walked most of the way from Frenz, with my '03 ready. We would have been an easy target for a Jerry patrol.

It seems that things were pretty hot in Lamersdorf that night. The CO decided that it was too much of a risk to feed the first and second platoons so he ordered all the food to be dumped in the street. I can still see those big piles of hot, steaming potatoes, peas and hot dogs on the ground. None of us had had a hot meal for more than twenty-four hours. That is to say that I had not eaten during the last twenty-four hours or more because those K rations were poison to me. I always made use of the soluble coffee and sometimes could take a bite out of the cheese or D bar but that was my limit. Eddie had a squad cooker back in Frenz and we made plenty of coffee during the day. We could have eaten supper back in Eschweiler but didn't take the opportunity. Now my meal was there on the ground. I must have looked like a hungry dog around a full garbage pail The food was piled so high there was plenty that never touched the dirt. I circled around and picked up some bread and then when I thought no one was looking I snatched up a couple of frankfurters and stepped back into the shadows to gulp down my supper.

Headquarters was located in a big building in the center of town, about fifty yards from a church. I stumbled in there in the darkness and tried to find a place to sleep. Naturally, all available sleeping positions were already filled. The only lighted room was a small cellar and that was already taken over by the first sergeant, the officers, and some wounded.

Life was at its lowest ebb during a situation like this. To find yourself cold, and hungry, and sleepy but not being able to get food or warmth or rest is about the toughest situation you could ever run up against in the front lines. Being under fire comes suddenly. But I knew I'd be shivering and stumbling around that building until at least daylight, which didn't come until about eight o'clock in December. But in all the darkness and confusion they were able to find me and put me on guard for a couple of hours that night. Outside of the uncomfortable position, it was otherwise a quiet and peaceful night.

There were rumors flying the next day that Love company must send a patrol cross the Inde River to determine the strength and positions of the Jerries and also to locate a good spot to cross. Announcement of a patrol was always a signal for all riflemen to start shaking with the jitters. Most patrol actions take place at night. And it was bad enough wandering around on your own side at night let alone crossing over into enemy territory. There were all kinds of ugly possibilities. Beside enemy personnel there were booby traps, mines, trip flares, and natural obstructions to worry about while on a patrol.

Red White's name was soon mentioned in the rumors. He was going to lead the patrol. Red had gone AWOL from the hospital in order to come up and rejoin the outfit before we had even left Stolberg.

Still being a comparatively new man in the company and only a basic in headquarters, I never did get any real information on that patrol. I understand that it did take place that night and that they found the trenches on the other side of the river empty. The resistance we were to meet did not come from empty trenches, so I doubt that the information obtained was of much value. They probably did determine the depth of the water, which of course is an important point.

Williams, Reed, Effley, Helmut Hebish and Carl Zurcher, our 300 radio operator and a few others, spent most of the day converting the rooms on the first floor of our building into sleeping quarters. The attic was filled with mattresses and pillows that supplied our entire group.

We had an opportunity to do some letter writing that evening. In one to my wife dated December 1, 1944, I wrote, "I got two yesterday and was very happy. The big surprise though was your radiogram which took about a week to reach me. It was swell to hear that a week ago you were all well and that you were writing regularly.

"Everything is just fine here. The only thing, I need a bath and a shave at present. You know if you don't hear from me regularly it is because sometimes we don't always have the time to write. Sometimes I have time but then I have to clean up. Anyway, darling, I love you and just can't wait till this is over and we can be together again.

"We all can't understand how the Jerries keep going but they do just the same. They (the Jerries) tell us the same thing and generally say the war will end in anywhere from one hour to a few days. (One Jerry had come through our platoon guards one night in Weisweiler and surrendered to a man in the Weapons platoon. He said the war would end in one hour.)"

We were plenty busy the next day but I found time to write again to Jean: "I want to write again to you today because yesterday's letter was too short and snappy. And so I'm taking this first chance, hoping I don't get interrupted.

"First off, I am still in the best of health. And also the weather is okay. But sweetheart, I don't see how I can go on not being with you. It seems so long now and there is no prospect of any quick decision. I may sound downhearted, darling, but it is only because I miss you so. I don't dream so much of our future anymore but just pray and pray for our reunion. When that seems like a near possibility then we can make our plans together. And I am not worried about that part of our future because I know it will be a grand and successful happiness with both of us working and trying as hard as we can for that attainment. I hope you understand what I mean darling. Anyway, to put it briefly, I love you very, very much and my whole future depends on you.

"All the news of my activities are about the same, most of it of course being unprintable. However, we are doing okay and we still have a roof over our heads.

"Our friend Jennings is here making us all laugh. Most of the time he is in a cellar somewhere. He just said, 'If my wife ever asks me to go down to the cellar, there will be a headline in the Inquirer the next morning, 'MAN KILLS WIFE FOR REQUESTING HIM TO GO DOWN TO CELLAR.'

"Our boy Williams, a bazooka man from Washington state, is playing a xylophone. One boy from York, Penna. (Saylor) and a boy from Indiana (Zurcher) are writing letters, too. I am smoking a Harvester cigar after having a lunch of hot chocolate and meat and beans. (K rations) The big clock on he wall is chiming noon. You would never guess where we are and what is going on outside,"

Outside P-51's were making near vertical dives into the very front positions of the enemy, their multiple machine guns and cannons drumming a beautiful tune to our ears. I had to stop writing with such a show going on outside our front door. The planes followed one another in single file and during the course of the dive they passed within few hundred feet of the church steeple. This was the closest support by aircraft that we were to witness during our months in the lines. It was welcomed support, too because we were to attack in that very direction within a few hours.

CHAPTER V
Trouble at the River

Love company was given the mission of taking a huge new factory building to their left front, in the direction of Pier, another small town along the Inde River. Quite a large group of company and battalion officers assembled in the church steeple to witness this movement.

The Second, Third and Weapons platoons moved out in skirmish formation across open fields. Our 81 mm mortars were firing in support and it is said that the lieutenant leading the Third platoon was wounded by this fire. He was a regular army man that had been stationed in Iceland for several years and had come up to Love company as a replacement while we were in Eschweiler. This incident was the beginning of an ever deepening fear of our 81 mm mortar section. Several similar incidents followed this one and it was often debated as to which side Mike Company was fighting on.

Shellfire was the only apparent resistance that our boys met and they soon had control of the factory. Intermittent fire continued to land on Lamersdorf all day and the church steeple was one of their main targets. It was soon after we all had left the church that a shell made a direct hit on the steeple. There was not much damage from this one shell and it is doubtful if we would have been hurt even if we had been in the belfry. During our days in the front lines we were always comparatively safe as long as we were in a building. An AP shell was the only thing, including a rocket of course, that could penetrate those thick stone and brick German houses. Another exception would be a very big shell such as those fired from a railway gun. And these were seldom aimed at front-line troops.

The Letters of a Combat Rifleman

Darkness fell early and quickly and we all wondered if we would get much sleep. The night before the Jerries had made a false attack on Lamersdorf and as a result we were all in need of a good rest.

They had started out by whizzing machine gun bullets up and down the main streets. This sudden sound of German automatic fire in the middle of the night was something that we came to dread. It was a signal for anything to happen. Most of all it meant that we would get very little sleep the rest of that night. Perhaps someone would be killed or captured. You had to face an open window or door and you never knew whether or not the next burst of fire would be at your opening. The tension mounted, too, as the minutes and hours went by. And as the tension mounted the thermometer dropped, until your feet were like two cakes of ice. You couldn't move without danger and to stamp your feet was almost like throwing a spotlight on your position.

I made the second floor that night without anymore noise than an elephant going through a china shop. That was the trouble with moving about in a shell torn house at night. You never knew what you were going to run into or step on next.

An upper story position is always best during almost any attack. The higher position usually gives better and longer avenues of vision; it is harder for the enemy to throw grenades in the upper stories; and it makes grenade throwing easier for yourself.

From my position I could see down one of the main streets in the direction of the church. The German fire soon ceased and all was quiet. Every man in headquarters and for that matter, every man in the company, continued to stand and watch.

It was nearly two hours later that the First sergeant gave the signal for all men to turn in and get some sleep. The two guards on the doors remained at the positions.

Perhaps I had been terribly frightened by the German fire. At any rate, Mother Nature told me that I should relieve myself. All inside toilet facilities were naturally out of order so that front-line riflemen generally used the best available spot. This often enough was in some room in the house that was not being used. However, for some reason or other I decided to go outside into the back yard for my detail.

After informing the guards at both doors, of my mission I stepped out into the open. It was about a minute later that I heard a sizzling noise directly over my head. Immediately I knew it was a grenade!

It landed right in front of me before I could even stand up. Without waiting to pull up my trousers, I whirled and took off in the opposite direction. I wanted to run as far and as fast as I could before the grenade went off. I couldn't see where I was going so after I covered about fifteen yards I flung myself on the ground.

While I was running I shouted at the top of my voice, "Who the hell is throwing grenades?" I yelled because I was sure it was one of our own men and I didn't want him throwing another grenade or firing a burst at me.

While lying on the ground I kept wondering when the grenade was going to explode. Apparently the thrower had not held it after releasing the lever, or else it was a dud.

"Wam-o!" she finally went. I stood up and tucked in my shirt tail and walked back into the house. Miraculously I was unhurt. The grenade tosser turned out to be my young friend, Helmut, who had not received the first sergeant's order. He thought I was a German!

Since three of the platoons had already shoved off, we more or less realized that our sleep would be broken up again. I don't believe that I even got into bed. It was early in the evening that Lieutenant Danowski ordered me to get ready to leave with him at any moment.

The lieutenant and I left Lamersdorf about 10 P.M., heading across the fields toward the factory containing our Second, Third, and Weapons platoons. I was plenty scared and could just about keep up to Danowski who was a very big man and a former track champion. On top of these handicaps I was traveling with full equipment and the only thing he had was a rifle and cartridge belt.

The building was big and modern. We had difficulty in getting through a wire fence that surrounded it. Once inside the grounds we walked about trying to find an entrance or a guard. Everything was deathly silent. The moon must have begun shining brightly because the whole side of the factory seemed to be lit up.

We were greatly relieved when we finally located a guard near a stairway. He gave us a complicated series of directions on how to get to the CP but we located it without too much trouble. The CP was in what looked like the living or sleeping quarters of slave workers. There were tiers of bunks lining the walls and things looked plenty small and crowded.

Lieutenant Thompson, who was leading the Weapons platoon, appeared to be in charge. He was in communication with headquarters, but I can't remember whether it was by wire or radio or both. As long as you are in contact by wire your radio should be turned off in order to save your batteries.

After a short time Lieutenants Danowski and Thompson and I left the factory and approached a small building in the direction of the Inde River which was less than two hundred yards away. Everything was quiet and apparently the officers decided this was the time to cross. We returned to the factory to get the three platoons and they lined up in single file, extending out into the open in the direction of the river.

From the information that I had gathered it seemed that there was the remains of a bridge across the water at this point. What was left of the bridge as far as I could find out was only a steel cable and the Weapons platoon boys were wondering how in the world the machine gun squads were going to get across with their weapons.

The Germans must have been watching us all the time. The column moved out but we didn't move far before all hell broke loose. I never came under such a heavy, concentrated fire before or after. It was here that the good Lord performed another miracle. Not one of our men was even scratched. I was somewhere near the head of the column and we seemed to be walking in and around a lot of piles of steel. I fell flat on my face and up close against a steel pile.

The barrage lifted quickly and the men started coming back. I still hugged the ground and finally a passing form stopped long enough to ask, "Are you hurt?"

"No," I replied and got up on my feet and hurried back into the factory with the rest of the men.

In review of this situation it might be well to mention a few items in a critique. It is best not to deploy your forces but it seems that the Weapons platoon would have been of greater service if they had mounted their guns on the factory side of the river, giving overhead and supporting fire as the riflemen attempted to cross the destroyed bridge. We studied fire and movement back in the States, but many times it was forgotten in the excitement of battle.

It seems, too, that from our advantageous position in the factory we could have had some of the bigger stuff farther back lie in on the area around the other side of the bridge. A preliminary barrage is a giveaway to an attack, but many times it disrupts communications and then the enemy is unable to call for help. Once the opposing riflemen are at grips, a mortar and artillery barrage can't very well be used. Certainly a unit trying to cross a river should be able to call for and receive artillery support.

Anyway, I'm glad we didn't get across the river at this point. I was in the neighborhood of this area about a month later and from the trenches, foxholes, and dugouts that I saw it was apparent that we would have walked into a hornets nest.

The overall strategy was that we were to cross the river at this point and follow down along a railroad in the direction of Lamersdorf, where we were to hook up with the First platoon. The First did successfully cross the river at Lamersdorf, and I believe they made it without the benefit of a bridge because later I was to learn that they lost all their bazookas while crossing the river.

Item (I company) successfully crossed the river at Lamersdorf and I am sure they made it before the bridge was blown up. Another miracle was that Item managed to get all the way up into Lucherberg, a small town on very high ground about a mile or more from Lamersdorf.

From the factory on the edge of Pier we got orders to return to Lamersdorf and try to cross the river there. About this time the First platoon, after crossing the river had sent a patrol up along the railroad tracks toward Pier in order to contact us. This patrol naturally ran into trouble and one of the men was seriously wounded. A boy by the name of House made the rescue. House was later to become a squad leader and then platoon sergeant.

When we reached Lamersdorf we were welcomed by Jerry machine gun bullets flashing into town along the main street leading from the bridge across the Inde.

The platoons got settled in some houses along this street and Danoswki and I proceeded toward the bridge to determine where the machine gun fire was coming from and also to find out if we could possibly cross at that spot. The engineers we met in Lamersdorf said that they had found it impossible to work at the bridge due to the gun fire that was coming in.

The dark earth was ploughed up all around the bridge due to the shell fire. The engineers' tools were lying there on the ground where they had abandoned them. We looked across into the darkness but could see nothing. Everything was quiet.

"Davis, you stay here and watch for that machine gun," Danowski said. "I'm going back into town." He took off and there I was alone again. It didn't take me long to find a partially dug hole to get into. With so many shovels handy I couldn't resist the temptation to make the hole a little deeper.

It wasn't very long until I heard the noise of approaching men. There must have been about thirty engineers and they were dragging along some wire mesh that they intended to throw across the river just above the bridge. I suppose this wire would enable men and machines to cross easier, but of course, it still meant that you had to go through the water.

Either the noise of their digging carried plenty far or else there must have been a Jerry at the other end of the bridge. The engineers were not there more than five minutes when that dark earth started to erupt all over the place. It was more accurate and concentrated Jerry fire. I wasn't down deep enough to hide my entire body and I started to dig with my hands because I couldn't handle the shovel without exposing myself. At the same time I called on God to save me. And He did. And on top of that He performed another miracle. Not one man there was hit.

The officer in charge told the men to start moving back again and then he came over to me to ask if I was going to go back. I explained to the officer who I was and told him I would stay up at the bridge.

After about twenty minutes of silent watching I decided to go back and find out what the score was in Lamersdorf.

"It's okay that you came back," Danowski said, "I was just going to send for you."

It was a dark and dirty cellar we were in and of course it was very crowded. Some of the men had found room to lie down. I just stood and waited. And it wasn't long until I got another assignment. This time I had to go back to battalion headquarters which had advanced already to Lamersdorf.

At headquarters, about three blocks away, we got new orders again. This time we were to go further back and try to cross the river at Frenz.

It was daylight before we reached Frenz, Lieutenant Danwoski and I taking a short cut across the fields while the rest of the men went by the roads. We could see plenty of tanks lined up and waiting for a bridge to be put across the river.

The Letters of a Combat Rifleman

Danwoski was as usual setting a hot pace and somehow or other I lost him as he entered a building. I waited and finally he reappeared and told me to head the column down toward the river. It was stretched out like a snake and ran all over town, the men standing almost asleep on their feet. They wouldn't even answer me when I asked them where the head of the column was and refused to turn and go in the direction I instructed them to move in.

We were all plenty exhausted when we reached the other side of the river across a narrow foot bridge, and then to make matters worse, Danowski gave the order for everyone to get down and crawl on there stomachs. Believe it or not, those men crawled all the way from Frenz to Lamersdorf, paralleling the railroad bank that followed the river. I got enough of it and I only went about two hundred yards. All the time Danowski kept shouting for everyone to get lower and lower. My arms and my back and legs felt like they were being pressed down by one hundred pound weights. My neck wanted to drop my head into the soft thick grass. To top it all, I was hungry but I didn't have the strength to push my hand under my cartridge belt to get into my jacket pocket where I had a D bar. I don't know how the BAR men and machine gunners made out. The mortar men and ammunition carriers likewise suffered a lot more than us riflemen.

It is inconceivable that Danowski ordered this long-distance crawl. The men were tired and hungry and it was an effort to just walk, let alone crawl. From information that he had just received from battalion he must have known that the ground along both sides of the railroad had been taken, up as far as Lamersdorf.

It was a relief when he told me to get up and follow him. And he immediately took off over the railway embankment and headed in a two o'clock direction away from the head of the column, which meant that we were now in the opposite side of the railroad right of way. He surely knew that area was safe.

We passed plenty of empty trenches as we approached a group of farm buildings about six hundred yards away. There was plenty of German equipment lying around and as we entered the enclosure formed by the buildings, we saw some of the owners of that equipment. They were cold and their blood marked the stone paving.

This building turned out to be a CP of a Second battalion outfit. Danowski took about a half hour to confer with the officers present. I was standing in the doorway of one room filled with quite a bunch of riflemen when suddenly an explosion and flash sent fragments of steel into all the four walls and ceiling. It was a hand grenade set off accidentally. The owner was severely hurt but the other dozen or so in the room were untouched. I sought out another room to get away from all the blood and confusion. My biting appetite had disappeared.

The two of us took off in a direction toward the bridge that spanned the river at Lamersdorf, continuing to pass many foxholes and trenches, all empty. As we neared the railroad, which was about three hundred yards from the river at this point we came upon a covered foxhole. It was a two-man affair. Danowski ripped off one end and I opened the other. There were two "supermen" crouching down beside their machine gun. The same one no doubt that had been spraying Lamersdorf the night before.

"Hands up," we ordered and out they came with their hands above their head. It was at this point that I made a big mistake by suggesting that I take the prisoners back. I headed them toward the bridge and immediately a barrage of shells started to fall on us. The zinging steel fragments finally forced me to hit the dirt and of course the Jerries immediately followed suit. That was all right but then they started to crawl for a shell hole. I started to shout and motion for them to stop. We hadn't taken time to search them and undoubtedly they were still carrying grenades. They stopped.

After this fire lifted I turned away from the bridge and headed the two prisoners upstream toward Frenz, figuring on crossing at the first shallow part. The engineers had not made any progress that I could see so there was no point in trying to get across the river at the bridge.

Danowski joined the head of the column. Glancing to my left I could see that he had them up on their feet now and they were moving along the railroad toward a small factory about four hundred yards up the tracks, in the direction of Lucherburg.

The River Inde was not much more than a creek but the prisoners were very reluctant to get wet. I couldn't blame them for that and if they got wet that would mean, of course, that I would too. I was afraid also that the current, which seemed to be rather swift all along, would knock me down and that I might come up minus my rifle.

Keeping the two Jerries about ten yards in front of me we finally reached a group of houses near the foot bridge where a bunch of GI rear echelon boys obligingly stood the prisoners up against a wall and searched them for me. Some questioning disclosed the fact that they were both only seventeen years old.

The M.P. at the PW station in Franz recorded the capture and asked me to stay while he searched them again. I was embarrassed a little when he produced another hand grenade from one of their pockets. He striped them clean of all their possessions and I doubt if they ever got anything back, including the personal stuff. As far as I noticed they had nothing of any value or special importance.

Walking from Frenz to Lamersdorf along the trench system I witnessed the familiar battlefield rubble. There was all kinds of equipment and personal effects strewn along the trench system. It was there that I acquired my first white phosphorous hand grenade. Ever since Munsterbusch, I had been pestering Max and then Eddie to get some WP grenades. At least seventy-five percent of the American equipment was inferior to the German, but in hand grenades we had the edge. Every rifleman should carry at least two hand grenades, one fragmentation and one WP. Neither grenade is apt to stop a good man but the WP is more likely to hit its mark. The WP grenade of course cannot be used in situations where the shower of sparks may spray over into the thrower or his comrades. As I never had an opportunity to throw that WP that I picked up, or any other WP for that matter, I cannot state their true value in combat.

In Lamersdorf, I stopped for about two hours for some rest and a cup of coffee. Eddie had taken over the building that we had occupied. I also reported our prisoner toll at battalion headquarters and gave some information to a tank captain concerning the bridges across the Inde.

Lamersdorf was under spasmodic shellfire and one of these bursts almost ended my combat days. I was crossing the street from the old Love CP to the building containing the battalion command post when a small mortar shell landed and burst within five feet of me. Fragments hit two men standing in the hallway of battalion headquarters but miraculously I was untouched. I knew then that I must have a guardian angel.

Gene Bailey and Max Delrogh walked into town just before I left. Max was just out of the hospital and was anxious to get back on the job as company supply sergeant.

With a squad cooker under my arm I started out for the river. These Coleman gasoline stoves, small enough to put in your jacket pocket, (if you weren't wearing a cartridge belt) were or should be rated as one of the best pieces of equipment that was ever issued to the infantry during the war. Hot coffee was the one thing that kept us going during that winter on the German front and the Coleman gasoline stove made that hot coffee possible. It was also good of course, for cooking bouillon, hash, beans or what have you.

Just before I reached the bridge I passed a barnyard where I witnessed one of the most heart-rending scenes of my combat days. There were about a dozen crying, squealing little pigs running about the huge body of their dead mother. The mother pig had been killed by shell fire. And all those little ones were doomed to die of starvation. The German civilians had fled. Soldiers did not have time to stop and feed starving animals. And what value did the lives of a dozen baby pigs have when men were dying every minute. But I was touched and my heart cried out for an end to this death and destruction.

The engineers had succeeded in stretching the wire netting across the river. Nevertheless there was a Sherman tank stuck right in the middle of the stream. The current was swift and the water was cold but I didn't hesitate. I knew that any minute another barrage might come in and so I started across. I had the squad cooker under my left arm, my '03 gripped at the balance, held just above the surface of the water.

The current swirled around the tank and almost caused me to lose my footing. The water was chest high and so cold I was gasping for breath. And to think that it could have all been avoided if I had only had sense enough to force the prisoners to wade the stream at the bridge and order them to keep going to the rear. They could not have escaped on the other side because there were plenty of engineers in the vicinity.

As soon as I reached the other bank I took off on the run toward the factory building along the railroad. It was about an eight hundred yard dash and I had to hit the ground a couple of times in order to rest and catch my breath. I could have made it walking, but I didn't want to take any chances.

Just inside the building, several GIs had a big bonfire burning and I got as close to this as possible in order to try to dry my uniform. The men standing around the fire couldn't tell me where Love Company was located.

With water still oozing from my shoes I started a dash up the road toward the next building, about three hundred yards away. I no sooner hit the middle of the road than a barrage of WP shells started to come in at just the spot I was headed for. Some shells landed about two hundred yards to my left and it seemed impossible for a two-man wire team working there to escape the spray. I slowed up and hoped and prayed that the barrage would lift before I reached the building. Once again my prayers were answered.

Those WP shells must have been some short rounds from our guns. I never knew the Jerries to use WP.

The building I now entered turned out to be a briquette factory. A briquette is a block of compressed coal. Almost every home in Germany burned briquettes. Only a fine powdery dust remained after the coal burned.

Like most German factories it was big and modern and well built of brick, stone, and concrete. A regiment could have been housed in its vast spaces. And a million artillery shells could not have shaken its foundations. Its smoke stacks were perforated but still standing.

Long conveyors tracked back and forth and up and down. The briquettes in the conveyors and those piled on the floors were all afire and gave me the feeling of floating through clouds of mist and fog. For a change, I was warm but the smoke and dust clouded my eyes and choked me. There were plenty of men about including some gravely wounded. But nobody could tell me where Love Company was.

After a short drying-out period near the burning coal, I started to explore the vast factory. Entering an office I noticed some shotgun shells lying on a desk. They were like magnets to me. I reasoned that there might be some firearms about and so I started a systematic search of the big roll top desk. After a fruitless look I walked out just in time to see several men placing satchel charges of TNT against another door of the room. Close calls were becoming an hourly occurrence with me!

I finally located Captain Hallahan and a few men of company headquarters. The CO was on a sort of balcony peering through his binoculars in the direction of Lucherberg. It was raining now and starting to get dark. Captain Hallahan disappeared in the falling darkness and there I was, lost again. It was midnight when I finally heard that a wire team from our battalion headquarters was going to go up into Lucherberg in order to contact Item and Love Companies. During the interval I had been trying to get dry and had managed to crawl under a stove and get about an hour's rest.

CHAPTER VI

Lucherberg

The distance to Lucherberg was one mile. We started out with two and one-half miles of wire and there were about ten men in the column, including several who were supposed to know the way. There were about five stragglers from Love Company beside myself.

You can judge the size of the factory and the sense of direction of the guides when you consider that we laid one and one-half miles of wire before we left the factory area. It seemed that we unrolled a mile of wire before we even got out of the building. Since we came out on the wrong side, it took almost another half mile of wire before we were headed in the right direction.

Crawling under freight cars and crossing several railroad tracks we went up over a very steep embankment. There were more steep embankments all around and a wooded section just ahead. The wire spools were squealing and sending out a terrible disquieting racket. I couldn't stand the noise so I finally urged the column to stop while I poured some oil from my oil and thong case onto the rusty spindles. The oil did the trick and we were all greatly relieved.

About this time the leaders got to arguing about which direction to move in. After some anxious moments they came to an agreement and we started off again, entering the woods soon afterward. It was tough going through small closely grouped trees and several times we almost lost some of the men at the end of the column. I often wondered how I reached the top of the cliff that we encountered at the other end of the woods. Once on top of this cliff we were on the edge of Lucherberg. The nearest house was a less than three hundred yards away and we were soon safe in the cellar. The wire men were so anxious to get into the cellar they dropped the spool of wire at the front door and company headquarters didn't know they had a wire connection with battalion unit the next afternoon!

The cellar was full of men but I didn't recognize anyone. I knew of course that they were Love and Item men. One fellow was sitting at a table and there were others grouped around him, listening and talking. The stories that followed on the Battle of Lucherberg were as varied and wide ranging as the fighting that took place on this cliff.

From various sources during the next year I was to hear about ten different versions of I company's battle to take and hold Lucherberg. From the information that I gathered it seems that Item would have been pushed out of the town had not Love company arrived just in the nick of time. King company and units from the Second battalion entered Lucherberg, too, and helped beat off the counterattacks. But it was Love company that bore the main counterattacks and inflicted the most damage on the attackers.

Item did arrange and carry out a truce with the German paratroopers that they were grappling with. This truce I understand was requested by the Germans so that they could pick up their wounded. There were many Item men wounded, too, including Lieutenant John J. Olson. commanding officer.

Somehow or other the Germans disarmed fifteen Item men during the truce. It was at this point that a German paratroop officer threatened to shoot the wounded Lieutenant Olson and then proceeded to do so. The Item men were helpless but demanded their rifles. The paratroop officer then refused to live up to the truce and he demanded that the Item men be held prisoners. However, there was a German colonel doctor present who overruled the paratrooper and insisted that his side live up to the truce. The Item men received their rifles, but when they went to use them, which was immediately, they found them empty. They rushed from the building but twelve of them were killed or wounded before they could get outside. Three men escaped to tell the story.

Soon after this episode, the Germans gave Item just ten minutes to get out of town. I have been told that eight men from Item immediately took off toward the rear. According to the information that I received there were only a handful of men left in Item and there were no officers at all.

The following is a publicity account of the action, handed out by division. I know that some of it is false. For instance, Love company did not wade the rive three times.

"Lucherberg, a citadel town perched on a five hundred foot high hill with a steep cliff on its northern approach, became the next objective after Inden fell Dec. 3. Striking again in pitch darkness, Co. I, Third battalion 415th, led by Lieutenant John J. Olson, crossed the river, headed for Lucherberg as the Nazi garrison slept.

"By scaling the cliff, Co. I riflemen knew they could surprise the defenders. Climbing upward, the raider pried three houses from the rim of the silent town before they were discovered.

The Letters of a Combat Rifleman

"It was then that the lieutenant radioed back: 'We are very close to them now; they are firing with everything they have; I am going to rush them.'

"When enemy counterattacks threatened to overwhelm the company Lieutenant Olson, laying long odds, called for fire on this position. Artillery promptly responded.

"Almost six hours later, Lieutenant John D. Shipley, Appleton, Wis., who had taken over when Lieutenant Olson was wounded, reported, 'We have so many dead Germans in front of us that we can't see to shoot!'

"Co. L. had been stopped outside the town at daylight by heavy fire. Refusing to give up, the riflemen now retraced their steps, wading the river they had crossed, and moved south. Splashing in the cold waist-deep water a third time, the company angled in from the south to aid Co. I which still defied frantic enemy attempts to be dislodged. Other companies implemented the attack. By late afternoon, the 415th had taken Lucherberg. The cost had been only thirteen casualties while more than four hundred Nazis had been killed or captured.

"Reluctant to relinquish this strategically located town, Germans countered with ten tanks and supporting infantry. A seventy-ton Tiger Royal tank fired point blank into Co. F's Command Post. Sergeant George E. Burns, Findlay, Ohio, rushed from the building and fired his bazooka—only seven feet from the tank. The bulky tank waddled away in flaming retreat.

"The Corps Commander sent the message: 'Congratulations to the 104th Division on its superb performance in capturing Lucherberg,'" The performance was good enough to merit a Presidential Citation for our battalion.

It must have been about 2 A.M. when I finally lay down to sleep. Every available spot on the cellar floor was occupied except the coal pile. It didn't feel like a feather mattress, but it was a welcome spot after almost thirty hours of continuous movement.

Before daylight I had my next assignment. Delakas, a tall, young bespeckled runner was ordered by Lieutenant Danowski to guide the five riflemen who had come up with the wire team over to the First platoon. The First had some difficulty in getting into Lucherberg. Hence the stragglers.

It was still dark when we left for the First platoon area. Delakas took the lead and I brought up the rear. I went along in order to accompany Delakas back to company headquarters as it was the policy to always travel in pairs during the hours of darkness.

Daylight wasn't far off. We could plainly see a mortar crew beside their gun as we circled a huge shell crater. Another half block and we entered 1st platoon headquarters. It was a big house and most of the First platoon was located there. There was a guard at the front door and one in the kitchen. I stood and talked with the guard at the door while Delakas took the men down to the CP in the cellar. He also had to warn the platoon leader of a dawn attack. This information had been obtained from one of the prisoners taken during the night.

When he returned to the front door, Delakas suggested, "Let's stop across the street here and pick up some rations." My answer was, "No, let's get back to our building. We don't want to get caught outside if they start a counterattack." We were still arguing several minutes later when the guard in the kitchen rushed out into the hallway and whispered. "There's about fifteen Jerries going by outside!"

I hurried over into the kitchen and just then another squad started to file past. Instinctively, I raised my rifle and was just going to squeeze off a shot when someone grabbed my arm and whispered, "Don't shoot yet."

That was right. And so I lowered the '03, waiting until they could alert the other men.

Two or three of us opened up on the next bunch of supermen. Several hit the ground and the rest disappeared. The range had been only about ten yards but there was a stone wall and trees intervening. Two small sheds were also available for cover and protection.

As the smoke cleared I saw two men looking around the corner of the church, which was next door. Unknown to them of course, was the fact that I was on the same side of the building as they were and they were facing me in line. They both fell with one shot. Later in the day the Germans were to duplicate this trick against us.

Another man sneaking along the church wall was the next victim. At least he fell forward on his face and remained motionless. Searching the area later we found only a few bodies and one seriously wounded man. This wounded man started to shout and cry as soon as he was hit and he kept it up for several hours.

About this time at least one of the Jerries became aware of our location and he fired a rifle grenade at the kitchen window. It hit the corner of the frame but nobody was hurt.

This is when I became a second story man. And from here I progressed up to the attic. During the next two hours there was intermittent rifle fire from both sides. Due no doubt to my high position I was doing about fifty percent of the firing from our building.

The chain of events that followed may not be in proper sequence because so many things happened that cold, wet day in December. The weather conditions were very adverse for good shooting. Every now and then we had bursts of hail and some light rain. However, at no time did I have any trouble seeing through my Weaver 330 scope. I had GI toilet tissue in my upper left-hand jacked pocket and the few times the scope did get wet I wiped it off quickly with the olive drab color tissue. It would have been suicide to use white paper or cloth.

The Jerries were shooting back and some of them were very close. It was about this time that they made a double on us, killing Sergeant Evans, squad leader, and wounding a man who was standing in back of Evans. They had been shooting out a window directly below me. Evans' body was lying on the second floor landing when I went down to the cellar to report more Jerries coming in across the open plain to our left front. The wounded man was lying on a bunk in the CP, his head swathed in bandages. I believe Evans was hit in the neck. It is my firm belief that a cigarette was their downfall. There was a newly lighted one just below the window.

It was suicide to be anywhere near a window, especially since some of the Nazis were in the next building, only twenty feet away. To light a cigarette near an opening on this dark December day was like putting a match to your funeral pyre.

An enlisted man named Fisher, I believe, joined me in the attic and he got in plenty of shooting, too, He appeared to be an Indian and no doubt inherited his good fighting qualities from his ancestors. However, Fisher missed a couple of shots due to the fact that his M-1 action snapped on an empty chamber. The rifle no doubt needed cleaning. The bolt failed to go back far enough to pick up a new round after it had ejected the old case. A new M-1 or one that is dirty will very often fail in this manner. This is why a man should never be issued a new rifle when going into combat. This applied to all types of rifles, including bolt action. This latter type will not fail to function because it is new, but it will operate one hundred percent easier if it has had a couple of thousand rounds fired through it.

The Jerries coming in across the open fields worried me plenty. There they were, slowly walking into the town and I couldn't do a thing about it. The range was one thousand yards or more, and after a few shots I told Fisher we might as well quit because we were only wasting ammunition. And every time we fired we were taking an awful chance of being spotted by the Germans next door.

There was a lone haystack about seven hundred yards in front of us just like in those landscape targets we used in the Pennsylvania national guard training. I knew that some of the supermen were stooping behind this, and so I decided to try to set it on fire with a tracer.

Much to my disappointment I never saw or heard of any other riflemen ever using tracer ammunition in combat. Also, there were very few machine gunners that used the tracers that came spaced every fourth round in their ammunition belts. They took the tracers out and replaced them with ball ammunition. The only advantage to this practice is that it offered me a source of supply. Tracer ammunition was never issued to riflemen in the ETO.

I don't recall ever seeing German riflemen using tracers but then don't forget that we were facing the leftovers from a four year war. Most of the men in front of us were old men, young boys and a lot of non infantry soldiers. One young German officer, wounded by us that day, said that he had just graduated as a pilot officer but that he had to spend four months in the infantry in the front lines to complete his training!

But don't think that we were having any picnic. The fact that their equipment and leaders were so superior to ours just about made things equal.

Their machine gunners, more experienced men, no doubt, never hesitated to use tracers when the situation called for them, and with good effect.

According to army training, tracers are used primarily for target designation and also for observation of fire or range estimation. With such strong emphasis in training on cover and concealment, American infantrymen naturally reasoned that they were giving away their cover and concealment by using tracers.

The psychological effect of tracers was never mentioned in training. Yet that perhaps is the most important feature concerning their use. Perhaps I am different from the average person, but when I could see bullets and projectiles flashing across the sky or over my head, I was more impressed than if I had seen nothing at all. Also I was more apt to duck or hit the ground when tracers were fired in my direction. Remember, when you duck or hit the ground in combat, you are immediately out of action and you become a sitting target. That is exactly what the enemy wants to do, pin you down and then lay mortar and artillery fire in on top of you.

A tracer could flash five hundred yards away and I would immediately become hesitant and detracted from my main mission. Sometimes I hit the ground. From my experiences in combat and on target ranges, a bullet must pass within three or four yards of you or else you do not know that a bullet has been anywhere near. Within this short radius you can hear a crack, like a whip. In the noise and excitement of combat you very seldom hear the report of the rifle. Hence it takes very close or accurate fire with ordinary ball ammunition to stop advancing infantry while with tracers the fire can be inaccurate and less heavy and still obtain just as good if not better results.

Perhaps you will say that I have discounted the fact that you give away your position by using tracers. My answer is that the Germans used tracers very often and we were never able to locate accurately the guns that fired them. Even the artillery with their college mathematicians and flash and sound apparatus were only able to pick up the locations of a very small percentage of German artillery. Contrary claims of course can and will be made but proof of these claims can never be shown. The only knocked out German artillery pieces we ever saw were those abandoned along the road during a breakthrough.. These in most cases were knocked out by our armored columns.

My first two shots penetrated about the middle of the stack, but did not set it afire. The third round struck the top of the stack and ricocheted off at a ninety degree angel. You can bet I wondered what I had hit! Later we found a lot of personal equipment in back of that haystack.

As the Germans moved in closer they got in line with a building directly across the street from our house and consequently we couldn't get a close shot at any of them. There was one row of houses between us and the edge of the town. The First platoon had made a mistake common with inexperienced troops. the CP was located correctly. It was a big building, a rectory and was formerly the German CP. But the other half of the platoon should have been in the houses on the edge of the town instead of in a barn to our rear.

The Germans were making plenty of mistakes, too, and they had suffered heavy casualties during that first hour at daybreak. They didn't employ any fire and movement tactics and had no support from any other units. One lone tank would have spelled our doom. Our bazookas were all lost in the river crossing! I was informed of this fact when I first became acquainted with the platoon leader, Sergeant Smart. The sergeant made his way up to the attic just a few minutes after I heard a burst of fire from the second floor.

"Who is firing that machine gun?" I shouted from the attic. "Cut it out."

Sergeant Marion D. Smart came up the stairway and I was a little surprised to see that the machine gun was a Thompson. It never occurred to me that Smart was the platoon leader or that he was even a noncommissioned officer. It was very seldom that rank insignia was ever worn. Our Timberwolf shoulder patch was occasionally displayed. However, the submachine gun was usually the mark of a squad or platoon leader. It was with no thought of rank that I proceeded to tell Sergeant Smart just how to employ his weapon. I believed I was right in telling him not to use it against single targets, but he naturally ignored me as I was a perfect stranger to him and he no doubt felt and could see by my uniform that I was a replacement. Replacements had no netting on their steel helmets and, of course, did not wear the division insignia.

It was not long before I realized that Smart was the leader and also that he was a good one. He ordered the telephone line to be run up to the attic and then proceeded to have mortar fire placed upon the advancing Germans and also tried to hit the haystack. But this effort proved fruitless, too; the small 60 mm mortar shells dropped in the big open fields like small pebbles in the ocean. The Germans across the street continued to get reinforcements. With some good fire and movement tactics I believe they were now strong enough to take our building. We kept pecking away at every chance, especially Fisher, Smart, and myself and perhaps this is what discouraged any movement on their part.

It was just about at this point that a German stepped from a side door of a house to my right front. He was tall and erect and looked as if he were dressed and groomed for a parade or review. The range was less than one hundred yards. He was standing still and appeared to be looking around and trying to decide just where to move next. The shot from my '03 ended his indecision. But that's all it did; it was a clean miss! He leaped like an antelope into the doorway and disappeared before I could eject the empty case. It was just a short time later that another German darted from behind a shed and entered the same doorway. It was impossible to get a shot in.

But I missed other good shots that day and also later. The boys in company headquarters never heard about the misses. I was giving them a shot by shot description over the phone, omitting all my mistakes.

Analyzing my misses is not an easy job. It must be remembered that conditions vary greatly, especially between target ranges and actual combat. I don't mean to say that range practice is worthless. Everything is the same in the course of firing the rifle except position and of course the natural strain of knowing that someone is also shooting at you. Since I was a very careful man, this knowledge of the fact that someone was also trying to hit me, did not add anymore butterflies to my stomach or "bring the lump up" anymore than if I were on the firing line in an important rifle or pistol match.

The firing positions are different because you do not have the opportunity to assume those positions that you learned on the target range. It is absolutely foolish to suppose that a rifleman would take time to adjust and use his rifle sling in combat.

During wartime, men should be trained to fire the rifle without the sling. It would save hours of time. Also, they should be allowed to assume any position they want while learning to fire the rifle. A box or bench or pile of sandbags should be provided for the beginner. Then he would be learning under near combat conditions. Also, he would be learning how to shoot the rifle properly and not how to assume a correct position. America's best riflemen attend the N.R.A. registered matches. Watch the positions of our best riflemen and you will notice that very few assume the standard army position. Teach position shooting, yes, but don't insist on a perfect position. Insist on a perfect sight picture, proper trigger control, and breathing. Fire fifty percent of all practice and match shots from the off-hand or standing position. Have more courses in searching fire. It might even be better to start rifle training with the standing position, allowing the rifle to be rested of course. Recoil is felt less in the standing position and this factor enters very much into the picture in regards to new trainees. Off-hand is one of the easiest positions to assume, especially if you have a rest, hence nearly all of the time could be spent in obtaining and emphasizing proper sight alignment.

Perhaps my misses were due to incorrect sight picture. I had had very little experience with rifle scopes. As I found out later, the point of impact was low and to the left. One of the wounded Germans had been shot through the right hand. A man that I had fired at several times was hit in the right side of the head. Another German got hit when he cut sharply to the left as he was running away from me. We can add to this the fact that all of my shots were in the standing position, most of the time half bent over in order to shoot through the small attic window and the holes in the roof. The blowing curtains added to the hazy picture.

The Germans were closing in on us from three sides. The point that worried me most was the house directly across the street from my attic window. It had a steep slate roof and it was practically intact and therefor we could not see if there was anyone in the attic. The muzzle of a rifle could be placed right up to a small opening, the shooter could take careful aim and one of us would be kaput. This, of course, is the situation where I called for a bazooka man and found that the bazookas had all been lost.

Sergeant Smart sent up a rifle grenadier. Here was a fine example of the training in the States. The man did not even know how to put the grenade launcher on the end of his rifle. I could see that he was scared to death and this made me plenty mad and I let the man know that he was a sad sack. But after all it wasn't his fault. He probably had had about twelve hours instruction three of four months ago on rifle grenades and had experienced shooting three dummy rounds. If he went through Camp Wheeler, Ga., he also had the benefit of seeing another man shoot two or three live rifle grenades. So how could you expect this man to come confidently up the stairs, whip out his grenade launcher and without hesitation, place it on the end of his rifle, and with eager anticipation ask for the target to be designated?

It is easy to figure out his reasoning. He was almost as much afraid of the rifle grenade as he was of the Germans. He no doubt figured that he would be a sitting duck for the enemy. Perhaps he feared that he might hit the window frame and have the grenade burst in his face.

Sergeant Smart came upstairs again and ended the boy's fears by grabbing the rifle and launcher and proceeding to pour two grenades into the middle of the slate roof. There was no hesitation or sign of fear. Like a good, intelligent soldier he stood so that the muzzle of the rifle was about three feet away from the window. I shuddered as I stood and watched and prayed that he wouldn't hit the frame.

Since we had only two antitank grenades, I asked the sergeant to fire just one, but he used his own judgment again and fired both. They opened up a good view of the interior of the attic and so that ended most of my fears in that direction

Some lively action followed this grenade launching. Three Jerries were crawling up a ditch toward a double house right next to our building. They had plenty of guts. But a little more grey matter would have gotten them a lot father along that road. We met their first appearance with a hail of lead. That is Smart, Fisher, and myself. I don't believe that any of the riflemen on the lower floors could see them.

The Jerries were good soldiers. They fired right back at us! Their fire was just as inaccurate as ours, unless they were shooting at the windows on the lower floors. We were shooting from holes in the slate roof and they probably did not suspect the fire was coming from the attic. If a piece of slate had dropped on the floor I know I would have covered it and no doubt Fisher and Smart would have ducked, too. A little more fire and some quick movement, instead of crawling, would have placed the three Germans safely in the house beside us.

When they stopped crawling we could not see the third man and so we assumed he had been hit. The other two still exposed their heads. Either they could not get lower behind the bank or else they did not know that we were in the attic looking down on them. We all fired at the two men several times and they remained motionless. Naturally, we assumed they had been hit, too.

About five minutes later, the unseen German suddenly jumped to his feet and started to race down the middle of the road. The range was less than one hundred fifty yards. All three of us opened up but the Jerry safely made an opening between two houses. I don't know why he did not run directly across the road and into a house just opposite him. There were no houses on the side they were on except the two just ahead of them that they were trying to reach. It would have been practically suicide to run for those two houses because that would mean that he was running right into our fire. But we couldn't hit them standing still so he might have made it.

About this time I began to feel hungry. It was no trouble to loosen and drop my cartridge belt and reach for that D bar, the one I was too weak to reach for just about twenty-four hours earlier. Remember, my last meal had been eaten about two days ago. During this time I had had about four hours sleep. That D bar sure tasted good. And despite the rain and hail I was thirsty enough to almost empty my canteen of water.

It was almost half an hour later that another one of the "dead" Germans leaped up and took off down the street. I was the only one to fire at him. It was no trouble to get him in the scope. The cross hairs centered in the middle of his back and I squeezed it off just as he started to cut to the left to make the opening between the houses. At the same instant he stumbled, fell over a pile of bricks and disappeared from sight. Sergeant Smart later reported seeing the body.

German machine gun fire was the next annoying factor. It came from the same direction as the three crawling men. Fisher said he knew where the gun was set up. And I had a good idea. There was a thick hedgerow and a much higher bank along the road about two hundred yards away and this combination offered excellent cover.

Through my Weaver scope the area appeared much brighter and enlarged but it was impossible to pick up any target. With the rifle scope focused on the head of the man one hundred twenty-five yards away it was impossible to determine whether he was dead or alive. This is where a good pair of binoculars or a small spotting scope would have proved very valuable. Either one of these glasses would have disclosed the fact that this last "dead" German was really dead. A bullet had entered his right temple. Of course we didn't know this at the time and the fact that this third man might jump up and start running kept me on edge until the very end of the fire fight.

There was only one thing to do to quiet the Jerry machine gun. That was to pour plenty of lead into that hedgerow. Fisher passed the news around downstairs about the probable location of the gun and told the boys to get ready to fire on that spot on my signal.

"Watch my tracer," I shouted as loud as I could. Taking aim I sent a red streak right into the hedge at the middle section. The responding fire was just about typical of the average Timberwolf outfit. Fisher and I were the only riflemen who opened up!

During this fight it was impossible to judge time but I began to get worried for fear that darkness would come and the Jerries would still be lodged in the houses around us.

From our experiences at Munsterbusch we all knew that as soon as the shadows started to creep, the Jerries would follow suit.

"We gotta do something to put those Jerries out of town before dark." I suggested to Sergeant Smart.

"They're sending a squad from another company up along that row of houses to clear them out, was Smart's reply. Smart, of course, was still in telephone communication with company headquarters.

It wasn't long before I looked down and saw quite a group of men standing on the street corner right beside the house into which we had fired the two rifle grenades!

I shouted a warning right away. "Get off that street! There's Jerries in that house right beside you!"

Casually they entered the house. I counted twelve men.

About five minutes later a man dropped out of a side window and preceded to walk across the interceding plot of grass toward the next house about fifteen yards away. He had to go over an eight foot wall to get into the next yard. As he reached the halfway mark I shouted, "Throw a grenade over the wall!"

Almost at the same instant two hand grenades sailed over the wall, but in the wrong direction! They landed almost at the feet of the GI. And at the same time an automatic weapon rattled off a burst of fire from the house right beside ours. The muzzle blast raised quite a cloud of dust and smoke and I knew the gunner's exact location but I would have had to have a one hundred and eighty degree angle gun to get him because he was on the same side of the street that I was on. To top it all there were several rifle shots from the house that the GI was approaching. This was the same house that the two men entered after I had fired at the one standing in front of the door.

Of course the GI fell. And I later heard that he was an officer and had been killed. Despite the fact that he was apparently dead, the two other GIs dashed out and picked him up and carried him back into the house on the corner. For some strange reason the Germans did not fire on the rescuers. It would have been perfectly legal as they were combatants and not aid men. Where were our aid men? German medics had been busy all morning.

Here was a perfect example of the lack of training in the States. That American officer had practically committed suicide. He used none of the tactics he had been taught, probably for the simple reason that the teaching had been piecemeal and insufficient. How could he automatically do the right thing when he received such little training in fire and movement and other related subjects. What good did all the jumble of subjects do him when he needed weapons and fire fight training and not ju-jit-su, parades, long marches, aircraft identification, bayonet drill, malaria control and grenade throwing?

The time spent trying to learn aircraft identification could have much better been put to use in learning how to move against and take a group of heavily defended houses. Even anti-aircraft gunners could not tell the difference between our planes and the German planes. What good did it do riflemen to spend twenty or so hours on this subject over a period of months what the AA boys couldn't learn even with years of training?

Five or six men should have all made for that house at the same time. The other men should have opened up with a heavy fire on all openings. Against good troops this plan may have still failed but against the enemy we were facing it could not fail. And it did not fail.

Realizing that the outfit across the street was of little help, Smart and I worked out or own plan. The sergeant organized a force of six men and moved out toward the double house right beside us. On my signal the men remaining in our building opened fire. This time there were not dissenters. As soon as the first man had entered the ground floor, I started on the windows on the upper floors, putting at least one shot into every opening. From here I progressed across the street, keeping my fire always a little ahead of Smart and his men.

In less than thirty minutes this small force reached the last house on the edge of town without a single casualty. Many bodies littered their path and the roundup included about ten prisoners. The plan did not fail. It was a great success! The battle of Lucherburg was temporarily over.

We moved about the streets and searched all the houses. The dead bodies came in for some searching too. As I felt the wrist of one man for a watch I suddenly realized that he was alive. His arm was warm. I grabbed his shoulder to turn him over and he started to scream and cry. He was pretty shot up and so we left him there with the idea of letting some of the German prisoners come and pick him up. After all my searching I ended up empty handed. Most of all I wanted a German pistol. One body that lay about thirty yards from a farm building had a pistol holster with flap closed, plainly visible on the left side. However, there were reports that one of the antitank men had been just hit by a sniper in this area and so I hung close to the building and finally decided not to take the chance. Another GI stood there debating the same question. He, too, decided to wait.

I located most of company headquarters in a building just up the street from the first platoon CP. In short order the company CP was moved to the priest's home and the platoons moved up to positions along the edge of the town. Some of the Third platoon occupied the house just across the street from the CP, the same one that we had fired the rifle grenades into. One antitank gun crew and headquarters located across the street from us and a little to the rear. Another gun crew was right up on the edge of the town and to the left of the Third platoon. Also in the town were units of the Second battalion as well as most of our battalion.

This was the situation as darkness fell that cold day in December. There were two rooms and a hallway in the cellar of the CP. There was no heat in the building, not even in the cellar. Besides the eighteen or twenty men in company headquarters, there were also crowded in that hell hole, forward observers from Mike company, Cannon company, Division artillery, and an artillery flash and second outfit. These observers had either radio or wire men with them. Altogether there must have been about thirty men trying to live in this small space.

We started out with three men on guard, one on the telephone and one on the radio. That meant that each man had to stand two or three times each night because the officers, First Sergeant, and communications sergeant never took turns on the phone or radio or on guard. Naturally none of the men from the other outfits pulled any guard duty.

White, the first sergeant who had made us police the soccer field back in Holland, was now pulling the same duty with Love Company. He had joined us in Munsterbusch. He was a regular army man and had only a few years to go to retire on a pension. Being a southern man it was only natural that he pick another rebel to be his assistant. This assistant was a tall lanky man and rather nervous. He was in charge of making up the phone and guard schedules and managed to exclude his own name from the list. This left White with nothing to do but sleep, rest and eat, if he could find anything to eat. It also meant that he did not have to leave the cellar at any time. The lists and schedules were all fouled up and there were plenty of arguments.

Chapter VII
Counterattack

The events that took place during the next forty-eight hours are sort of all jumbled together now. I was not keeping my diary any longer and of course there was no time to write home. I can't remember whether we had one or two counterattacks or maybe it was three.

It must have been about 11 P.M. the first night that I was standing guard near the dining room door when all of a sudden the whole town seemed to explode. There was one long continuous burst of shellfire and it was time on target fire.

I dropped down on my stomach and started to crawl for the cellar stairs. I was so scared that I even started to crawl down the stairs, head first. But I stopped in the middle and got up on my feet and said to the other guards, "We'll have to get right back up there as soon as the fire lifts because the infantry will be coming right in,."

The barrage lifted shortly and up we went to take positions on the first floor. It wasn't long before we heard some rifle shots and now and then a burst of super rapid automatic fire that sent cold chills chasing the other cold chills up and down our spines. The Jerries were in town and they were using their machine pistols.

I had Delakas's Thompson sub and it wasn't long before I had my first opportunity to use it. I am lucky I lived long enough to use the Thompson. I made the mistake of standing in the moonlight where a big shell had torn a hole in the attic roof. Suddenly a rifle spit flame from an archway just across the street. It was the exact location of one of our .57 mm guns but I didn't hesitate when the bullet bounced off of the bricks at my feet. Up went the Thompson and I let go with a burst of about five or six rounds.

This was just the beginning. Things kept getting hotter and livelier. One building housing a squad or two of the Third Platoon looked like a flaming fortress. There seemed to be fire coming out of all openings. It was a concrete house and apparently the Jerries considered it an important location.

"Hands up, Americans, a German would holler. The reply would be a burst from my Thompson and multiple flashes of exploding grenades from the Third Platoon, plus grease gun and rifle fire. Good old Love Company was in the groove. From now on we were to be a rootin', tootin', mostly shootin' son-of-a-gun of an outfit.

Suddenly two forms started to move through the shadows between our house and the weapons platoon buildings. "Halt!" I shouted, but on they went. My Thompson automatically went to my shoulder and started to speak. The moving objects stopped and apparently hit the dirt. There was silence. And then up again went the two shadowy forms. "Halt!" I shouted again and they disappeared as they hit the ground. There was still no password.

Lieutenant Danowski was in the attic and he came over to ask what I was shooting at. I explained the situation and Danowski replied, "You better not shoot at them anymore. They might be GIs."

Just as he finished speaking the two men started to move again and this time they entered the moonlit front part of the yard and we could plainly see they were Americans. We were never able to establish the identity of these men but it is possible that they were from the antitank company. It wasn't long before I emptied my first clip. And there stood expert rifleman Private Charles Davis with an empty gun in his hand and without the necessary know-how of reloading. This was the first time in my life I had ever fired a submachine gun. It was the latest model Thompson, the M-1, with the straight line box magazine holding twenty cartridges.

Reaching for the extra magazine I had in my pocket, I called down the stairs for instructions on how to insert it. After some fumbling in the dark I was ready to open up again. Things were pretty noisy about that time and that is why I was able to shout down the stairway to the first floor.

Things quieted down eventually but not until after I had thrown a fragmentation grenade down into the yard along with several others tossed from the lower windows.

The quietness only helped to accent the running of motors that reached my listening ears. I thought, "It must be a half-track or maybe a jeep." It wasn't a loud roaring sound like our Sherman tanks made. It wasn't even loud enough to be a truck. It seemed that the vehicle had reached almost the intersection, coming in from my left, without my hearing it approach. "It must be something light and it must be one of our vehicles," I reasoned.

I headed for the cellar to report to Captain Hallahan. "Do we have any half-tracks up here, Captain?"

"There isn't even a bridge across the river yet," was Captain Hallahan's reply.

"Well, there must be a Jerry tank outside," I answered.

And it was a Jerry tank and perhaps two. I returned to the attic and continued to listen and watch. Now the sound seemed to come from down the road behind the two buildings on the other corners, the ones housing the Third platoon., That is where the Jerries really were as we found out later. It was never determined whether or not there was one or more tanks but it is possible that there were two. Anyway, they pulled off the road and entered the field just in back of the red brick house across from us, the one holding Red White's squad of the Third platoon. Two men finally got through to inform us that a German tank had the nuzzle of its 88 almost sticking in the window of their living room. There was a bazooka with the squad but naturally it would have been suicide to use it on the Jerry's front armor. That, apparently, was the excuse for not using it. While coming up the road the Tiger had fired one shell which hit a man standing in a doorway of a house occupied by the First platoon. They later found his right foot.

After I thought I had the tank located I returned to the cellar. Captain Hallahan was talking with Lieutenant Taylor, the officer in charge of the two antitank guns in our sector.

I can't remember the conversation now but Hallahan could not convince Taylor that it was advisable to go out and fire one of his 57 mm guns at the tank. Taylor's story was the usual line— "I cannot penetrate his (the Tiger tank) front armor." That made me pretty angry. Here we are fighting a war but nobody wanted to do the shooting. It was the same old story—hold your fire—don't give away your position—cover and concealment. How were we ever going to win by digging foxholes and cowering in cellars?

But this was not worrying me then. I was just good and scared. Just afraid that the next 88 shell was going to have my name on it. And so with my life practically hanging by a thread it was without any hesitation that I almost shouted,

"What the hell do you have a gun for?"

Lieutenant Taylor never answered that one. Captain Hallahan gulped, and quietly said, "You better get out of here, Davis."

Lieutenant Taylor never was very friendly to Private Davis from that day on.

I didn't go far. And it was with great pleasure I heard Captain Hallahan say in loud, firm tones (and he pointed at Lieutenant Taylor) "I'm giving you a direct order to go out and fire that gun."

That was the best order I ever heard issued during my days on the front lines. It was the order that perhaps saved all our lives.

Lieutenant Taylor went to the attic with me and I showed him where the tank was sitting on the road, just a little the other side of the two corner houses. Well, it looked like a tank and Lieutenant Taylor even said that he could see it, too. So off he went to join the gun crew across the street. He said he would fire five rounds right down the middle.

The Letters of a Combat Rifleman

I cannot blame Lieutenant Taylor for hesitating. One of his gun crews had been chased away from their gun. As a matter of fact both gun crews were chased from their positions. The lieutenant was taking a chance by just stepping outside the house. On top of all this it was absolutely true that the 57 mm shell would bounce off the front of the Tiger like a golf ball off the end of a club. It was sort of like committing suicide to gain nothing.

The 57 was wheeled from the archway (the same archway from where the rifleman fired at me) and the first round went barreling right down the middle of the street, across the intersection, past the two corner houses and on out into the countryside, finally hitting a house in the next town, (Pier) about two miles away. Either the tank had backed off the road or else it never was on the road. The four remaining shots followed the first. I had no difficulty observing their fiery trail. The muzzle blast from that small gun was really terrific. It shook the house worse than the concentration of artillery shells. The concussion made me wince. It might be possible that the Germans thought we were using a .155 self-propelled gun. Whatever their thoughts or reasoning the Germans never made use of that tank during the time that they faced us.

There were other German tanks that entered Lucherberg that night. Division publicity pamphlets said, "Reluctant to relinquish this strategically located town, Germans countered with ten tanks and supporting infantry. A seventy-ton Tiger Royal tank fired point blank into Co. F's command Post. Sergeant George E. Burns, Findlay, Ohio, rushed from the building and fired his bazooka—only seven feet from the tank. The bulky tank waddled away in flaming retreat," They neglected to mention the casualties, which included several officers.

In the meantime we took precautions against an attack by the Tiger in our area. Roy Williams, our tall, young choir boy from the state of Washington wanted very much to get a shot with his bazooka. Roy looked like a choir boy, but he fought like a man. We couldn't determine just where to place Roy in order that he could get a rocket launched and at the same time be safe. Finally he set up his position by a window on the second floor at the corner of the house nearest the intersection. There he had excellent vision and the range was less than forty yards. The tall, nervous southern fellow was his assistant.

The next important incident took place in the cellar. A tank captain swaggered into the room and started to inform us that we were now safe. He and his steel steeds were our salvation.

I never saw a man change his manner so quickly as that armor expert. Captain Hallahan broke down his wagon when he spoke about the Royal Tiger prowling in our front yard.

Another argument ensued. Despite the fact that he had six Sherman tanks in back of the church the armor commander refused to move one inch. He gave the exact same argument as Taylor. "It would be impossible," he said, "to penetrate their armor. And all of my tanks would be knocked out."

We were helpless. Captain Hallahan could not overrule another captain. We finally had to be satisfied with the tanker's promise. Before leaving he said, "I'll go back and talk it over with my officers, And then I'll contact you by radio." He went back and turned his radio off.

It was just about daylight that the mighty Royal Tiger quietly turned over its engines. There was no loud, rancorous roar like our Shermans made—just a soft, powerful purr.

I was in the attic waiting, listening—and shivering. There were several officers there with me. Williams was just below us with his finger ready to release the rocket.

Suddenly we saw a gun barrel coming up the street. It was unsupported—just seemed to be traveling in space. There was a muzzle brake on the end of it—so it was Jerry. As the muzzle brake part reached the center of the intersection it began to wave at us. It moved rapidly from side to side and up and down—just like it was searching for a target. The gun kept coming and coming but there was nothing to support it!

"Was it suspended in space?" I wondered. But no, it was just the first 88 I had seen in action. Of course the tank finally reached the corner too. And as it did we all made a rush for the stairway. I was first but I stopped on the landing and told Danowski I was going back to try and button the tank up. It was, however, buttoned up but I figured I would try to hit some of the opening slits. Before I could get back to the window, the tank had backed up and turned into the archway of the house-barn on the opposite corner. I could no longer get a shot. It was really amazing how that tank turned around so fast. I was away from the window only about thirty seconds, or less. And yet General Patton and other high ranking army officials claimed that our tanks were more maneuverable. I don't believe a Sherman tank could have turned around in that street and I know that it would have taken at least two or three minutes for it to turn if it could at all. The Sherman would have needed a man on the outside of the tank to direct the driver also. The Tiger was tightly buttoned up. The barrel of the 88 was as long as the street was wide, if not longer.

Our first question was, "What happened to Williams?" The answer—he had a bad connection on his battery to trigger wire. I wonder if the tall, nervous, first sergeant's assistant fixed it that way. We must give Roy credit for trying. He pulled the trigger but nothing happened. Danowski had an M-1 with an antitank grenade on the launcher but when he ran down the stairs he left the rifle propped against the wall by the attic window! The Royal Tiger roared and took off toward Pier. Red White ran out of his house with a bazooka and fired one or two rockets. He claimed he hit the tank in the motor and that it entered Pier burning.

Were our tanks superior to German tanks? That question has been asked many times by Americans. The answers have all been supplied by men like General Patton and other high ranking officers, "Yes," they all said, "We have the best tanks."

The Letters of a Combat Rifleman

I was only an enlisted man. I was in the infantry. But what I would like to know is, "Why wouldn't six American tanks attack one German tank?" Why not get the tank crew men, the ones that were up there slugging with the Royal Tigers, to answer that question. Why not ask them, honestly, "Who had the best?"

For them to say that the American tank was better would be the same as admitting that they themselves were cowards. And I wouldn't accuse our tankers of being cowards. Would you take a BB rifle and walk out to fight a man holding a 30-06 and wearing a suit of armor?

Well, it wasn't long until all the little Shermans were deployed behind different buildings right along the edge of the town. Everything was quiet. Even the chickens came out from their hiding places and began to scratch for food.

Everything was muddy, sloppy and wet. I counted twelve direct hits on our house. The stone wall surrounding the house was almost flat on the ground. The gardens and graveyard were well ploughed. Many bodies still littered the area. Very few were Americans. Sergeant Evan's body was still on the landing. It was there more than two days. Many times I walked over the still form as I made my way from room to room during the hours of darkness.

The search for watches and pistols continued but I still had no luck. The first sergeant came up with the suggestion that I search the dead Germans for money for him. He had only a few years to go and he would be retired. Said he wanted to buy a mule for his small farm in Mississippi. Well, that one nearly killed me.

Darkness fell early again and back we went to the crowded cellar. I had looked over the upper floors for a suitable place to live but there was only one small room on the second floor that was any good at all. It was still clean enough to walk about in and there was a couch that would make a nice bed. However, a completely broken window faced Pier and I thought of the remote possibility of a shell dropping in that window. Most of all I wondered how I would keep warm. Finally I joined the rest in the cellar.

A few candles were burning. My Coleman gasoline stove was going on almost a twenty-four hour basis. That was a life saver. We had hot coffee. The men were so hungry they were eating the contents of the German knapsacks which consisted mainly of black bread, butter, fish paste, and bologna.

Zurcher had his 300 radio going all the time so that we could keep in touch with Blue Three, our battalion headquarters. The tall nervous man was making out the guard schedule, omitting his own name again. As usual, I couldn't find a place to sleep. Too add to my misery, I had the GI's.

Tom Jennings was in a bad way, too. He just about made it up over the cliff into Lucherburg, arriving about two hours after the others. The physical strain was too much for a man of forty. Tom's eyes were watery, his face dirty and unshaven and his shoulders hunched. He had a very bad case of the GIs. But Tom took his post just like all the rest.

I was up in the attic when the Jerries started coming in again. It must have been about midnight. I had a telephone and I could hear the platoons calling for artillery. They had outposts and the outposts said that German infantry was coming in.

Our artillery opened up. The observers had arranged George points (firing areas) during the day and they knew just what to call for. The crash of bursting proximity fused shells rent the sky like bolts of thunder. It was concentrated fire and it did not let up after a minute or two like the German barrages. The crashing noise seemed to shake my body and I could hear particles of steel hitting the slate roof. I crouched beside the wall, the phone still to my ear.

Many of the shells were bursting right over our outposts. The men were getting frantic. Their foxholes offered no protection from the air bursts. "Call off the fire! Get them to extend the range!" the men were shouting into the phone.

The artillery F.O. immediately got on the radio and ordered the fire lifted. But it still continued. "Stop that fire," shouted the platoon headquarters, all three of them.

I started to complain, too. "The shells are bursting almost over my head," I told the operator. "Why in the hell don't they stop that fire?

The barrage must have been going for about fifteen minutes now and still there was no letup. The German infantry on flat, open ground must have been completely dispersed.

"They have called to lift the fire," the telephone operator kept telling the outposts and platoon. Finally the artillery F.O. said that it must be German fire. "Our barrage must have been lifted long ago," he claimed. But I knew better an I told them over the phone. It was bad enough up there in the attic. I knew those boys in the outposts were under a terrific strain. No doubt they figured their time was up.

After nearly twenty minutes of concentrated fire, the barrage finally stopped. A few enemy infantry men may have entered the town. Things were quiet around headquarters the rest of the night except for an occasional short burst of fire from the German artillery or mortars.

We were glad to see daylight the next morning without it being heralded with a burst of burp gun or artillery fire. I spent a lot of time watching our forces advance toward Pier during the day. Our CP swarmed with forward observers and rear echelon sightseers. The quartermaster men appeared and started to collect the American dead. Riflemen did most of the collecting. I helped remove Sergeant Evans. He wasn't to be the last dead man I was to handle.

We came in for some shellfire again during the day. And some of it was American stuff landing on us—or else the Germans had radio controlled shells. One of the FO's had placed his big radio on a window sill on the side of the house away from the enemy. This was hit and knocked apart. My friend Helmut Hebish was busy in the second floor toilet when a very big shell hit the window of the small room.

I was on the stairway between the first and second floor and I shouted, "Are you hurt, Helmut?" There was no answer so I called again. I couldn't see anything due to the cloud of dust. Finally, Helmut answered quietly, "I'm okay," He didn't seem at all scared or shocked, but there is no doubt that the explosion helped his movement. This shell also hit on the "safe" side of the house!

Before dark that day I counted the hits on our house. There was evidence of twenty-five hits since we moved in! But not one man was killed by shellfire; and not even one man was injured!

I felt I couldn't bear another night in that packed cellar so I went up to look over my small room on the second floor. The window opening was now twice as large as before. Fragments of steel had perforated the couch with tiny holes. There wasn't one square foot of space that had escaped a shower of steel. God was still answering my prayers and guiding me in a safe way.

Germans entered Lucherberg again during the hours of darkness. Mike Susskind, Third platoon BAR man let two of them walk past him as he stood on outpost duty by the corner of the barn where the Tiger tank turned around. I never heard the explanation for this action. Mike nevertheless was one of the best squad leaders ever turned out on the western front. He was to prove himself many many times later during the battle for Germany.

But young Irwin Schwartz, Brooklyn's exception to the general rule, did not hesitate. Irwin laid a heavy index finger on the trigger of his M-3 grease gun. The fire was concentrated. The range was short,—less than twenty-five yards. The .45 caliber slugs hit the mark. The next morning they found the mark to be two Germans, one an officer with a large artillery radio. The radio had been hit, too, but battalion managed to salvage some parts. It was generally believed that they were coming into Lucherberg to direct artillery fire the next day. The Germans tried this stunt many times during the war. It is a smart trick if it works. And it will succeed many times because an army cannot occupy every building in a town. The entire operation depends on plenty of guts and even more luck.

I got up the next day with an excellent breakfast waiting for me. We always had hot chow in the morning as long as the kitchen men could make it up to the lines. They prepared the food in Eschweiler and brought it up on a jeep and trailer. Staff Sergeant Kwilosz got the Bronze Star for getting that hot food up to us, and he really deserved that award. We had breakfast in the dark so the Jerries couldn't spot the activity. We never were served a noon meal. Supper was brought up after dark.

Right here is a good tip for laying in artillery barrages, if you have the extra shells. Start firing just an hour before daylight and keep up intermittent fire until it is light. A shell every five or ten minutes into different parts of the town you are facing would be enough to interrupt all chow lines and if one hit near a chow line there would be plenty of casualties. Men must eat and they must get some sleep if they are going to continue fighting. If you interrupt or deprive them of this supply of food and sleep you will weaken them and their will to fight. Sickness and disease would deplete their ranks. It all adds up toward victory for the army that uses the weapons it has instead of just deploying these weapons along a line. Artillery fire just aimed at a town can bring some splendid results sometimes. You must play the law of averages in combat, especially when your means of observation may be limited. One big shell that didn't even explode landed many miles behind our lines and killed our assistant division commander as well as the C.O. of one of our other infantry regiments. That one shot caused a lot of interruption in communications, uncertainty in division and lower headquarters and loss of contact between many units. A lot of changes had to be made quickly, and it is very unlikely that any of these changes helped the combat ability of the division.

It seems that everyone was busy trying to remodel our home as soon as it was light enough to see. The living room and the priest's office on the first floor were habitable without too much work on blocking up the windows and cleaning out dirt and rubble. With some help I brought my steel studded couch down from the second floor and put it in the living room. Williams decided to make his bed here, too, because there was a piano in perfect condition standing against the north wall. The other men to move in with us were Orrie Saylor, weapons platoon runner (Orrie was from York, Pennsylvania), Carl Zurcher, Tom Jennings, and Henry Bailey, also a platoon runner and also from Pennsylvania.

The traffic was getting pretty heavy so finally our officers decided to put a guard on the door. It was just another way to keep us busy. As if we didn't have enough to do trying to make a place to sleep and trying to get cleaned up as well as going over our rifles and equipment.

I stood my hour or two on the door and then went back to work. I left my '03 standing in a corner near the door. In a short while it was missing. From the story I got, I assume that an officer picked it up as a German souvenir. The guard said the last time he saw it, an officer was examining the scope and he heard him remark, "This is a German sniper's rifle." That's an officer for you—he couldn't even read "Weaver 330" on the scope or "Remington" 1903 on the receiver. Of course the little the average American knew about weapons you would naturally expect any of them to think that the above identification marks were German and not American.

But Max Delrogh was on the job. He was noted for getting what he wanted. And he got it in the fastest and most expedient manner even if the method used was a bit shady. Within four hours I had a brand new '03, a duplicate of the one I lost.

I was again faced with the problem of sighting-in. It may seem strange but you can't go shooting a .30 caliber rifle just anywhere even though you are in the front lines. But I finally found a spot in the barnyard where

Schwartz and his boys were located. The longest range I could get without going too out into the open, was about forty yards. It wasn't hard to knock off tin cans at this distance, but the men watching me were actually thrilled by the demonstration. I was still plenty dubious myself and I wondered what I would do with a target at two or three hundred yards.

Sickness hit our ranks continually. We all suffered from colds and the GIs. Finally Tom Jennings had to go back. He was in bad shape. Also the big tall southern boy went back with a case of combat fatigue. He just couldn't take it. That was the last we ever saw of him. The old marine fighter, Tom Jennings, was to return in a short time.

It was about this time that I got back to writing letters again. On December 7, 1944, I wrote my wife: "I received your two telegrams and may I thank you for such a timely and kind thought. Also received a letter addressed to my regular outfit. It only took about twelve days to reach me, which is very good.

"I have been busy. That is why I don't write as much or as often. It will certainly be wonderful now to receive mail that is recent and to receive it regularly."

Jean complained about the lack of endearing terms in my letters. Actually I was afraid of the censor. My answer was, "Regardless of how my letters may sound I am still very, very much in love with you and I want you and the world to know it. Perhaps the thing that makes me happiest here in Germany is the knowledge that you love me, too, and that you keep saying you love me."

My letter ended by saying, "It is getting dark now. The days are so short and we really hurt for candles. They are so hard to get. The last batch we got from a church."

Chapter VIII
Letters and Christmas Cards

Things started to become routine around Lucherberg. Pier had been taken by the 414th Infantry and our First battalion moved at night on Merken and cleared that town. That put us right up on the Roer River. For some reason or other there wasn't much talk of us moving out and I don't remember that anyone mentioned crossing the river. We came to fear rivers. And it always seemed that we were bumping into rivers that ran north and south.

I wrote to Jean again on the Ninth: "I've just been wondering all day today how you and Bill are. Your last letter sounded quite sad but I wrote the day before yesterday to reassure you of my constant love for you. I hope you get it soon because I know you will be wondering all the time. I know how it is to keep waiting and waiting for an answer to a question.

"My mail from you is quite regular dear, but I do not receive one every day. Don't ask me why. It must be the mail system. Anyway, I usually get them in batches.

"Things are about the same here. I am getting over a slight cold. Otherwise I'm in good health. The weather turned colder last night and it was snowing some this afternoon. I know it is getting cold in Pennsylvania now. It usually does after Thanksgiving.

"It is so hard to think of things to tell you. That goes for Billy, too. Perhaps he would be interested in hearing about the snow anyway.

"Dearest, I hope you are not too much disappointed in these letters. It is not that I don't love you because I do, just as much if not more than ever before. It is hard at times to write and conditions are not ideal. The candle I have now, I made by melting wax in a can and using a rifle cleaning patch for a wick. I think I told you we found a lot of them in a church but we used them all or lost them.

"Anyway, sweetheart, you and Bill just keep praying for me and I am sure the Lord will soon bring me home safe to your side because that is where I belong. Keep writing, darling, and keep praying."

It was a great help to receive recent mail. My family needed and wanted the latest news more than I. When Jean received a letter dated two weeks previous, she naturally couldn't help wondering what had happened during those two intervening weeks. Of course I never told her of the real danger I was in, but I never said that I was in a safe zone as some of the boys told their loved ones.

The next day I wrote Jean: "I must write to you today. I received six wonderful letters from you this morning and they made me very happy. One was written December 1, which means it took less than ten days to reach me!

"You spoke of getting my letters in reverse. I have received many of yours the same way and no doubt there are quite a few old ones that I didn't get yet. But I am so happy now dear because I am getting your recent letters. I don't think you are that lucky. I do hope however, that it does not take more than two weeks for you to receive my mail. I certainly would like you to get this letter before Christmas so that you will know I am safe.

"When you spoke of the weather getting cold in early November it made me rather homesick. There are four other boys writing at this table with me and two are from Pennsylvania. One is from York. We were just talking about hunting and running dogs and it sure reminds me of many a November day back in Pennsy. I remember how well you always took care of me and made me such nice lunches, too."

I mentioned the Lord and praying many times in my letters because I really felt that He was guiding me and that He was the only one that could see me safely through.

In the same letter I said, "Let's hope darling, I can soon be home again with you. It would be so wonderful to again hold you in my arms. Keep praying as we do here, and I am sure the Lord will soon answer our prayers. I don't think the Jerries can hold out much longer. But that is what we have always been saying. I know the Lord is on our side though and He will bring us through.

"They sometimes make us so angry and then again I feel sorry for them. I wish I could understand their problem so we could make this a better world to live in. One came in last night and gave up. They do that quite often, nearly always telling us they are some other nationality. He said he was French and as usual it kind of provoked us. So just to make him hurt a little I made him watch me while I ate breakfast. And it was a good one, too, and probably made his mouth water. We had apricots, hot cakes, syrup, bacon, oatmeal, and coffee. I asked him if the German army fed him like that and he said, 'Nien.'

"I'll have to close now, darling. I have a weapon to clean before it starts getting dark and it gets dark quick now."

It was while we were in Lucherberg that I had my first chance to inspect some of the German infantry weapons. Young Gasch of the weapons platoon got a Jerry machine gun going and fired off plenty of rounds. I had a burp gun and we disassembled it to learn the nomenclature. Effley and Sugar Reed helped with the experimenting. There were more ninety-eight Mausers lying around than you could count in a week. The Jerry that had fired the rifle grenade at us from the vicinity of the church had a large wooden box full of grenades. It must have been an awful load to carry along with the rifle and his other equipment. It is possible however that the grenades had been there since the Germans had occupied Lucherberg.

About this time we also started to practice with some of our own weapons. I took the .50 caliber air-cooled machine gun off of the jeep and we hauled it down the road on a little cart to a lake on the southeast edge of the town. It must have been an old quarry. It certainly offered an ideal spot for small arms practice as we were able to get up to at least a range of one thousand yards.

Roy Williams helped me move the gun and ammunition. It was quite a load and we had to make a couple of trips. We had fired it in Munsterbusch, but we never did get full automatic fire., After some experimenting I finally got it going completely automatic. Then we tried different ranges on the rear sight. We had to estimate the range to the spot we wanted to hit and then we put that on the sight. It was plain to see that sand bags would be necessary to lay in on a small target or area that was more than two hundred yards away.

We were beginning to think about Christmas now. On December 14, I wrote Jean, "I keep thinking of you and Billy at this Christmas season and it makes me so homesick. Our boy Williams from Washington state is quite a musician and he has been entertaining with Christmas carols on the piano.

"But by the time this reaches you I suppose Christmas will be over. I sure hope you try to have a good time and enjoy yourself both at home with Billy and at church.

I ended with: "Give my love to our Happy Chappy boy and tell him I'll be home as soon as I catch up to the Germans and give them a good spankin."

My next letter on December 16, carried some good news: "The day before yesterday I had a hot bath back where our kitchen is. Maybe I didn't miss you then! Of course my back never did get washed so you will have a lot to make up for when I get home. Then the shower deal came through yesterday and so I went there, too, and also got clean clothes. It was the first chance I had to bathe in about seven weeks."

The men in the kitchen worked hard for us that day. It was an extra special favor to carry and heat all that water for us just so that we could have a real honest to goodness hot bath. Of course only a few men benefited by the deal and we had to wait our turn to get in the tub. And also we had to jump back again into the same old dirty clothes.

The Letters of a Combat Rifleman

The showers were back at division headquarters in Brand, southeast of Aachen. We managed to get some clean clothing there after a lot of confusion and standing in long lines. Surprisingly enough we did not smell too bad even though we had worn the same clothes for seven weeks.

My December 16 letter had other good news: "The packages are still coming in but none of mine have arrived yet. I am glad to say, however, that I am not eating so much anymore so that I get sick. Last night we had a snack of fried chicken before bed time. Three of us went out and picked us the best chicken we could find and then one of our kitchen boys helped us prepare it and we fried it in butter. Sure was delicious."

Lucherberg was swarming with chickens when we first went in but it didn't take long to clean up the whole lot. Sugar Reed and Gene Bialey helped in catching the chickens and several others also joined the chase. We finally had to shoot one with a carbine in order to get it. Lyons was the kitchen man that cleaned the bird.

"Now for some more good news for my darling wife," my letter continued. "I have been promoted to private first class! Also, dearest, I am now a combat infantryman as of November. I can now wear the badge I always admired the most, a Kentucky rifle with silver leaves.

"I am just about out of news now, sweetheart, and the boys want me to go out and fire some of our weapons for a little practice.

The target practice consisted of shooting our rifles and automatic weapons down by the lake. However, we had received complaints from the outfit on our right and so we had to contact and inform battalion headquarters every time we were going to practice fire.

There was a four day lapse in my letter writing, the next one being dated December 20: "It has been a couple of days or more since I've had time to sit down and write you so I hope you are not worried. Everything is just fine here.

"I had one experience that I can mention. However, the details must wait. Last Sunday I was lucky enough to win a drawing for a trip to a rest camp in Belgium. That is about as much as I can tell you. Perhaps you can get the rest of the idea from the headlines around this date. Anyway, the trip didn't last long and I can say I was glad to get back to my outfit."

It was a mistake to say that I was lucky. We left the front line just twenty-four hours after the Germans had started their final offensive of the war. They (our command) pulled one-third of our battalion out of the lines so that we could go back to Verviers, Belgium for a rest. Of course it didn't matter as far as the high command was concerned that Verviers happened to be right in the path of the German drive. If our high command planned the Bulge or knew about it like they claim, then they ought to all be court martialed for torturing us GIs the way they did that cold, ill-fated day in December.

The torture started when we had to get up at 4 A.M. in order to leave the lines and walk back and get aboard the trucks for the long, cold trip to Belgium. In typical U.S. Army fashion the convoy drove right through

Vervies without knowing that they had passed the city they were looking for. The trip took about eight hours. Just try riding for eight hours in an open truck in December without anything to eat. We had brought our rifles with us so perhaps the high command had finally figured that the Jerries might reach the Meuse River, in which case they would have a rest camp to protect Verviers. That's what I call grand strategy. Our unintelligent corps was really on the ball! Despite the fact that the infantry patrols brought back reports of heavy troop and vehicle movement, no precautions were taken. If they knew that the Germans were going to strike with twenty-four divisions, ten of them armored, like they claim now that they did, why did they put a brand new outfit like the 106th Division in that section of the line? And why did they place the 28th Division there when they were under strength from their recent fight in the Hurtgen Forest?

These facts should make it absolutely clear that the high command did not know that the Germans were planning an offensive. It was another Pearl Harbor. The GIs, the doughboys in the lines knew that something was coming but their warnings went unheeded.

When we arrived in Verviesr we immediately began to witness signs of the German activity. Buzz bombs were sputtering overhead; Sherman tanks racing through the city made it difficult to cross the streets. However, we gave no special significance to these activities.

I got into the currency exchange line quickly and turned my shillings, francs and German invasion marks into Belgian francs. Some of the boys were trying to exchange regular German marks into Belgian francs. They met resistance, but if the sum was not too large the exchange went through. First Sergeant White asked me to get some of his marks changed over. I refused. The Bulge was just about ready to knock White's farm-mule plan over the traces.

It was Sunday in Verviers. The weather was cold and damp so that the saloons offered a place to rest and get warmed. The American soldiers outnumbered the Belgian civilians both in the saloons and also on the streets. The evergreen-covered Shermans were about the only vehicles moving. After two beers I wandered into the Red Cross canteen and sat down to await the afternoon show that was to be presented for the benefit of the resting GIs.

It seemed kind of odd when an M.P. walked on the stage. I more expected a burst of band music and a flock of beautiful chorus girls.

"Everybody in Section so-and-so report back immediately to the rest camp." he said.

Back at the old Belgian army barracks that constituted the rest camp, our outfit gathered rather quietly. No one seemed to know what was up but we all sensed something serious. By this time the Germans had been pushing ahead two full days and yet nobody seemed to know about it. We waited for the trucks to take us back up. After supper we attended chapel services. We prayed in earnest. By now we sensed that the Germans were putting up a new offensive and that it was very serious. We expected an announcement from the chaplain, but he had nothing definite or official.

It was almost twenty-four hours before we were back to our outfits. It was a terrible night, More important convoys pushed us off the road and German planes dropped flares and bombs along our route. Our part of the front was quiet.

The next day we went immediately to work in setting up elaborate defenses. Our patrols, guards and outposts were doubled. New guards were placed on the roads. They checked every vehicle that left or entered Lucherberg. Mine fields were laid and booby traps set out. Love company strung out and circled the entire town with foxholes and machine gun emplacements. Mike company set up positions and antitank company and the TD boys picked out additional gun positions and more carefully camouflaged the old ones.

Lieutenants Danowski and Thompson and I walked over the fields and inspected the new positions. We went on as far as Pier to find out the position of the outfits on our flanks and where our fire tied in.

I dug a two-man foxhole in an orchard on the northeast edge of town and placed the .50 caliber machine gun in the position. From here I could cover the road into Pier and all the expanse of mine fields in between the two towns.

As soon as the positions were finished, Danowski ordered an early morning alert. On this first alert I accompanied Danowski around the town as he inspected each position. The lieutenant was thorough and efficient. He was a capable successor to our great Captain Hallahan who had been transferred to battalion headquarters where he took over the G-3 job.

During a later inspection after I had my .50 caliber position completed, Danowski walked by without even noticing the gun or hole. He was surprised and pleased when I called after him to get his attention. A newly fallen snow had aided in the camouflage.

The Bulge did not slow up our plans for a real Christmas celebration. My letter of the 20th continued:

"Today Williams and some of the rest of us went out and cut our Christmas tree. We have some real decorations and some makeshift ones too, like the tinfoil the Nazis drop to jam the radar equipment. I'll enclose some of the leaflets the Nazis drop for us to read. I wonder who they think they are kidding or if they believe they can influence us into giving them easy peace terms so they can get ready to start another war. They may put that stuff across to some boys and that is where the trouble starts. After being raised like they have been for so many generations it seems like an impossible tasks to ever change the nature of the German people. Regardless of what happens to them they always say they like and believe in Hitler."

The Christmas leaflets dropped by the Germans showed a young child looking at an angel on the Christmas tree. Underneath in large letters it said, "YOU SHOULDN'T SEE THIS PICTURE."

On the back of the leaflet in red and black letters was:

ONWARD CHRISTIAN SOLDIERS!
Forget those many millions of little kids who
will have no Christmas.
Forget those children who are waiting in vain
for their fathers to come home, those innocents
who will never look into their father's face.
Those poor ones who even at Christmas, living in
ruins, will hear the crashing of bombs.
Forget them! Don't think of them, it breaks the
morale of a soldier.
War goes on. Murder is still legalized and
there is no end in sight.
ONWARD CHRISTIAN SOLDIERS!

Another leaflet was the second edition of a small single sheet newspaper. It was dated December 19, 1944. Among the news items were the following: "During an air raid on November 27, the Cologne cathedral has once again been hit by bombs. One bomb exploded in the interior. The high altar and the vestry suffered irreparable damage." We were to enter Cologne later and learned that this was purely propaganda. Under the subhead, USA we read: "Colonel Elliot Roosevelt, second son of President Roosevelt, has married a Hollywood actress. Sometime ago, he has returned from the European battlefront." It wouldn't take an English teacher to tell that the above tripe was written by a foreigner.

Another interesting story appeared on Page 2: "The following American POWs want to send word home that they are safe, not wounded and well treated: Second Lieutenant James M. Gillespie, 01297521 (Conn.), Tec. Sergeant Howard A. Wolpert, 6893313 (Penna.), Tec. Sergeant Albert T. Maudice, 33161440 (Penna.) etc. etc. with twelve more sergeants and privates."

The third leaflet I picked up in the fields surrounding Lucherberg was an out and out invitation to surrender. It was titled "They are all alike!" Then followed two pages of writing: "Good soldiers are all alike. You'll find them in all armies, in yours as well as in ours. A good soldier is brave, gallant and a good fighter whether he is American, British or German. And a good soldier expects to be treated well, even by his former enemy should he ever get captured. This is what we expect from you and you've got right to expect the same from us. The Germans are not only good soldiers but also good winners. You may rely on this:

GERMANY IS STRICTLY OBSERVING GENEVA CONVENTION.
"If you should ever face a situation when fighting on would mean senseless self-destruction keep the following points well in mind: After

your having spent the first few days in a Dulag (transit camp) right behind the front you will be transferred to a Stalag (permanent camp). The Stalags are up-to-date camps with all conveniences. The food is prepared in modern kitchens. It is ample and of the same quality as the food of the German soldier. Besides, you are allowed to receive a package every week through the International Red Cross. If you are wounded or sick you will immediately receive the best of medical care exactly like a German soldier.

"In the Stalag you will be housed in clean airy rooms. Lavatories and toilets are of high sanitary standard.

"If you wish to work, your qualifications will be taken into consideration. You will be given opportunity to learn a trade, to improve yourself in your own profession, and you can even acquire university degrees. All Stalags have athletic fields and modern sporting equipment. There are motion pictures and plays for your entertainment. You may receive any amount of mail. The forwarding of letters and packages by the International Red Cross is swift and reliable. You yourself are permitted to write four postcards and three letters every month. "The dreadful war will be over for you and you will return safe and sound.

"DON'T FORGET THE MOST IMPORTANT THING ABOUT THE WAR IS TO COME BACK HOME ALIVE."

There were some Americans, too, who walked over to the German lines and surrendered. I know of only one case but there must have been more. Others gave up too easily, no doubt when they were in a tough spot. The Russians look with disfavor, to say the least, on the Red Army men that were PWs. American PWs should be open to suspicion, too, and accorded less honors and attention than what they receive.

On Christmas Eve I wrote to Jean: "The mail hasn't been so regular lately and you should know why by just looking at the headlines. I think I told you I went to Verviers, Belgium last Sunday for a three-day rest, but as things started to happen it got too hot there and so we were all glad to get back to the front. It was Sunday so I didn't get a chance to buy anything. However, I wanted to get you a nice present and also have my picture taken. Let's hope I get back there again sometime.

"I'm glad you are still buying bonds, darling, and you can be proud you are giving your blood for the boys who are wounded. The biggest problem is the evacuation of the wounded and no doubt the blood donated by the people at home saves many a soldier's life.

"Billy must be going to be a big boy. I do wish I could get home to see him. Did he have a nice Christmas?

"It is Christmas Eve and things are quiet so far. We are making it as near to a Christmas at home as we can. We have a tree and have been singing carols. I want to go to church if I can make it. We are lucky to have all this when you realize where we are.

"I never liked the type of celebrations they have back in the States and I don't ever want to spend another Christmas Eve in a drinking bout. Of course we even have a few barrels of Belgian beer here, but it means only a cup or two apiece, which is just something to wet the throat with. It would take twenty cups of that stuff to make you think you had a drink.

"Don't worry, darling, if you don't hear from me for several days. I can write almost every day but there are times of trying to find a place to live as you probably know the weather is too severe to live in a foxhole. Of course there are men who come back so keep faith in God."

My second letter the same day mentioned some aerial action and a message for my son:

"Here I am writing again today. It must be the Christmas spirit! I did go to church and guess what the chaplain talked about? The way some people celebrate Christmas! He spoke of some of the things I mentioned in my other letter.

"It was a beautiful, clear day and it reminded me a little of the Christmas Day we were married. It was quite a bit colder, however. There was a very heavy frost on the ground.

"It is now Christmas Eve and so far everything is quiet. As we held our church services today, a German fighter plane was shot down close by and the pilot parachuted to the ground. We are hoping that there will be no more activity tonight or tomorrow. The radio is going now and mixed in with the propaganda we get the season's carols and hymns.

"Pray God, next year at this happy season we will be together, living happily and in peace. The strains of Silent Night, Holy Night just faded away and now we hear the guttural sounds of German. Perhaps it is easier here for us because we are not reminded like our loved ones at home. But we know it is hard for all and we should all do everything in our power to make sure that peace will reign over the world at the next Christmas season.

"I'd like to send you a message for Bill. He will be among the leaders of the nation when the sorrows and sufferings of this war are a faint memory. At that time perhaps similar terror groups will be trying to gain world control. It is up to us to make the right peace. It ii up to Bill and his generation to keep that peace, appease no groups, just be guided by the gospel of truth and goodwill.

"In his own life he will be happiest if he follows the Golden Rule. His uppermost idea in life should be to get understanding. We should try to understand the other fellow's problems. To gain this understanding may be hard at times. It entails listening more than talking, reading the opposition's viewpoint and being able to admit the other fellow is right. By following God and 'doing unto others as you would have them do unto you,' little Billy and his generation can make a lasting peace and bring goodwill to men. If we are good parents perhaps our children will achieve this goal.

"Jennings keeps us laughing. He just remarked, 'I better take this ammo belt along on guard tonight since things are hot. I'd hate to get caught with only a clip (eight rounds) and a carton of cigarettes.' (Jennings is a big smoker and usually carries his ammunition belt full of cigarettes instead of ammo).

"Darling, I wrote this letter at this time because I've been thinking so much of you. I love you and I want the whole world to know it. There is no better time of the year I think to reassure you. Tomorrow is our anniversary and marks another milestone in our lives. At this time I like to think that all future anniversary dates will find us happier each time, with our love of each other more deep and everlasting.

"Anyway, darling, happy anniversary and a very Merry Christmas. I love you now and forever. As always, Your loving husband, Charles."

The weather had cleared and as a result we had plenty of aerial activity. We walked back to Lamersdorf to attend the church services and the boys with the Bofors and .50 caliber machine guns were busy tracking the clear, cold sky with puffs of white smoke and tracer shells. German planes were almost constantly in sight, flying perpendicular to the lines. Always the AA gunners seemed to be at least five hundred yards in back of the target. When the firing was heavy, I ducked into a doorway if there was one convenient. To us doughboys it was a great show and most of the time we stood in the open and cheered and shouted for a hit. The Jerry fighter pilot that bailed out of his smoking plane must have landed somewhere between Lamersdorf and Lucherberg.

As I stood guard during the long hours of darkness the Jerry planes continued to shuttle back and forth. Their motors were loud. I looked up many times as it seemed that they must be only five hundred feet off the ground. Our battery of .76 tank destroyer guns in the orchard fired every night, the shells whistling over our house as the muzzle blast shook the ground. We were on the border of the toughest fighting of the war, a relatively safe position.

"How is everything at home?" I asked Jean on December 27th. "I trust you and Bill are well and that you both had a Merry Christmas. I am just fine and have nothing to worry about. According to the *Stars and Stripes*, the people back home had a somber celebration due to the news of the Nazi offensive. There isn't much I can say now about it but I do want to reassure you that everything is okay where I am. You have no need to worry. As I told you before, I was at Verviers the day it started but we soon got out of there. That isn't very far from some of the towns mentioned in the late news stories. And just think, we went back there for a rest!

I'll never know what caused me to take a walk out across the snow covered farm land extending quite a distance beyond the edge of Lucherberg that Christmas day. Perhaps it was my hunting instinct. Or maybe it was my idea of filling the larder for our kitchen. Why I went alone is sure a mystery.

I ended up looking down over a steep bank, into a deep quarry filled with water. There, sitting on the water near the bank from where I looked down was a large raft (flock) of wild ducks.

Charles Davis

Instantly I thought of the idea of making a big kill by throwing a hand grenade down over the edge of the bank but holding the grenade two seconds before throwing it so that it would go off just a few feet above the ducks.

I released the grenade from the lapel of my combat jacket, was about to grasp the ring to pull the pin when two fighter planes came roaring directly at me——and only about 100 feet above the ground.

It was an American P-51 chasing a ME 109 German fighter. The bullets were hitting in the snow around me.

As they banked over my head they made a sharp left turn, flying almost parallel to the front line.

Our Bofors opened up. Tragically they hit the American instead of the German. Major George Preddy, the leading ace in the ETO made a gradual shallow dive to the ground, hitting a farmhouse that burst into a huge ball of fire and smoke.

Though the crash was only a short distance away, I hastened back to my outfit. I later heard that they only found his dog tags.

The Letters of a Combat Rifleman

Clipping from condensed version of TIME magazine issued to front line troops. (Jan. 1945 ??)

U.S. AT WAR

save this clip. I saw

HEROES

Major Preddy shot down. He went right over my head

In One Week

Seldom has the Army Air Force had to announce there such tragic losses as it made public last week. *the FW 190.*

¶ Brigadier General Frederick W. Castle, who continued combat flying even after he got his star, was piloting a Flying Fortress on a mission over Belgium when seven Messerschmitts attacked. Bullets ignited an oxygen tank, which threatened to explode the Fortress' bomb load. Lean, young (36) General Castle refused to jettison the load, because U.S. troops were underneath. With two engines afire, he leveled out, and stayed at the controls while his crew bailed out. He was still in the plane when a fuel tank exploded, sent plane and pilot to the ground in flames.

¶ On Christmas Day Major George E. Preddy Jr., son of a freight conductor and top U.S. ace in the European Theater, was shot down by his own comrades. Shy, stocky George Preddy, P-51 fighter pilot, had 25½ enemy planes to his credit (plus

PREDDY   McG
In one week, rarely

five destroyed on the ground) when he climbed into the skies over Belgium that day and tangled with two German fighters. He knocked them both down and took off after a Focke-Wulf 190. U.S. troops on the ground opened up with ack-ack, trying to get the 190. Instead they shot down 25-year-old Major Preddy.

"But just to show you how we have it now,—I just came in from hunting rabbits! I went out with a boy from Minnesota and we kicked up three of them but we couldn't shoot because we only had rifles and we didn't want to take a chance of hitting a GI. However, we set a snare for one and perhaps tomorrow we may have rabbit stew."

"In our house here we have a nice set up that includes a radio and electric light. There are seven stoves going to keep us warm and we get two hot meals a day. Not bad, eh!

"The weather here has been real nice lately. Of course it is quite cold but there is plenty of warm sunlight and the moon has been almost as bright as it was in Georgia those nights we spent on the lawn. Remember? Yesterday the vapor trails from the airplanes made some beautiful patterns across the clear, cold, blue sky."

My buddy on the rabbit hunt was "Sugar Reed," our great communications sergeant. newly promoted. We used trip wire from flares and booby traps to set the snare. We had received quite a few mines and material for setting up the booby traps but were warned not to use any of the latter. After the extensive mine fields were put down Love company drew a detail of opening and closing one point on the road every morning and evening. Like that great percentage of all our casualties during combat the only men that I knew of that were killed or injured by mines were the men from the mine laying detail. One sergeant was killed and two other men were seriously wounded.

The electric light was supplied by Gene Bailey's jeep by running wires from the battery to a small light bulb in our room. The other occupants of the house had to be content with candles, flashlights and Coleman lanterns. The lanterns were scarce and the officers always nailed on to the few that were available. Later, one of the companies was to set up a generator and we secretly cut into their line, covering up the evidence with snow.

The seven stoves were kept going with briquettes, the compressed coal that was very plentiful, due no doubt to the fact that we were only about a mile from the briquette factory. They burned very well and left only a fine dust. It was not difficult to keep the fires going all night as the guard was changed every hour or two.

There were six men that lived in our room. It had been the priest's office and was rather small. Only one bed was available and I shared that with Lou Effley. A big roll top desk filled one corner and the stove took up the space in the middle of the floor. Hebish occupied a spot near the door and it was difficult to leave and enter without almost stepping on his head. Lyons, Reed, and Bailey covered the remaining space. I had moved over to the smaller room in order to be with Reed and Effley, who were now my beet friends.

Things were running rather smoothly. Our meals came up on schedule. At noontime we made our own coffee and toast. Lyons, a kitchen helper, set up and cleaned the GI cans and stoves out in the hallway. Chow was served to the whole company in the dining room, the men taking their full meat pans back to their squad quarters. When we were under fire, platoons were served individually and mess gear was washed as best the men could under the circumstances.

Lyons was a great kid. He was always full of fun and could take a lot of kidding. He saw that we had plenty of bread and butter and whatever else was available or left over.

Chapter IX
More Letters and a New Year

It was during this long stay in Lucherberg that I found time to write to others beside my wife. I wrote to Pete Downs, one of my best friends and many times president of the Broomall Sportmen's Club. I was not surprised when I received a letter from Broomall's pistol captain, Mrs. Alice Matthews.

"Last night I was down to the range as we had one of our regular monthly shoots and Pete let me read the wonderful letter you had written to him from somewhere in Germany. So I asked him for your address so I could write you a few lines."

"I was very much surprised to hear you were across and you have one of the most dangerous jobs any army man could have so take good care of yourself cause we here back home want you to give us a few lessons when you get back. I bet your rifle means as much to you as your right arm and you're the fellow who knows how to use it right." (Alice was national women's pistol champion in 1947 and 1949 and could teach me a lot about handgun shooting.)

Alice continued with some club news and that interested me most. "The pistol activity is just about all that now transpires in the club. Now we shoot pistols twice a month like we used to do with ammunition for sale to members. The fellows are all working long hours and don't have a chance to get in any shooting or the scarcity of ammunition makes the situation uninteresting. You have to walk from store to store to buy one box of .22s.

"I have been loading my own .38s as I need them and I have become pretty experienced at it now. However, I've run short of lead so will have to ask some of the fellows who work at defense plants like Bendix to snag me a couple hundred pounds."

Well, I composed the "wonderful" letter to Pete Downs all myself. But part of the one that I sent to Alice in answer to her letter, I copied out of a small overseas edition of Time magazine. It was good copy and it was "real" because I had witnessed similar scenes,—such as "Flying Fortresses towing vapor trials across the sky."

Alice wrote back again and said, "you would make a wonderful war correspondent. I showed your letter to the girls at the office and we all cried."

That Time stuff was sure good. I couldn't have described combat conditions on the western front any better.

"Dearest," I wrote to Jean on December 28, 1944, "Today I received a letter you wrote December 16, The mail is 'on the ball' again and am I glad! "That was the night you were writing, sitting on the couch in your pink silk nightie. I do certainly wish I could have been there to take the place of my picture. That picture is sure out of date now, darling. I wish I could have a new one taken. It seems so strange now to think that I once wore a light cotton uniform with garrison cap. Can you picture me now with rough combat shoes, leggings, olive drab trousers, combat field jacket covered with dirt of England, France, Belgium, Holland, and Germany. 'Longhhandles' underneath, plus two wool shirts and the olive drab wool sweater you made for me. I use a Nazi paratroopers belt that I want to keep as a souvenir. Add to this, dirty hands and face with about three days' growth of whiskers and long hair like a South Philadelphia jitterbug, only of course not combed or slicked down. If I should suddenly appear beside you, just like that, wearing my steel helmet, it would be kind of shocking to say the least. However, I guarantee you, darling, that with a bath, ten hours' sleep and some new clean clothes I could again look something like the 'man I left behind.' You must have been beautiful, honey, to the eyes, nose and touch.

"Glad to hear you are buying war bonds. It was good to read that the people back home over subscribed the last bond drive goal. It sounds as though they are taking a different view of things now back in the States. It seems that it is hard for all Americans to understand the Germans. Their military leaders are superior to ours and the average German, including the women especially, are real fanatics who back the Nazi leaders one hundred percent. Even though we as soldiers see and hear first hand some of the outrageous crimes they commit, it is hard for us to turn around and treat them in the same way. However, if we are to win the war and make a lasting peace we must really get tough with these fanatics first and then try to make the next generation understand as well as ourselves trying to understand their point of view. As I said in my last letter, to be able to understand the other fellow's point of view is not easy but to make a better world we must all strive for this understanding. I can understand why the Germans like Hitler. He made Germany a strong and rich nation. We can see that. Their military highway is like the Pennsylvania superhighway. They had fine clothing and fine furnishings for their homes. Their factories are tremendous; they are a great industrial nation. They really are powerful and with the inspired leadership of fanatic nationalistic devil it is no wonder they think of themselves as superman. However, we know they are not supermen. Their industrial might is something to be proud of but it was not built by free workers like ours nor can it even match ours. We have read how they made slaves of the other peoples of Europe and we as soldiers have seen it with our own eyes that this was true. But despite Hitler and his propaganda of lies, the German people stand convicted of all the crimes and atrocities, too. And this we must not forget. We must make them understand. We must be hard but we must be truthful. We must force them and teach them what the right way is. This is our duty to future generations.

"Hope you are not bored to death, darling. The subject seems to occupy our minds quite a bit. In fact, it seems to be the main topic of conversation for most of us."

That last paragraph may sound like an exaggeration but it was not. Some of the younger A.S.T.P. boys were vitally interested in the subject of world affairs. Our talk, too, was often centered about fighting tactics and past fighting experiences, mostly the comical situations. Other topics were our hometown and families, army experiences in the States, our former jobs and for a few of us, hunting was a popular topic.

It was with some pride and knowledge that I talked of military tactics. I had in some way or other been connected with military organizations for fifteen years. It started back in Girard College where I learned the old manual of arms and was taught how to shoot a .22 rifle in the prone position. Major Kearnigan, who coached teams at Camp Perry for the Pennsylvania National Guard, was my first instructor.

The more than seven years that I had spent in the Pennsylvania National Guard were far more beneficial than my I.R.T.C. training or any other army training that I had received. I knew what fire and movement meant. I knew something about estimating range and designation of targets. Through our limited days in combat I was able to point out to the younger boys that we needed more firepower to support our movements. It wasn't right for a platoon or company of men to move out toward the enemy without any overhead fire or supporting armor. It was basic to say that you shouldn't get too close to an opening when you are firing and I cited the case of Sergeant Albert J. Evans. Jr. and the newly lit cigarette. We all condemned the supporting branches. However, the fellows spoke with satisfaction and pride of Lieutenant Moffett and his assistant who were F.O. boys from our Cannon company. This combination was broken up about this time when Lieutenant Moffett was hit by a shell as he came down the road by our church.

Williams, Zurcher, Henry Bailey and all the other young fellows were right in the midst of all our discussions. They very often asked my opinion.

The Letters of a Combat Rifleman

As New Year's Eve drew near I wrote to Jean and expressed my thought again on joining our Jane. It comforted me to say:

"I received two letters from you yesterday and also the Christmas card which I prize and the dearest. sweetest one I ever got. When I opened it and looked at the pictures of the hallway I could feel the tears gathering in my eyes. Jane's name was not there but her spirit was.

"I am resolved to lead the best life I know, darling, and then if Jane should need me I know the Lord will see that I join her in heaven where we know she is now. If anything should ever happen, dearest, just remember, I went to join our daughter."

To more complaints about the mail and the Bulge I answered Jean: "I can't understand why you are not getting my mail. I write at least three letters a week. Of course, the German offensive slowed up the service somewhat. There are a lot of questions I would like to know the answers to, just like some of the newsmen back in the States and I guess a lot of other people. If the quality and quantity of everything we have, from hand grenades to big bombers, is supposed to be superior to the German stuff, how is it possible for them to make such a breakthrough? I'm not worried but I would like to know the answer to that one. There is no doubt that we are amateurs bucking a line of professionals when it comes to leaders who know what it is all about."

Other notes under Sunday, December 31, "We had church services today. As far as celebrating New Year's Eve, it will be just another cold night for us. There is a barrel of Heine beer sitting here but nobody is drinking it. You may as well drink water.

"The day has been clear and cold with the vapor trails of the planes streaking the blue sky. Evening chow has arrived. We get two meals a day. They are good, too, and that makes a soldier happy. Last night we had steak and french fried potatoes."

I stood guard by the door that night as the old year faded. The clear, cold night air was split at midnight with a thunderous roar of guns and big whistling projectiles. I stood and looked toward the East as the T.D. boys sent flashes of flame over the tops of the houses. It was my most thrilling New Year's Eve. I smiled and was satisfied. I felt secure and safe. Jack Frost was the only one that could penetrate our section of the line. The new year would find us ready for the greatest offensive of all times. When we were to get started we were to roll on and on into the heart of Germany.

It was a few days later that I had a shower again and this always pepped me up. The Red Cross girls were there passing out coffee but it was the young, brightly dressed German girls sledding in the city streets at Brand that reawakened my interest in the opposite sex. They sure were cute.

On the Third, I wrote to Jean, "Yesterday I had another shower and got some more clean clothes. I feel like a new man after a hot shower. You ought to see me in a pair of tight fitting "long handles!" After getting warm again and getting my blood circulating, I really get thinking of you and how I'd like to be getting in bed with the one and only girl in the world for me—you. As for it being harder for me, you are wrong there. We seem to need every moment we have to just keep living. We don't have much time for thoughts or actions in regards to relations with women. Under combat conditions, women from the sex angel become almost like money under the same conditions. You can't take it with you, so it becomes a forgotten commodity.

"A woman is broadcasting from Berlin in English. (Berlin Sally) She sends messages to relatives of British POWs. She puts out plenty of propaganda for the Nazi cause. She asked, 'How long will it be until you hold your loved one in your arms again?' Trying to make us give up the war, they are singing, 'I Don't Want To Make History I Just Want To Make Love.' That's how I feel of course but you realize I can't throw away my rifle and come home. I like some of those sold songs. 'Always' was always one of my favorites. I was surprised to hear it on the Hit Parade. We have the radio again and I'm hearing those songs you mentioned. Christmas Eve, Dinah Shore sang. 'I'll Walk Alone,' (Christmas version)."

The big offensive move toward the heart of Germany was still many weeks off, however, and we still concentrated on defense. The platoons were pulled back one at a time to dig defensive positions near Helrath. We did not like the idea of giving up the high ground at Lucherberg in case of a German drive in our sector but we had to carry out orders. It seemed that all the armor that had been in our section had been withdrawn and consequently the big boys no doubt thought that we could not hold our ground without armor support.

But our immediate leaders were not thinking in terms of defense. Lieutenant Danowski was now company commander and he soon was promoted to captain. He organized schools in radio communications, explosives and weapons training. He secured the town of Helrath as a practice battlefield and we went into maneuvers firing live ammunition. I learned the proper procedure in radio communication. There was little classroom work. We stood out in the snow and cold and called one another over the little handy-talkie (536) radios. If I wanted the first platoon the call went something like this: "Hello, One Love One, Hello One Love One. Message for you, Over."

Company Headquarters, in order to remain unidentified, did not have a number. So the First platoon would answer, "Hello, One Love One, Hello, One Love One. Send your message, Over.

It was surpassing how little the men knew of the proper procedure and the difficulty we had in learning this simple routine. Like weapons training, it had no doubt been quickly passed over back in the States. Next to weapons training, communications should be the most important subject for all infantry men. Knowing who is on your right and left is one of the most important factors in the forward movement of attacking forces. Better radios are one of our greatest needs.

The Letters of a Combat Rifleman

The bazooka school used a real target, a knocked out self-propelled gun just on the edge of town. A lieutenant that had just come up as a replacement was acting "brave" or perhaps I should say stupid one day at a bazooka demonstration and got a piece of flying steel in his knee cap. I generally stood in a nearby trench as the bazooka was fired. It was more of a test of the bazooka than practice at hitting a certain spot and consequently the operator stood only about twenty-five yards from that tank. The officers in charge and also all the men witnessing the demonstration stood just a few feet away from the man firing. It was just another example of army training methods. At times they were over cautious and then they turned around and exposed the men to unnecessary hazards. We were to bump into a very fatal example of this after we reached Cologne. All the rockets penetrated this middleweight German panzer.

The following action took place several times during the first week in January:

The enemy was coming through the church, just two hundred yards away and only Gene Baily, our jeep driver and I were there to hold them back. They started to blast their way through the row of houses on our right front so that it was unnecessary for them to cross the open ground directly in front of us. In no time we would be surrounded or else we would have to take off out of town and cross the cemetery into the open fields at our left rear.

Gene and I had plenty of ammunition and our weapons included a Thompson sub machine gun, and automatic carbine, a P-38 pistol and a semi-auto carbine. The barrel of the Thompson was plenty hot because I had poured hundreds of rounds into the church windows. Gene was calmly plinking at fancy chinaware set up on the window sills of the house across the street. Gene was a good shot with the P-38, but every now and then I took time out to even up the score in tea cups and saucers. We weren't trying to kill the "enemy" because they happened to be some of the boys in our own company. Gene and I were the "enemy detail."

It was good practice for all. The live ammunition made it realistic for the attacking force. I made it safe by making sure that all shots went over their heads. I learned that you must hold a fully automatic weapon down if you wish to get a concentrated fire on a small object. To put every shot of a five shot burst into a small window or opening in a house just across the street means that you must rest the barrel of the gun on some firm object and hold on tight. Naturally, you shouldn't rest it on the windowsill like we did during these practiced maneuvers, but on some other support away from any opening.

Each platoon took its turn blasting a path through deserted Helrath. The men who were new needed the experience of "enemy" fire and everyone needed the practice in fighting from house to house. There should have been some problems worked out where in the attacking force fired live ammo and practiced plenty of fire and movement exercises. It is all right to blast a hole in one house and crawl into the next one but they didn't practice going from one block of houses to the next. Regardless of the criticism, it was wonderful training, better than anything ever conducted in the States.

By January 9, our mounting aerial thrusts were beginning to turn the tide in the Bulge. This mighty, visible striking force rode forth almost every day and certainly filled a doughboy's spirit with exuberance. I wrote to Jean on that date:

"Things here are about the same. It has been snowing for a few days, which isn't good for us. However, we don't mind it too much in the present situation. We have foxholes but we don't have to live in them. The planes sure give us riflemen a thrill when they go over. It makes chills run up and down you and makes you want to cry with joy. I saw hundreds go by the other day in perfect formation, like silver fish, far, far up in the blue. The fighters buzz around them like silver gnats. It must be terrifying to be on the receiving end."

Some of our planes were on the receiving end at times. And in turn, some of our rear echelon elements were on the receiving end. It happened when some of the big fortresses limped back in distress. At least seven parachutists were in the air that day. One air man landed near the river and he got his directions mixed up and ran toward the Jerries and consequently was taken prisoner. One of the damaged planes dropped its bomb load and they plunked down right on top of a group of houses and factories between Eschweiler and Weisweiler, causing great damage to a unit of division headquarters and killing many officers and men.

It was the same old story of our own side inflicting more damage than the enemy. The only difference this time being the method. I do not know of anyone in our division who was killed by enemy planes. Everyone in the American armed forces needed more training and experience, from the infantry on up to the air corps.

My little family kept complaining about the poor mail service and I had to keep making excuses. So I wrote on January 10:

"Billy certainly must be disappointed when the mailman doesn't have a letter for you and him. You tell Billy that you don't get a letter from me every day because the mail trucks have a hard time getting through the snow over here and the ships have to sail through rough seas."

To interest Billy I wrote, "We have something here Billy would like. Carl (Zurcher) just opened a gallon can of hard candy. It is GI candy and helps some."

As usual the planes came in for mention again: "The air corps thrilled us again today. It was a beautiful clear winter day. The sky was blue and the sun was shining. The planes were towing vapor trails but they were much shorter than usual."

In the next paragraph I told of some of our hunting expeditions and hinted at our location: "Reed, our communications sergeant and Williams and I went hunting for rabbits. The snow is two or three feet deep in places and we could see the bunny tracks running all over the fields and fence rows. However, we didn't see any bunnies. Reed flushed a big covey of quail. We also have quite a few wild ducks around so you know we are near water. Perhaps you can guess the name."

It was a long and varied letter I wrote on the tenth. More followed: "Williams just showed me a Dagwood comic. It was about Mrs. Bumstead trying to join the Minerva Club and Dagwood was experimenting with his radio invention. Sure was funny.

"Homer (Jean's cousin) probably had a good time in Paris. From what I hear, there is plenty of wine, women, and song there. They say you are approached on almost every street corner with the question, "Zig-zig?'

"We have sleeping bags now and some of the boys have an awful time getting in and out of them. If the zipper ever sticks we will probably have to start shooting from the prone position.

"The boys want me to write to Clare Booth Luce. She is in Congress and just recently spoke up for the infantry saying they should get a break like the air corps by having a furlough in the States after so many days in combat. We all liked the idea. However, I guess it would never work."

Apparently Mrs. Luce had an understanding heart. Her idea may not have been practical but it made us feel that someone, even if it was a woman, could project themselves into our position and understand our problems, which was more than the biggest general could do, including Eisenhower.

I wrote and thanked Mrs. Luce.

My letter to Jean ended: "I still keep faith in God and I know He will answer our prayers so don't give up. We do at times feel like Representative Luce said, 'wondering when our time will come because that is all that we seem to have to look forward to.' But God has brought me through so much I feel that He wants me to join you and Bill again, so keep faith, darling. If He should ever change His mind you will know I went to join our Jane in heaven. It brings tears to my eyes but I am happy, knowing I am safe whatever His decision. Without a doubt, your waiting and hoping is a greater sacrifice than I am making so do not worry, darling, about the 'little bit' you are doing. I love you and I will be with you soon. As ever, Your loving husband, Charles."

The wild ducks on the lake at the edge of town were targets that I could not resist. It was a question though as to how we would get them. The Springfield was still not sighted in to my complete satisfaction and even if I hit a duck with it I wouldn't have anything left to eat. Reed and I wanted shotguns but we had no hope of finding one. By this time every house in Lucherberg had been looted. It was apparent that the German civilians had taken the few firearms that they owned with them.

It was a great temptation for us when two officers from another outfit drove up to company headquarters one day, parked their jeep and went down into the cellar to the CP. In the rear seat lay two beautiful European double barrel shotguns. Reed and I debated. We finally decided that we couldn't get away with stealing them.

I decided to try something new in the way of duck hunting after exhausting every normal approach. Why wouldn't hand grenades do the trick, I reasoned. Without consulting anyone I started out for the lake one bright day with a couple of fragmentation grenades. The bank on the north side was very steep and if the ducks were near the north shore—well, they would never know what happened.

Going down along the road to get into position, I could see the ducks close up against the bank. There were at least twenty in the flock and they were close enough for me to heave a grenade right down on top of them. It would be unnecessary to hold the grenade very long after the handle flew off because the throw plus the fifty or sixty foot drop to the water would take up a couple of seconds.

As I drew near to the edge of the bank almost opposite the ducks I was just ready to pull the pin on a grenade when suddenly I looked up and saw two planes coming across the lake no more than two hundred feet in the air. To me they looked like two P-51 fighters. Quite a flurry of bullets hit in the snow around me and in seconds the two pursuits were banking almost over my head. It all happened so fast I never hit the ground and I never even saw what insignia they had on their wings. However, I realized that one must be chasing the other and that was more than the AA gunners knew because just after they banked and turned to the left, some .50 caliber AA boys or Bofors 40 mm's cut loose. Both planes were hit. One plane threw out a smoke trail and nosed down directly into a house. There was a terrific explosion and the plane and house exploded in a cloud of black dust, smoke, flame, and flying debris.

They later found the pilot's dog tags. Said he was an American captain with twenty-three enemy planes to his credit, the leading ace in the ETO. It took an American ack-ack crew to bring him down.

It was later that I read in an overseas edition of Time magazine: "Major George E. Preddy, Jr., son of a freight conductor and top U.S. ace in the European Theater, was shot down by his own comrades. Shy, stocky George Preddy, P-51 fighter pilot, had twenty-five and one-half enemy planes to his credit (plus five destroyed on the ground) when he climbed into the skies over Belgium that day and tangled with two German fighters. He knocked them both down and took off after a Flocke-Wulf 190. U.S. troops on the ground opened up with ack-ack, trying to get the 190. Instead they shot down twenty-five-year-old Major Preddy." This, undoubtedly was the tragedy I witnessed. Needless to say, it ended my duck hunting.

It took quite a bit of effort and time to get our first rabbit. There were plenty of them about. We saw some big ones and we also saw many tracks in the snow. Many were caught in the snares but all managed to escape. We thought someone was getting around in the morning before us. I soon found the trouble however. The wire was easy to break and apparently the rabbits pulled and jumped around until it gave way. It didn't seem right to me that you could break our trip wire with your hands.

All managed to escape—except one. I was a proud hunter the day I brought in that nice, big, prime bunny. It was delicious, fried in butter.

The box trap filled with corn that Reed and I rigged up to catch quail never produced. We were rather disappointed hunters. We had plenty of firepower but not the right kind.

We had plenty of time to write letters now and I sent one home almost daily. January 11, I wrote to Jean: "There was no mail or packages today. I'm looking forward to tomorrow morning now, as it is rather late at night. We all go to bed quite early whenever we can. Tonight I was sitting up talking to a new man that just came in. He kept saying how he missed his wife. All us married men just smiled to ourselves. Like us, he will have to get used to being without his loved ones.

"We are still having snow and it is about zero out. The trees are all silver with the ice and snow. Quite pretty, but nothing like Pennsylvania.

"I have to crawl in my sleeping bag and get some sleep, darling, so goodnight and pleasant dreams."

Two days later I wrote again: "Things look gloomy at times over here. Tremendous things are happening and what the future days of '45 hold for us no one knows. But above everything we know we are fighting for what is right and we know in the end we will win. Many die every day for some cause or other. We believe firmly in our cause and if necessary we are prepared to die fighting for what we believe in. In the meantime we are all "sitting it out" hoping and praying for the best.

"Everything is about the same with us here. Outside of dreaming of home and the future, we are still occupied with the problem of just staying alive. We live from meal to meal and our only other interest is getting some sleep whenever we can. Our only relief is talking to each other. Sometimes we get a chance to listen to the radio. The fellows I am with are all amateurs at war but they don't lack anything in courage and they sure are a swell bunch to get along with."

Things were looking brighter on January 14, when I wrote: "The war news is much better now so I do hope you are not so worried. Perhaps we may all be surprised someday to wake up and find the war is over. Anyway don't give up hope, darling.

The next day it was more good news: "All is well here. We still have it pretty nice considering. It was a wonderful clear, cold winter day today. It is evening now and it sounds as if another great air armada is going over. It is a continuous roar and lasts for about a half hour or more.

"Some of the boys received some more packages today so perhaps some of mine will start arriving. However, don't worry if I don't receive them, honey. I got the one with your picture and that was the one I wanted most."

The news in my January 16 letter sounded like anything but the front lines: "We are still holding out here. However, we had a little entertainment for a change. After a five mile hike we saw a show, 'Rhapsody in Blue.' with Paul Whiteman. My feet became useless about the middle of the picture so I got up and went back 'home.' The biggest news is—I just had coca-cola, the first one since I left Camp Kilmer. It sure tasted wonderful.. We were each rationed one, and I guess we are lucky to get one, where we are. I just wonder if the Krauts opposite us, get to see movies and have soda pop to drink!

"The biggest kick we get around here now is to sit and talk for hours on end. We have a swell bunch of boys and I sure have fun listening to some of their stories. They come from all parts of the States. Their ages run from twenty to forty. They are the best, too, because anything but the best doesn't last long here. Of course, their knowledge of tactics and weapons is another story."

My last paragraph struck a sad note again: "We don't seem to have much to live for over here but we never give up hope. We'll spank those Germans good, one of these days and then I'll be home and I hope you are there waiting for me with open arms."

CHAPTER X
Front Line Garrison Life

Five mile hikes were now becoming a daily occurrence. It was good training and it helped us to keep in condition. The trend, however, seemed to be more and more toward the old, stateside, garrison routine. Reveille was the next step.

First Lieutenant Thompson was now the executive officer and his influence had a lot to do with the new set up. Weapons training was again near the bottom of the list.

Even though reveille wasn't until 7:45, it was still dark when we formed a single line in the street outside of the company CP. Lieutenant Thompson always took the report and always made a front and rear inspection. The lieutenant practically rubbed noses with each man as he peered through the darkness to see whether or not we had shaved the day before.

Thompson showed his lack of good sense one day when he marched the company too close to the Roer River. The Jerries cut loose with mortar fire. But this didn't deter the lieutenant. An army officer could never let the men know that he was wrong, that the marching company less than one thousand yards from the river had attracted the German guns. The next day he marched us all back again! I sweated that hike out—in more ways than one. Luckily, we were not shelled.

The movie was shown back in Lamersdorf in the building that had been our company CP. It was so crowded that I had to sit on the floor and couldn't move in any direction. Naturally, the film broke several times even though it was supposed to be a world premiere. I was feeling low and "Rhapsody in Blue" didn't help to make things brighter.

Jean showed her anxiety and jealous temperament when she asked in one of her letters about the salesgirl who sold me the perfume in Zambre, Belgium. My letter on the seventeenth addressed her doubts: "I received the letter you wrote December 29, today, darling. It was a real long one and just as sweet and loving as ever. You mentioned again how you like the perfume. Thanks, sweetheart. As I recall, there were two salespeople, one a woman and the other a man. I told them I wanted it for 'Madam—in America.' They were all smiles and very helpful. I even forget the color of the girl's hair in case you are still interested."

Lieutenant Thompson had not as yet started a close inspection on our quarters according to my January 17 letter: "Things are still the same here. Did I tell you we were in a priest's house again, that is, what is left of it. I'm sitting at his desk writing this letter. We are lucky enough to have two lights. One is a lantern and we have a small electric light with the juice furnished by a jeep. There is the usual pile of junk around. I'll just give you an idea. Here is a partial list:

A Kraut beer mug full of coffee
wire cutters
pencils
cigarettes (enough to last a month)
pipe tobacco
several pies
a mirror
toothpaste
many bars of soap
ink
old copy of S. & S.
hard candy
hand grenade
scissors
stale loaf of bread
pair of gloves
ammunition clips

writing paper
four cans of evaporated milk
a clock
adhesive tape
several shaving sets
flashlight
canteen cup
deck of cards
kerosene lamp
stuffed owl
K rations
D rations
canned butter
pair of socks
old undershirt
field telephone
etc., etc.

"That is just some of the stuff piled on this desk. Louis F. Effley, a boy from northern New York just placed a can of string beans beside me (he first heated them on the stove) but I like steak with my beans. Reed just turned a piece of bread over on the stove (he is making toast) and Effley said, 'Watch out, you'll break that stove.' Over all this scene is a crucifix and a picture of the owner of the house with Pope Pius XI's signature on it."

This letter ended with a good note, too,—"Someday soon I'll be crossing the ocean again to return to my loved ones. The news is very good today so we should all feel happy. I'm taking care of myself to return to you, darling. Keep faith in me, please, and keep writing."

On January 18, I wrote, "It is warmer but we have a strong wind blowing. In fact it just knocked the church steeple down.

That practically ended all enemy shelling of Lucherberg. It was now apparent that nearly all their shots were aimed at the steeple. No wonder our house had received twenty-five direct hits!

My letter continued, "I'd sure like to be home with you tonight, sweetheart, in our own little home. We could let the wind howl outside and we could be warm and happy together by our fireside. I could just go to sleep in your arms now, darling. Someday soon we will be together again, the happiest family in the U.S.A. Billy and I can run his trains to Macon and a lot of other places. We sure will have a lot of fun.

"Eugene Bailey, a lad from Arkansas (by way of California) is going to make some coffee and then I'll hit the hay. I can't say whether the days go fast or slow. Anyway it seems ages since I held you and loved you, darling. I sure have saved up plenty of loving for you—and only you."

To keep up the home moral I also reported, "The Russians sure are going to town. It looks like they are giving the Germans a good spanking."

On January 20, 1945, I wrote to Jean: "We are all glad to see the Russians making headway. We would just as soon wake up some morning and see the Reds on the other side of the river.

"It was a beautiful clear day today and we riflemen were glad to see the big air fleets going over again.

"Reed is having a lot of fun. He has a big gasoline torch and is heating a gallon of coffee. He looks like Superman with a flame thrower.

My letter to Jean on the twenty-second recalled a repeldepel buddy. "Remember," I wrote, "Bobby Delach, the South Philadelphia iceman whom I became acquainted with in the replacement camps? I saw him yesterday for the first time since Holland. He has the Purple Heart and is now an M.P."

Bobby and I did some traveling together through Belgium and we had a few experiences with the black market in that country. We would have sold the shirts off our backs in those days and we sometimes did. Bobby got a nice price for a pair of corrective shoes that the army had made especially for him. He told the Belgian gentlemen that they were paratrooper boots and they paid a handsome price. It was about this time that we found out we could put in a claim of lost property with no questions asked, every time we moved, even if it were only from one woods to the next field. The Belgian merchants began to canvas us right in our camp sites.

Bobby was especially interested in getting enough francs together to buy his sweetheart in South Philly a beautiful gift. The price of the shoes and a couple of wool shirts enabled him to send home a lovely compact.

There was another reason we went into Namur and this one had blondish red hair and was pretty as a picture. She tended bar in her father's place despite the fact that she was only seventeen years old. Nelly was her name and Bob used to great her with a loud, "Who hit Nelly in the belly with a flounder" The best Bobby could do was to leave for the front with a picture of Nelly, inscribed, "To Bobby, toujour my love."

It was a pleasant surprise to march past regimental headquarters that day and see Bobby standing guard at the main entrance. We were on our way to a rifle range that had been set up in a field just across the road and so I had an opportunity to stop and talk with Bob. He had been assigned to a rifle company until he was hit. The MP job suited him a lot better as he had had extensive experience in that line back in the States.

The rifle range was a temporary affair and we did not know the distances that we were shooting. But I estimated the range at less than two hundred yards. We started out to zero in at about seventy-five yards, and I found my rifle shooting at seven o'clock in the three ring. After a correction and then some practice with our automatic weapons, we moved back another hundred yards or so. I got down on the snow and into the sling and although I was very uncomfortable I managed to place a very nice group in the black. The sling is a good aid in sighting in a rifle but taking all into consideration a sling should be used only as a means of carrying a rifle, the same as is the case with a sporting arm. A sling should not be used even to sight in a rifle or to train a rookie. In actual combat you do not use a sling, and consequently, you are holding the rifle differently, and as we all know it will group differently or the point of impact will change when the hold is changed or when the tension on the barrel is varied.

It was about this time that I made my second visit to the aid station since I came up to the lines. My January 25 letter mentioned the trouble: "My jaw was giving me some trouble a few days ago so I went back to the aid station. The doc said he thought I had the mumps but I told him I had them before so he was undecided. Today he said it was an infection of the same gland, not the mumps. I've been taking some pills and I go back each day and he paints the inside of my mouth. The doc said there was nothing to worry about and it feels a lot better now."

While at the aid station in Lamersdorf one day I witnessed the usual handling of a case of the GIs. The man complaining was a tech sergeant in our weapons platoon. He was a good soldier and would not put on a sick act. However, he got the usual treatment. I heard about it often before but this time I witnessed the whole show. The sergeant said he was sick and he looked sick. The captain-medic gave the standard answer, "Go back and wash your mess gear."

There was some good news in the letter, too: "We had another PX ration which is always welcome. Got some candy bars, fruit juice, one cigar and a box of Weston's New Yorker assorted cookies. We always have plenty of coffee. Reed has the gasoline torch going and has boiled two gallons of Java in the last hour.

"The room is full of smoke,. Someone dropped a brick down the stove pipe. There is always something going on around here to keep you 'nervous in the service.' We take pictures and use the glass frame for windows and then someone goes and fires a gun nearby and we have to start looking for another picture."

It was generally a volley from the tank destroyers in the orchard that blasted our picture glass window panes. Pictures were getting hard to find. That was what had us worried.

There was more good news in my next letter: I was "blessed with two lovely, most welcome letters" as the mail service had been very bad during the last two weeks. Also, "I was glad to hear that Carl (my brother-in-law) is home. Give Carl and Dorothy my best wishes. If he must come across, tell them not to worry because we will have the war over by then. If we don't, the Russians will. The S. & S. today said they are ninety-one miles from Berlin. We are going to start teaching the boys in our outposts how to speak Russian. The latest one we heard was that the Germans were collecting boats across the river in order to escape from the Reds!

My face is feeling much better. The captain told me I bit myself! Anyway, I have an infected spot on the inside of my cheek.

"We had our hot shower yesterday and got clean clothing. Got a new pair of leather and cloth mittens with woolen liners. We are supposed to get some more Arctic clothing according to S. & S."

The mittens had a trigger finger section separate from the rest of the glove. They had very long cuffs that went halfway up to the elbow. I wore them and found them to be satisfactory for the weather conditions we experienced. It is doubtful that they would be sufficient in colder zones. The standard GI glove is wool with leather palms proved to be excellent.

My letter continued, "Reed is entertaining with some knife throwing. He has two trench knives. a pair of scissors and a pocket knife. Just now he stuck all four of them in the door. He reminds me of George Marnhout (big game hunter and knife collector).

"We have a barrel of beer on tap and I have to set my canteen cup on the stove to warm it up.

"This afternoon we saw the movie, "Our Hearts were Young and Gay." It was funny , but I would have fallen asleep if I didn't have to keep balancing myself on my steel helmet. There were no chairs, except for the officers. There were two girls in the picture seeking a little diversion in Europe. All the boys cheered when they showed a billboard saying, Visit Germany and see the Beautiful Rhineland.' When they were sightseeing in Paris one said to the other, 'What are you staring at?' The answer was, 'Frenchmen.' You should have heard the boos."

My letter closed with, "The boys are making some toast now and then we will make sandwiches with the K ration cheese that we get.

"We are all hoping the news continues good. Keep praying, darling."

As I came off my post early on the twenty-ninth, I wrote: "It is five A.M. and before I catch another couple hours of sleep I thought I would answer the letter I received yesterday. You wrote it January 19, which means that I got a real recent letter (ten days) and I am happy for that."

My family complained of not getting my letters and I sure was a very unhappy soldier to hear that Billy, my Happy Chappy boy, looked forward so much to the daily visit of the mailman and then was so disappointed when there was no letter from his daddy.

I told Jean in my letter: "It must be an awful disappointment to Billy, too, when there is no mail. You tell my Happy Chappy that I write every day if I do not have too much work to do. And tell him that the snow must be slowing up the mail trains because he should get more mail than he does."

The chaplain had spoken to us about a subject that I had given little thought. I mentioned it to Jean, "Yesterday was quiet. I attended church. The chaplain told us we would be forgiven for killing. He said we were just like the law enforcement agencies at home."

When I was shooting to kill my only thought was self-preservation. I knew that if I did not stop the enemy from coming at me then I would be killed. There was no hesitation or trembling as I squeezed off the shot to take a human life. The misses or near misses that I made were not caused by buck fever. I attribute them mainly to tough shooting conditions and an improperly sighted rifle, plus my inexperience with a scoped gun.

In my last paragraph I complained to Jean about my bed partner, "Effey:" "I'm missing you so very, very much, sweetheart. That soft bed and fireside you spoke of was enough to drive me crazy. Instead of that I have to lie on a broken-down single bed and share ii with — a soldier!"

The next day I wrote again: "Here it is early morning again and I am going to take time to write you that I am well but still missing and desiring you. We have plenty of coal, the fire is heating the room just right and I have a bed waiting, but still I dream and long for you, darling."

My letter on February 1 had the usual report on the weather, which naturally always affected combat troops to a very great extent. I wrote, "The weather is not so good. It is much warmer and we are getting some rain, which makes things pretty sloppy, especially where we are. However, we are making out all right."

The medics were making things as miserable as the weather and more miserable than the enemy could and I sought comfort by saying: "I'm fine myself after recovering from a couple of 'shots' by the medics. You know how I dislike needles. I was supposed to get one for typhoid and one for tetanus, but by mistake they gave me two typhoid shots, one in each arm. They make you feel pretty miserable for a couple of days. I'm glad to say I feel better now."

I only hinted at the good news: "I haven't seen any news for a couple of days but I want to tell you that there is a very good prospect that the war will end soon. I can't give you any details, but we had something happen yesterday which gave good indication that it can't go on much longer."

The Letters of a Combat Rifleman

A German soldier had crossed the river during the night and had surrendered to our outposts, volunteering the information that the positions on the other side were practically unmanned and that the soldiers holding them wanted to surrender. This information was, of course, partially correct. However, the German army was far from beaten and the war was to last for another fourteen weeks. Most of my best friends would never see the end. The next day our outfit moved. We relieved the first battalion in Merken, which was much closer to the river. Lucherberg had become practically rear echelon during the last couple of weeks.

We made the march to Merken early in the morning and it was a slow, hard walk. The ground was covered with ice, snow, and water and the dirt road across the fields was full of deep ruts. My sore arms added to my discomfort.

It was dark yet when we entered the town and we were covered with mud and soaking wet with perspiration after our short, rough hike. Things were shipshape and we just moved into already furnished and blacked out building. Valenzuelo, Bogas, Eugen Bailey, Effley, Jennings and I took over a large room in a corner house. We were almost on the far west end of the town which was about three blocks wide and ran parallel with the river for a distance of about half a mile. The entire population which probably numbered less than two thousand had fled.

The main section of company headquarters bedded down in a large farmhouse building across the street. This group included the captain, executive officer, platoon runners, radio operators and communications men. Wire ran out to all the platoons and a man remained on the phone at headquarters twenty-four hours a day.

We made some changes in our quarters and expanded a little There was an excellent cook stove in the room that furnished the heat and hot coffee. plus some excellent toast. We brought in a brand new set of pots and pans from the local hardware store and we were all set up for housekeeping. "King" company was in town on our left and "Item" took over positions on our right. "Mike" supplied heavy machine gun and mortar support.

Security of company headquarters was maintained with a two-man guard post that had a roof and even a small stove. On February 3, I mentioned it to Jean: "Time out while I put some coal on the fire. (coal mark) That smudge is coal dust, all the way from Germany. Right now I wish I were shoveling some of that good old Pennsylvania anthracite on 'our fire.'

"I'd like to tell you where I am now but that of course is a military secret. It isn't exactly an ideal place to write a letter. There is just room here for the two men to stand up. We have a roof but it leaks some. However, as long as we have heat we can stand a few hardships.

My letter again mentioned the Russians: "The war news continues very good. Yesterday the S. & S. said the Russians were only thirty-five miles from Berlin.'

"Just for fun," I wrote, "I made a list of things I had in my pockets. It even amazed me so I'll enclose it to give you an idea of what a rifleman carries. Of course there are a lot of other things that I didn't list."

Among the forty-seven items were:

wallet D ration bar of chocolate	needles
gun part	German coins
scissors	Belgian coins
key ring	English half crown
map of Germany	Religious coin
pay book	matches
Red Cross coupons	rifle cleaning patches
letters	string
radio book	three pocket knives
mirror	safety pins
your picture (Jean)	nails
photo folder	cigarette lighter
pipe	thimble
Testament	tweezers
fountain pen	salt shaker
stamps	hellozone tablets
toilet paper	screw driver
German and Belgian currency	pencil
handkerchief	Christmas card
newspaper (S. & S.)	pipe tobacco

That was an awful bunch of stuff for a man that was trying to travel light. The important items for a rifleman were: matches, pocket knife, patches, salt shaker, screw driver, scissors, map, mirrors, and toilet paper (or S. & S.). The cartridges should have been in my cartridge belt.

My next letter told about the first P-38 I acquired. I shot this pistol and learned to like it and depend on it. It functioned well and handled nicely.

"I was paid again the other day," my letter stated. "It comes to four hundred thirty-eight marks a month now. A mark is worth ten cents so that's forty-three dollars and eighty-eight cents. I've invested thirty in a P-38, pistol with Bailey., It cost sixty dollars. It is only an investment as we can sell it back in the rear echelon for seventy-five or one hundred dollars. We have about five hundred rounds of ammo. too."

My February 5 letter was a long one, over one thousand two hundred words. Perhaps my second paragraph explained my writer's cramp. I wrote Jean, "I went through my pockets and found twelve of your letters, I'll read them again and answer them."

I had other letters, too, just recently received from my sisters, Victoria and Florence, and from an old friend of the family, Mrs. Annie Noonan.

The Letters of a Combat Rifleman

Jean told of the hard winter in the States in one of the letters so I assured her that we were a lot better off. "You sure are having a very bad winter," I wrote. "I hope you got your supply of coal. We never have to worry about coal here but the boys in the rear have to burn wood. Hardly any of the hotels in Paris have coal and the Belgians need fuel, too. I don't think the Germans ever hurt for coal or food..

Having been to church the day before I was in a "sermon" mood. On page two I wrote, "You always said I looked down on you but I can honestly say that secretly I always admired you as well as loved you and that I was proud of you. Please don't look up to me anymore, darling. You are so much more intelligent than the average girl I want you to go on loving me and helping me and taking care of me. And take good care of yourself as a present for me. You are such a precious gift. God made you and He was kind to us both. He made us equal, too, and He offers us unlimited opportunity. The chaplain told us about the 'rich, young ruler' in St. Luke. It was a wonderful talk and I wished you were there with me. We are like the 'rich, young ruler,' you and I. Between us we can make a better world, But if I am not here to help you I am sure you can do just as well. Remember, what happens is God's will. I love you, darling , and I'm proud of you. Be good and never loose faith no matter what happens."

My boy, Billy, had enclosed a piece of candy in one of the letters so I had to remember that: "I received the stick of candy Billy sent me and I thank him very, very much. It was just the kind I like. I gave a piece to Bailey, our jeep driver and he liked it, too, Billy."

I had to thank and remember him, too, for the big job that he was shouldering. "My Happy Chappy must have worked awfully hard shoveling snow. It is a good thing you have such a big boy around the house to help with such manly jobs. It sure is hard work shoveling snow isn't it Billy?"

Billy had received the big toy wooden locomotive that I sent him form England and he was asking for a duplicate for his pal, Joey. "Billy, if I get a chance I'll send Joey a locomotive. I only wish I could send you the bicycle I have. It took me two days to fix it up but I put plenty of things on it. It has a headlight, generator, hand brake, chain guard, bell, wheel lock, two taillights and a combination stand and rack. I'm putting large pedals on it with yellow caution reflectors. All I need now is a rear view mirror and a couple of foxtails."

The bike was assembled from numerous vehicles that were scattered about the town. It was a diversion in quiet, workless Merken. It was quiet because we sent out very few shells and we received even less. It was practically workless because we had no training program due to our closeness to the enemy. The bikes we assembled were also a great help in getting around to our scattered company. Every platoon except Weapons was up on the line. They were staggered, just like houses on the edge of a small town are staggered. Some squads were in back of others. The second platoon was practically in a reserve position. "Mike" company had a heavy machine gun squad right up on the line with us. Just in front of their house they had a German 75 mm gun and plenty of ammo to make it speak. And typical of the spirit of the company they were associated with, those Mike men ran out every evening and fired that 75, directly into the town across the river, Huchem-Stammeln. The Jerries in Huchen-Stammeln just took it. They were too tired and weak to fire back. And perhaps they had no guns to fire back. But I don't want to take away from the credit due the loyal men of Mike. The Jerries did have machine guns and rifles and mortars and rockets. They flashed machine gun tracers up the main street once in a while and we got samples of their accurate and efficiently used shells. Their 75 mm gun was right out in the open with no cover whatsoever. The distance to the nearest German position must have been less than eight hundred yards. We clearly had the enemy dominated. But this was only part of our domination plan. It developed every day until it mounted to a crescendo on the early morning of February 23.

My letter continued, "We have a big Belgian rabbit here now. Bailey caught him. He is almost black in color and weighs about five pounds." He was the biggest thumper I ever saw and boy how he thumped the bottom of the cage we put him in to fatten him up. It was a miracle to me how he survived the attack on Merken and the occupation by the First battalion plus other possible dangers. It was hard to believe that there were any living things in that desolate, destroyed town except American soldiers. We never saw any mice or roaches or even lice. But out of all the destruction and ruin hopped this big, black bunny, a wonderful supplement to our daily ten-in-one rations. Fried in butter, old thumper was a tasty morsel.

The light flickered as I ended with, "My candle is almost gone, sweetheart, and I must shave this beard off or I'll frighten the Krauts even. So goodnight and more wonderful dreams. Give Billy a big hug and kiss from his daddy. I love him too, and I want to get home and help him shovel some of that snow."

On February 7 I mentioned my first sale of a foreign handgun, the popular P-38: "Bailey and I sold the P-38 pistol. We got seventy-five dollars for it. That makes eighty-seven dollars I am carrying with me now.

That was profit for us of fifteen dollars. We were confident that we would pick up many more P-38s for nothing. However, we were both to be disappointed.

I often mentioned the amount of money that I was carrying because I never knew when I was going to be carried back by the quartermaster boys and from what I heard, little if any of a dead doughboy's personal belongings ever reached his family. I guess though the mention of a certain amount of money in my possession would not have helped my wife in recovering it if it were stolen from my body.

In this letter I mentioned one of my best friends, Claude Ansel of Upper Darby: "I received another letter from Claude. He is still sweating it out on

The Letters of a Combat Rifleman

Siapan. Hopes to get home soon." Claude was in the engineers and had been strafed by Jap planes during the attack on Pearl Harbor. He was starting his fourth year in the Pacific and I couldn't help but feel sorry for him and wish him the best of luck. Conditions in the South Pacific were no doubt twice as bad as the ETO, and I did not envy any of those boys in their island hopping. From what I heard and read afterward, they did have an easier fight. The Japs were not near as good soldiers as the Germans and their weapons were inferior to ours, whereas most of the German weapons were superior. The Jerries had no knee mortars or .25 caliber rifles and machine guns. They spoke with 88's and .31 caliber guns. The Germans had the best tanks in the world. The Japs had the worst. It's a good thing they were not fighting the Germans in the South Pacific.

We still talked tactics and once in a while we drank milk. "One of the boys is making milk with powder and water," I told Jean. "Bailey is writing and there is quite a discussion of mortars and tactics going on. The weather is still warm and wet.

The weather, mail delivery, and chow were constantly on our minds and nearly always the chief topic of discussion. Naturally, I wrote many times about the same subjects. As in my February 8 letter: "The mail hasn't come up yet. We get two hot meals a day and they bring the mail up after our evening meal. Our chow is usually very good. Tonight we had turkey, mashed potatoes, peas, string beans, spaghetti, filling, coffee, bread and butter and sliced pineapple."

No wonder I wrote, "I'm feeling fine, darling, never better."

My '03 came in for some mention, too, "I cleaned my rifle good today and tonight I must shave and wash up. I generally shave about twice a week."

In the last paragraph I finally got around to the weather: "The sky is a brilliance of color as the sun goes down in the west. If it were not for the shattered houses and muddy roads it would remind me of Lynnewood Park. Pray God we will soon be watching the sunset together again from the doorway of our own home."

It took a long time for any packages to reach me because of my replacement status and often the ones that did arrive were in bad shape. My blind brother, Bill and his wife, Annabelle of Pittsburgh sent the best wrapped and the most practical gifts of all my friends and relatives. I said in my next letter: "Got a box today from Annabelle and Bill: three pairs of wool socks. two hunting magazines and a nice box of candy."

Bill never saw or experienced army life or combat, but he couldn't have picked a better combination. There he had sent the most important item of a combat soldier's clothing; the food delicacy that we dreamed of and could use most and, knowing I was a sportsman, he picked the best possible medium for me to while away my spare time. The sightless may be blind physically but often they can "see" what you and I are blind to.

Jean had asked in her last letter if I was with our division commander, Terrible Terry Allen, so I replied, "I am not with T.T. as you can see by my address. That is all I can say. Perhaps Carl (Jean's brother) can explain. He probably understands APO numbers. As far as the army I am in, this often changes. I am in the same one now as I was in 1939 and '40. Do you remember that banner over the radio?"

My address was Co. L, 415th Inf. APO 104. The 104 identified me as being in the 104th Infantry Division and naturally the other part of the address indicated that I was not with the division commander but in one of the line companies. The banner over the radio in our living room, read, "First Army Maneuvers, New York, 1940."

Jean enclosed a Billydote, as follows, "Daddy (Billy's grandfather) bought a Varga calendar and Billy climbed up—took it down from the wall and sat on the floor looking at the girls. We could hear him say—mmm—that's delicious! Boy, oh, boy—she's beautiful! etc. etc."

"I wonder," Jean asked, "Just who he could take that from?"

It was getting plenty sloppy in Merken but in Philadelphia it was still snowing. I wrote, "I hear you still are getting plenty of snow. It is all water here. Pretty soon we'll need boats. The roof is leaking now and many of the cellars are flooded."

There would be no more snow in our section of Germany. We were definitely headed for spring weather. It was at this point that they started to issue arctic or winter clothing. The home front had come through all right and made the clothing but they forgot to tell the high command when to issue it. In less than two weeks it was collected, there being no further use for it.

Valentine's Day heralded the approach of spring-like weather, for on that day I wrote, "The sky is blue this morning with dabs of white, fleecy clouds moving east, low and fast, And taking advantage of the brilliant sunlight, a squad of GIs are snapping pictures on the corner. One of them looks like a Russian. His beard is big and black."

"May this be a Happy Valentine Day for you. And I hope you get the flowers I sent." The Red Cross had taken orders for the delivery of flowers to our wives and sweethearts back in January and I hadn't mentioned it to Jean before. She received the large bouquet of yellow roses, our daughter Jane's favorite, about the same time that I was writing the letter. Needless to say, Jean was very happily amazed and pleased. Later she wrote, "To think that you would remember me in such a way right in the middle of battle!" The Red Cross deserves a big assist credit on this noteworthy remembrance by the fighting male sex

CHAPTER XI
Roer River Crossing

We were alerted now for the Roer River crossing. Almost every day we attended chapel services to prepare us spiritually. It wasn't compulsory of course, but they were attended nearly one hundred percent.

The river was flooding due to the broken dams upstream. Also the heavy rains and thaw aided the enemy by increasing the speed and depth of the rushing muddy waters. The Three Wisemen, a patrol sent out from the Third platoon every evening, went down and measured the depth of the river and this information was relayed back by telephone to battalion and no doubt in turn right on back to Paris.

There was some excitement one night when another patrol composed of about ten men got split up down near the river and started shooting at each other. A replacement lieutenant was leading the patrol and he was the one mainly responsible for the mix-up although after the war he blamed it on "green" men. This lieutenant saw little or no combat and yet he was made an instructor at the division recruit training school.

One man was wounded in that fracas and he was lucky that the bullet struck his Thompson sub first. The two men that fired on the main body of the patrol were lucky, too, because one man went to fire back at them with a Thompson or BAR and it jammed. It seems the two men were stationed at a certain point and then the other men got wandering around until they bumped into the stationary pair. The main patrol was halted but did not give the password. What would you do? The two men opened up. Just another lack of combat training and no doubt lack of sense of direction. Guns were issued to shoot, not just to lean on or do the manual of arms.

Charles Davis

Captain Danowski and I were also preparing for the river crossing in other than spiritual ways. The captain was active in directing artillery and mortar fire on likely targets. And with his permission I loaded a .50 caliber air-cooled machine gun on a cart and pulled it up to Red White's squad, after getting his (White's) permission. It wasn't hard to get Red's okay because he was not one to withhold firepower. Red was aggressive, big, and brave. He had ideas and he was open to new ones. He wanted no delay. He wanted to fight the war every day in the week and get it over. Red was to go down fighting, grease gun in hand, facing an .88.

The house containing Red's squad had three stories. It was almost in the front line of houses and was completely open to enemy view except to our left front. It was about eight hundred yards over flat grassy ground to the edge of the sprawling river. In other sections the channel remained very narrow but the water moved very swiftly. Directly to our right at about fifty yards was the heavy machine gun squad from Mike company with their German .75 setting out in front of their house. They fired their heavy .30 from the second floor, through blanketed windows.

White and I decided to mount the .50 on the third floor in order to cover one hundred eight degrees to our front. We had a window facing the river, but it was too high for the tripod and we couldn't get a table big and heavy enough to support the gun. Then the fun began. We decided to knock out some bricks directly under the window, but we faced a slow and difficult job because of lack of tools. It was at this point that someone suggested hand grenades. They taught us how to use C-3 back in Lucherberg and then never issued any to us. So we had to use hand grenades. We had fun pulling the pin and then racing all the way down to the first floor before the explosion. We soon had a hole about eighteen inches square and put the muzzle of the gun almost up to the hole. There was a pump on the first floor so I got some water and wet down the bricks in order to eliminate any dust. We also nailed up a rug on the inside wall and covered the hole.

We were loaded up with air corps ammo. The cartridges were in metal sectioned belts and ran two white phosphorous, two armor piercing and one tracer.

There was quite a difference of opinion on the head space adjustment of a .50 caliber machine gun. The number of clicks suggested to back the barrel out, ran from two to fifteen. I can't remember now, but I think that we found four clicks to be satisfactory.

Naturally, as soon as we had one in the chamber we pressed the triggers. It needed plenty of sand bags to hold the tripod in place and even then there was a great variance in the area covered by our fire at the distance that we were firing. Our main target during the next couple of weeks was the church steeple in Hutchem-Stammeln. But as the distance was a mile or more the tracers burned out before they struck the church or other buildings in the area and so we were never sure that we were hitting our target.

The Letters of a Combat Rifleman

There is no doubt that the Germans knew our location. We always fired with the tracers in the belt and despite the water thrown on the bricks the muzzle blast created a cloud of dust on every burst and the hole kept getting bigger and bigger. After a couple of bursts the carpet we had nailed up was caught by the muzzle blast and whipped out through the hole and sailed about twenty-five yards through the air. We never bothered to cover the hole again. A pair of six by thirty binoculars should have been able to disclose our exact position.

After the first day that we moved into Merken there were a few reports of enemy activity across the river. To our left front there was a small woods and a factory. Directly to our front were fields, a few trees and some brush as well as a lone three-story house. This house came in for plenty of attention. I blazed some shots through its windows and doorways and I shot at other likely dugout positions up and down the far bank. I never once saw an enemy soldier and I was never fired on by small arms. During these firing sessions I often used several tracers, too, in order to estimate range and spot my shots.

It was while looking for targets that I bumped into a section of regimental headquarters that had an observation post and was studying the enemy territory. Their advantage over us was a B. & L. 20 power spotting scope But they were handicapping themselves by remaining too far back. They were in a big school building almost three hundred or four hundred yards back from the forward elements of our company. When I look back I feel it was a shame that I didn't steal that spotting scope from the regimental boys and put it to better use. Spotting scopes definitely should be issued to rifle companies.

During these last days in Merken I witnessed a demonstration by the artillery boys that convinced me they should never try to hit anything smaller than a small village. Our boys reported that twelve Jerries went into a certain lone house at the far end of the town, that is the north section of Hutchem-Stammeln. The artillery F.O. men were in the church steeple in Merken, which was just about in the middle of the town. I climbed up to watch the fun.

The artillery men didn't lack numbers. There were about six of them. Their communications with the guns was okay. But they just couldn't come within twenty-five yards of the house. After nineteen sighting-in shots they finally gave up and called for a concentration. No shells hit the house. It was good practice and they surely needed it. However, such demonstrations are otherwise a waste of ammo.

If they had hit the house twenty-five times they probably would not have killed one enemy. Those boys were no doubt in the cellar and it would be necessary to drop a shell into a cellar window to catch them. Certainly artillery men can't hit cellar windows at three or four miles.

On February 16, I wrote a letter to Jean that affected her more than any other letter that I wrote while I was overseas. I was worried that the impending river crossing might be my last. Anyway I wrote, "One thing, darling, if I don't get back I would like Billy to go to Girard, as I did. The training there would be wonderful and the opportunities boundless. At the same time Billy could be home with you for almost four months of the year on vacations, holidays and weekends. It would be like ten years of college for Billy and I know he would like it once he got used to his playmates.

"I didn't want to mention the above, sweetheart, because I am sure the Lord will bring me back home safe, but He may decide to take me as company for our Jane."

Girard College is a school for fatherless white boys. It was the biggest and the richest boarding school in the world and yet everything for the student is absolutely free. I had graduated from there ten years before, and it was only natural that I should want Bill to attend there if I did not get back.

My letter for that date continued. "There is no other news that I can write about except the weather and such other uninteresting items. It is still like spring and that makes me yearn for the U.S.A. and you, darling. It is sometimes so quiet and peaceful we hardly know there is a war on. Of course, there are always 'gentle' reminders to spoil our dreaming and you have to close your eyes to the sandbags, mud and torn buildings.

"I could use a bath again—with you doing the scrubbing. It is about five weeks now since the last shower."

A few "gentle reminders" had sailed into Marken that day. I was just emerging from the "two holer" in back of our house when a couple of shells landed just up the road about fifty yards. It was a very peculiar coincidence that two battalion wire men were working along the road at this point doing some repair work. One, or perhaps it was both, were now sprawled on the road, hit. Later I heard that the wounds were serious. I do not know whether or not they were fatal. My only thought, naturally, was to get under cover, and, too, the men were just a few yards from the building housing battalion headquarters or some unit from that headquarters. Therefore I felt no obligation to go out and help the wounded men.

A few other shells were lobbed into Merken that day and, naturally, everyone was a little alarmed. We had not been under serious shellfire for weeks. Lieutenant Thompson was more than a little alarmed. He came up with the theory that the Jerries had a spotter in Merken with a radio. Hence, we had to organize searching parties and go through all the empty houses. The results were nil. It could be possible that the battalion wire men were located from the church steeple in Huchem-Stammeln, as they were working on an exposed part of the road. Don't ask me how the German artillery men could hit that road with the first volley. They made other good hits that day, which testified to their ability.

My daily visits to the gun location at Red White's house proved interesting and lots of fun. Ten men living in one small house can always assure one of plenty of talk and rowdy good times. Before I went upstairs to flash a couple of bursts across the river, I usually sat down with Red and his boys for a cup of coffee and something to eat. After the firing session we had another bull session. Red talked about making a patrol across the river. There were rumors that he would lead one across in the near future. Lucky, perhaps, for us the patrol never took place.

In order to interrupt enemy patrols on our side of the river, Item company had booby traps set as well as trip flares. It was about the middle of the day when news came in over the phone on February 19 saying that several men in Item had been seriously wounded when they set off one of their own booby traps. I took off for one of the forward houses that contained one of our machine gun squads and a squad from the First platoon. The large factory where the Item men were hurt was about three or four hundred yards to the right front of this house. A jeep and two medics were looking for a forward position to go up and get the men so I directed them to the house that I was headed for. They parked the jeep in the back as the house was sitting out in the open and could be plainly seen from all sides by the enemy except the rear.

It was only natural for us riflemen to urge the medics to drive up to the factory to get the wounded men. The medics naturally refused to move any farther. What really made us angry, however, was that one medic's excuse was that he didn't want his jeep to get hit. It was better for those men to be up there in the factory dying from loss of blood than for him to risk getting the jeep hit!

It was not long before two stretcher teams came out of the factory and headed for our position. It was a long walk and they were exposed all the way to the enemy but not one shot was fired. Several times the men had to stop and rest. Every minute meant that those men were closer to death and it seemed like hundreds of minutes passed before they reached us. I stood at the side door as the carrying teams entered the yard and walked on back to the jeep. The stretchers were covered with blood and there was no doubt that the men were in serious condition. Like nearly all seriously wounded cases, we never heard the outcome.

Pedaling my bicycle back to our house I passed a very strange sight. White, our former First sergeant who had disappeared in Veviers, Belgium was walking near battalion headquarters. He was accompanied by two other GIs who carried M-1 rifles. White was unarmed. He was a prisoner. I had heard that White was under arrest but this was the first time that I had seen him since he asked me to exchange some of his German marks in Veviers.

The captain and I continued to make plans for the river crossing. Lieutenant Thompson was also very active and organized company headquarters into the necessary groups to aid the actual crossing. He appointed carrying parties and assigned specific jobs to everyone. I wasn't told but I assumed that I would go with the command group and accompany the company commander.

Our immediate plans were put in effect at least a week before the crossing. Captain Danowski arranged with Mike company to lay in a heavy mortar and machine gun barrage at the same time that we would open up with everything we had. The time selected was 5:15 A.M. The plan was carried out several times. The idea was to falsely alert the enemy and put them on edge. They knew that we were coming but the big question was when. We didn't know ourselves as the date was constantly being changed. It was a satisfaction to us that they let us know a day or two in advance when the crossing was to start. But the greatest news for Love company and the rest of the Third battalion was that the Second battalion was to go through us and make the initial crossing in our area.

Our early morning barrages continued even though we knew we would not have to face the river bank defenders. The fireworks included two fifty caliber machine guns in our company plus all our 60 mm mortars plus our light machine guns and a captured German mortar that was operated by the Second platoon. Everything let loose at once and the firing lasted for fifteen minutes. We lost some sleep but the Jerries never got back in their sacks.

To make the Jerries still more "nervous in the service," Major Hallahan, our former company commander, brought up a couple of truckloads of captured German rockets. They were unloaded in the middle of the day in back of a large barn, not very far from our most forward elements.

The rockets were really big stuff. It took four men to carry one, each man holding one corner of the wooden or metal crate that they came packed in. There were no sides to the crates and consequently it was unnecessary to unpack them. We used the crates as launching platforms.

It was in the evening, a day or two before the Roer River crossing that we gave the enemy a taste of his own medicine. Two launching sites were used, one on each side of the main street of Merken leading down to the river. Max Delrogh, now platoon sergeant in the Third platoon, was in charge of the left firing site. I worked with Max and helped carry the rockets forward to be launched. We made one mistake but luckily it was not fatal. Instead of carrying all the rockets up to the launching positions and then starting to fire them, we carried one rocket forward and launched it and then went back for another one. Consequently, our fire was not concentrated and worse than that, we left ourselves exposed to the return rocket fire put up by the Germans.

No wonder it brought some response from the Germans. Those rockets were really terrifying and terrific, right from the moment they started to hiss out of the crates. To add to the fire and noise threat to our sense of security a rocket fired on the right side of the road exploded about one hundred feet above the ground, just about vertically above Red White's house.

We were just about in the middle of the program when the Jerries started to counter-rocket us. And with the usual German accuracy and proper intelligence, they laid the big stuff right in around the barn where our rocket supply was piled. One German rocket landed right in the middle of the road exactly opposite the gate that we had to enter and leave to pick up the rockets. Our carrying parties continued despite this return fire, and luckily we received no casualties. Perhaps we harmed no Germans but we certainly did arouse them. We did manage to hit several houses with the rockets big enough to knock a small house apart. Several big fires were started in Huchem-Stammeln to testify to our beginners luck.

The Roer River crossing was no doubt the best planned and organized and also the biggest river crossing in the history of warfare. The sweep from the Roer to the Rhine River showed that it was planned and well organized. The activity that we witnessed and heard during the next few days testified to its scope.

We went to bed on the night of February 22 with anxiety in our hearts but with confidence that our well-rested force would make the river crossing, sweep the Cologne plain, and destroy the German armies.

A dull pounding roused me about 3:30 the morning of the twenty-third. It was our division and corps artillery opening up with everything they had. Everything was firing from 60 mm mortars back to the biggest stuff. It was continuous, with hardly a second elapsing between each thud. It was the first time that artillery fire had ever awakened me. I lay and smiled to myself. It seemed impossible not to go back to sleep with such a tremendous historical event taking place. It could be the beginning of the end of the war. That is what I hoped for.

We had our usual hot breakfast and then waited for reports from the river front. The first news was discouraging. Members of the Second battalion that were attacking in front of our positions had difficulty in getting across the river. Some of them just gave up and came back into the houses where our men were stationed. I did not venture down to the river because I expected a German counter-barrage at any time and I figured that I shouldn't take any more chances than necessary. For some strange reason the Germans never bothered to shell Merken at all that morning. If they shelled the town later, they certainly didn't catch any forward combat troops.

It was about noon when we shoved off towards Hoven, south of Merken. We marched in a double column, one on each side of the road with about five paces between each man. The command section of company headquarters was in the lead. As we neared open sections along the road paralleling the river, Captain Danowski instructed me to see that the men were the proper five yards apart as some were bunched up together.

As we drew up to a pontoon bridge across the Roer River in Duren, we finally witnessed the first signs of real active combat. Several engineers were standing on the sections of the old blown bridge that spanned the speeding river at this point. Several other GI forms were lying on these abutments and along the shore, parts of their bodies dangling in the current. They had died that morning. Just as few hours ago. They had died so that we could get across. It was a marvelous feat to put a pontoon bridge across that deep, swift river. It not only took courage, it took sweat and blood. The dead bodies, the tenseness of the scene and situation were nothing new now but I'll never forget it as long as I live. There was raw nature, there were living men, tense and moving forward and working to avenge the dead and to stop the slaughter.

I was glad to get over that bridge without having to race through an artillery barrage. The Germans must have been weak in numbers and short on guns and ammunition.

It was not long before we were inside Duren four or five city blocks and housed up in some solid, undamaged buildings. Little time was wasted before many of us were off on the biggest looting spree of modern armies. But as I recall, Duren produced little in the way of real or good trophies. The German army had been there first, and for some time.

I stumbled over the prone body of a German soldier in the basement of one building. He was badly wounded and apparently could not be moved. We notified a medic.

Generally the first thing we did on entering a new town was to build a fire so that we could make hot coffee. Next came an inspection of all nearby houses and buildings with our eye out for possible loot and also for a place to sleep. The large houses we were located in offered plenty of room but very little in the way of beds, blankets, etc. It was apparent the German people and possibly the German army had pretty well cleaned out Duren during the winter.

Entering the attic of this large house we could see through the torn roof and it was possible to make out some of the fighting that was going on in the direction of Arnoldsweiler, one of the key towns in the German defense of the Roer.

Our first battalion, with Baker and Charley companies abreast had jumped off toward Arnoldsweiler at 300. Some of our boys from the Third platoon were mounted on tanks to support the First battalion boys.

Arnoldsweiler proved to be a tough nut to crack and there was plenty of house-to-house fighting plus many enemy counterattacks with infantry and armor.

It was about this time that Danowski came up to the attic for a look and then Reed, Danowski and I took off for a more forward position. The first platoon formed a patrol and moved forward into the same area. We entered a house right on the edge of Duren and searched the open fields toward Arnoldsweiler. It was possible to see both German and American infantry out there in the trench-lined fields. Some of the Germans were retreating and some were walking to our rear with their hands up in the air. Our boys were advancing, ready to shoot.

This was close enough for me. But Danowski took off across the open ground with Reed and me running to keep up. We entered the German trench positions after walking through some protective barbed wire that crisscrossed the ground about ten inches high. Naturally, I was fearful of stepping on the wrong spot all the time as many of the attacking forces had run into extensive minefields, including Schu mines and regular trip wire and pressure devices. I felt better but not entirely safe when I walked along the trenches. It was easy to see that our enemy had been living here a short time previously. The Germans had dug into the sides of the trenches and had covered them at other places to form small sleeping quarters. There were calendars hanging on the dirt walls and one place there was a regular house clock, still running and showing the correct time. The deserted German weapons and ammunition was what interested me most. Most of the rifles were automatic weapons or machine pistols as the Germans called them.

After some scouting about and observing in the direction of Arnoldsweiler, Captain Danowski ordered Reed and me to take a dirt road back into town and check it for mines and determine whether or not tanks could move up that way.

Sugar Reed and I checked the road into the city and found it to be suitable for tanks to move on. Reporting back to company headquarters we found quite a commotion going on. We were told that a fellow in the Third platoon had been standing on a street corner with his M-1 rifle when a group of German prisoners were being marched by. This individual with the M-1 shouldered the weapon and fired right into the middle of approximately fifty POWs. A couple of Germans were wounded. The GI had already been demoted from private first class to private. What concerned me most was the fact that our officers were considering demoting Staff Sergeant White, who was the squad leader of the offending soldier. They were going to bust the best soldier in the company simply because he did not have complete control of his squad at all times.

Here was another fault of the present army setup. All noncommissioned officers were held jointly responsible for the mistakes or crimes of the enlisted men in their immediate unit. The officers know this is an unfair practice because they do not hold themselves responsible for a subordinate's conduct. It is a foolish and unsound principal that assumes a sergeant can be at a dozen different places at once or that he has such magnetic or supernatural control over his men that he can direct their every move even though he may be out of sight.

Within a few hours the incident was forgotten., Red White was still a squad leader, the best in Love company.

We were on the east bank of the river, but our kitchen was still on the west bank. Hence, we began to feel hunger. I toured a few nice homes on the outskirts of the city and managed to come up with a few bottles. It was all potent stuff. In fact we found that it made better cigarette lighter fluid than anything else. We settled for K rations and I satisfied my hunger with some soluble coffee.

Time was passing quickly. I wrote a letter home and picked up a nice book on animals for Billy which I put in my pack until I had time to wrap and mail it. With empty stomachs we were off to bed right after darkness fell.

It wasn't long before our sleep was interrupted by the crash of bombs. The night wasn't very dark and it was possible to see the low flying German planes which were evidently trying to hit the bridge and also do as much damage as possible to the large concentration of men and armor that was being assembled in and around Duren.

The bombs made the loudest noise that I ever heard during my combat days. One hit the building across the street and it seemed that an earthquake was taking place.

Just about the time that I was considering retiring to a lower floor (I was on the second), Captain Danowski ordered me to get ready to leave with him.

We hopped in Bailey's jeep and started off for Huchem-Stammeln, taking the road north through Birkesdorf. The road was lined with artillery, facing to the east. In the open field were rows and rows of tanks, light and medium. We went on up past the cloverleaf of the Autobahn as planes buzzed overhead. Suddenly, one was coming in very low and very close. Bailey slammed on the brakes and stopped almost in the middle of the road. Captain Danowski hit the right ditch and Gene was in the left one. I tried to get out of the back seat but couldn't move. My equipment held me down and the pack got stuck in the seat or on the roof so I just sat back and relaxed. A bomb dropped but it landed in the field on Bailey's side.

Flares were dropping all over Huchem-Stammeln as we entered the town. It must have been about midnight, about the time that King company kicked off for Ellen. Mike company was firing mortars. As one flare burnt out on the ground, I picked up a cord from the parachute that suspended it and put it in my pocket as a souvenir. Captain Danowski and I looked around for empty houses suitable to put the company in for the rest of the night. Bailey remained down on the road that ran parallel to the river as it was impossible to drive the jeep into the town as the Jerries had dynamited a row of trees for a long distance along the road leading east into Huchem-Stammeln.

Back at the jeep the captain ordered me to stay at the road junction and then lead the company up through the field paralleling the tree-strewn road.

It was a long and lonesome wait at that junction but I felt safer than riding along the highway with all those Nazi planes dropping eggs.

It was a miserable thing to sleep half the night in one town and then march to the next one to spend the remaining part of the night. It was especially difficult to enter a town at night and find a suitable place to sleep. You never knew what you would wake up to find in the morning,. Invariably, you had to lay on the bare floor. Of course, a dry floor was always better than the cold, damp ground and we were always thankful when we could make a town.

With very little rest I woke up to find about twenty-five men sleeping in the same small room that I occupied. In some places they overlapped but that helped the heating problem a little.

There was no hot breakfast but I managed to make a cup of coffee. I had little time to examine Huchem-Stammeln, the town that I had been firing at for the last few weeks. Most of the houses were standing and in habitable condition except for the windows, of course.

I was soon alerted to get ready to move up to the next town with Captain Danowski. We hopped in Bailey's jeep again and were off. The weather was clear and sunny and it felt good to be alive. Winter was on the way out. There would be an early spring.

Armor and cavalry vehicles were every where. It looked as if a big breakthrough was in the making. Perhaps the end of the war! Hooray!

We drove up to the edge of Ellen, passing through Oberzier, held by the Second battalion.

Ellen was supposed to be a key road center according to division, and its buildings were set on a ridge that dominated the eastern banks of the Roer. King company had jumped off in the attack at midnight and immediately ran into difficulty when a German plane dropped a flare just at the tail end of the advancing column. This halted them for about ten minutes and then they continued their advance over the open terrain. At the halfway mark of the fifteen hundred yards they had to go, the King men started to use marching fire. A burning haystack and some burning buildings lit up the area, silhouetting the men, and making the advance considerably more difficult.

According to the division history the town was cleared by 0800. However, we found the fight was still going on when we entered the town about 1100. Also, this book failed to mention the real difficulty experienced by King company on entering the town. The King men hit a rather large body of water just on the west edge of the town and had plenty of trouble getting through this obstacle. This water was not on the maps and apparently it wasn't noticed on the aerial photos. Some men were drowned and others were cut down by machine gun fire.

The division book did say that taking Ellen was a "nasty task," but they also omitted to say that one entire platoon of King company was killed or captured. It looked as if the annihilated platoon had struck the town almost at the middle and had reached the main road junction of the small town when they were probably counterattacked. The division history called Ellen a city, but actually it could hardly come under that classification as it had only one street running north and south and the few buildings seemed to be clustered mainly about the above-mentioned road junction that shot off toward the east.

There were almost one hundred prisoners coming down the street as we entered the town. Leaving the jeep we proceeded forward toward the road junction. The town must have been hit by planes as well as artillery and direct fire of self-propelled guns, as everything that once was a house or barn or church looked like a pile of rubble. In one house at the junction were the partially covered bodies of four or five GIs. There were M-1 rifles and a BAR and plenty of ammunition mixed in with the rubble. They had been counterattacked with infantry, tanks and SPs and no doubt the armor just came up close and pumped shells into the houses containing King men. This points up the need of big, heavy, slugging armor to support infantry in night attacks and also the need of plenty of bazooka teams.

It was apparent that the southeast end of the town had not been cleared as there were plenty of small arms fire down in that section and a couple of our Sherman tanks were still firing into some buildings about half a block away.

Captain Danowski contacted the platoon from our company that had come up to support the other companies and help mop up the town. We then moved through a large building on the east side of the north-south road to have a look out into the open fields to the east. The C.O. walked out into the field and it was just then that a GI standing in the building warned me that there were Jerry infantry out in the field. I went out to warn Danowski and just then a couple of shots whizzed over our heads. They were rifle shots and they came from very close range. We hit the ground and crawled up behind a very small pile of boards. The captain said he was going to throw a grenade into the hole on the other side of the lumber, and so I hugged the ground and waited for the bang. I raised up after the explosion and there were several Germans coming out of another hole only fifteen yards away. Luckily they wanted to give up.

"Bring them in here," Danowski ordered, and I ran toward them and urged them over toward the opening in the building. There were nine of them and apparently they were the crew of a large 88 that was standing another twenty-five yards out in the field.

They were well equipped with small arms and ammunition I noticed. There was quite a pile of weapons in the big hole that they had been occupying. One of the men had a Luger and the C.O. relieved him of it as he entered the building. We gave them a thorough searching on the street side, but I had no luck in my search for pistols.

Captain Danowski and I were proud soldiers as we marched our prisoners down the street to the northwest edge of town. There were all kinds of GIs standing about and they seemed surprised that we picked up the prisoners almost under their noses. Some of these onlookers had joined in on the searching project and were rewarded with a few minor souvenirs such as cigarette lighters.

Many of the prisoners that were taken at Ellen were carrying the "safe conduct" passes that were dropped by our planes. As they came in to give up they held these passes in their hands raised well above their heads. The English translation at the bottom read:

SAFECONDUCT

(Valid for one or several bearers)

The German soldier who carries this safe conduct is using it as a sign of his genuine wish to give himself up. He is to be disarmed, to be well looked after, to receive food and medical attention as required, and to be removed from the danger zone as soon as possible.

          Dwight D. Eisenhower
          (signed)
          Supreme Commander,
          Allied Expeditionary Force

    Another indication that the town was still occupied by enemy troops was the occasional rifle bullet or crack of a bullet that snapped through the air. It made me uncomfortable and I kept throwing quick glances toward the very tall church steeple near the center of the town. Finally, I decided to investigate and made my way to the back entrance where the steeple section was located. It was one of the largest churches that I had ever seen and there seemed to be unlimited locations for a sniper in its vast ceiling and towering walls and steeple. I was afraid to stand still on the main floor and just stayed long enough to have a look around. The stairway to the belfry was so littered with rubble it was impossible to mount the stairs. I have often wondered if there was an occupant in that steeple. Continuing my search I ran into a vast underground dugout next to the church. It no doubt had housed an important command post of the German army during the winter holding operation along the Roer.

    From the dugout I went forward to the positions occupied by our second platoon men, hoping to pick up some targets in that area. The buildings they occupied were mainly along the road running out of the village toward the east. Not far out of town along this road was a very large wooden barn, an unusual building for Germany. This presented some very good possibilities. And so did the hedge-strewn fields in back of the houses on the south side of the road. A light tank was standing out in the field and was raking it up and down with machine gun fire so that there must have been Germans there. I climbed into a loft for a better view but was unable to see any moving thing. The tank turned its tracer spitting machine guns on to the barn and almost immediately it went up in smoke and flames. A short time later it was just a skeleton of charred timbers, eliminating it as a hideout for the enemy.

    It must have been late afternoon when the remainder of our company arrived in Ellen. They housed up in the buildings on the northwest edge of town. We even had a garage for our jeeps. Living conditions did not look very good because we had very limited space to start with and they were about the dirtiest looking homes that I ever saw in Germany. In the room next to me was a dead GI and so naturally we did not want to occupy any space in there. It was not long, however, before I found myself going after a stretcher in order to remove the body. I can't recall now how I got the detail but I certainly did not want it. And further, I was burnt up because I had to do a job that should have been done by the quartermaster corps or the medics. It was a messy detail. The blood pooled up on the stretcher, soaked through and then dripped along the road as we carried the body up to the church where they now had some kind of medical unit setting up for business.

The Jerries poured some blood into the streets of Ellen that day, too. There were four German tankers lying beside their disabled vehicle near one small street corner. The street was so narrow the tank didn't have a chance. The whole crew had either been killed or captured by our King boys. Another victim of our attack lay near the dugout next to the church. He must have been killed in the line of duty. He still had a set of earphones on his head. By this time it had become routine to kneel down and feel a dead man's wrists. I got his cigarette lighter and watch. Then as I searched his pockets I noticed he had on two uniforms. The concealed uniform was black. He was a member of the dread S.S. Pulling back the lapels of his Wehrmach uniform I exposed the silver colored death heads, framed in a red rectangle, on each lapel. What a souvenir! I took my knife and removed a good section of the lapel, leaving the death-head insignia in place. There were several medics watching the procedure. One asked me to cut off the other lapel for him and I obliged.

Getting back again to the outfit I found things very crowded. It looked as if we would have to sleep about fifteen men in the kitchen. It was getting toward evening and already there were a lot of new outfits entering the town. Quite a few of them were cavalrymen, assigned to make the breakthrough in our section. It was not long before we heard that they would make a dash out of Ellen the next morning about six or seven o'clock. I was now witnessing and taking part in my first breakthrough. It made me feel good. Now we were to go forward by leaps and bounds. We would take miles of territory instead of yards. It was a new way of making war to me and I wondered just what it would be like for men to mount up on machines and just drive right into the enemy. It offered all kinds of possibilities. I often wondered what would happen in our rear area if the Germans ever got past our battalion headquarters. From there on it would be rather smooth sailing, especially with armored vehicles leading the way. These spearheads had their limitations also, and it was entirely possible that they might be stopped cold or that they would be cut off and wiped out by enemy armored columns that could travel just as fast as they could and had better supply and reinforcement setups.

It was a day and a half now since I'd had a meal. The excitement had made me forget my appetite to a certain extent. Also I am normally a man who eats little. Coffee and an occasional bite of cheese or chocolate had kept me going. I was in very good physical condition. The men who just had to eat found some consolation in the K rations. I would have to be without any food for about three days before I could bear the thought of eating some of the contents of these field rations. The stick of chewing gum I always used.

The olive drab toilet paper in the supper ration came in handy. The three cigarettes were useless to me. The biscuits were like dog food and so was the canned meat. It was the breakfast ration that became a premium. That always contained the small envelopes of soluble coffee.

The best news was the announcement that our kitchen was bringing up some hot chow. It was strange that up until chow time there had been little or no shelling. When it was time to eat we started to get a few rounds every minute. I saw quite a few burst among some apple trees in back of the houses. Some landed in the right place and there was at least one casualty. We were ordered to pick up our supper in an extended and staggered formation, a few men going over to the kitchen at a time. As I walked back with my full meat pan I saw an empty one and a canteen cup lying in the road. They were clean but there were signs of blood on the ground nearby. There was no body. The officer who had been hit had been removed. He was dead. The scattered, clean, eating utensils lying in the dust at the edge of the road made cold chills run over me. They told a story, a familiar story by now but they told it in a different way. It all reminded me, I guess, of how quickly I could die. It made me feel, perhaps, that I was never safe, that the German, even though he was reeling in defeat, could still reach out and strike and kill. Maybe I would be next, even before I took another step. That was one of the strange things about combat. You could be well and happy and even laughing one minute and the next minute you might be dead. The young dead American soldier, his blood now staining my trousers and clotting on my shoes had affected me less than those clean GI eating utensils writing there morbid story in the dust and pointing up the ever-present possibility of sudden death.

I fell asleep that night hoping the rolling wheels of the cavalry would awaken me at dawn. It so happened that I pulled guard early the next morning and stood by the door and witnessed the start of the breakthrough. There was no gunfire as the spearhead hurtled into the dawn-streaked east.

Chapter XII
Meeting Civilians

There was a beehive of activity at daylight. Hundreds of mechanized armored vehicles churned through the dusty streets of Ellen. It was almost impossible to cross the street. I ducked between a couple of tanks and went back to the spot where we picked up the nine prisoners. Selecting four different types of rifles, I made my way back to the garage where we had the jeep parked. Gene was busy putting the top down and I soon learned that Danowski wanted the .50 caliber machine gun mounted on the jeep. There were reports of German planes strafing the roads and there had been some casualties. We were going to be prepared. It was a touchy job getting the rifles hidden away in the jeep, but I managed it despite the objections of Lieutenant Thompson.

Soon we heard the news that we were going back to Duren where we would be in regimental reserve. I hung close to the jeep and prayed that I would not have to walk back to Duren. Somehow I made the grade. Danowski must have heard some awful reports about the German strafing. I would be ready with the 50 caliber machine gun.

Back in Duren we started to look for a place to sleep and make our home a while. The big apartment houses we were assigned to were roomy and clean. They contained some interesting items but nothing much in the way of beds and blankets. I stacked my four German rifles in the hallway until I could find cartons to put them in.

Just about mealtime we got news that we were to move again at five o'clock. This was only the beginning. We were to experience many more quick changes in our dash across Germany. I had to leave the rifles behind.

The Letters of a Combat Rifleman

After a big, delicious supper we were off again to a town east of Duren. We marched single file on either side of the street. It was dark when we reached our destination, Merzenich. We spent a miserable uncomfortable night.

We remained in Merzenich all the next day and night. The barn next to our house had burned to the ground. In the cellar we uncovered lots of German equipment, including one of the German machine pistols or carbines that shot the new necked down 7.9 mm cartridge. I had read good reports about this cartridge, and so I decided to experiment with the gun.

It functioned perfectly. That was enough for me. The cartridge looked a lot bigger and more powerful than other machine pistol cartridges. The main test was the rate of fire. It sounded slow enough to me, but I had to make certain. We were forbidden to use the burp gun because that had such a fast rate of fire you would immediately be identified as German, which naturally would cause plenty of confusion.

In the rate-of-fire test, I took a BAR and a grease gun in back of our house and I fired these two along with the German carbine. Several listeners on the other side could not distinguish the carbine from the other automatic weapons. That made it okay and I started to clean it up and to make it a permanent part of my equipment.

It wasn't long before both officers, Thompson and Danowski ordered all shooting to be stopped. They made sarcastic remarks about my acquired Jerry gun but did not actually order me to disregard it.

We had a chance to get cleaned up while we were in Merzenich and also to write home. In my letter to Jean I wrote about the good weather. I tried to give her an idea of my location when I said: "Everything is jut fine over here. You can tell the towns I am in by following the main stories in the papers."

We were eating good hot meals again but there were some food items we had not had for months. In one paragraph I wrote to Jean: "Those soft boiled eggs and toast Billy was eating certainly made me hungry. I forget the last time I had a breakfast like that.

There was plenty of aerial activity by the Luftwaffe during the day, which was a surprise to us. The German planes were jet jobs, the only type they would dare use in the daytime. The jets proved too fast for me. I had the jeep parked right by the side door of the house with the .50 caliber ready to go but every time a Jerry jet hove into sight it had disappeared again before I could even get into the jeep. They were flying low and, needless to say, very fast. The AA boys were throwing plenty of stuff. Some of it was hitting the buildings in our areas. It is doubtful if any hit the jets.

To lighten my load I had discarded my gas mask some time ago. Eddie, our supply sergeant, caught up to me in Merzenich and handed me another mask. I promptly stored it in the jeep, unbeknown to Danowski or Thompson.

I shoved out of Merzenich the next day around noon, accompanying Danowksi, with Gene Bailey driving the jeep. The weather was still clear and quite warm for that time of the year. We covered a considerable distance, testifying to the success of the armored breakthrough. There was little or no sign of battle along the route that we took. At one spot between a couple of small villages, a dead German soldier lay along the road with full equipment. We began to see civilians and quite a bit of livestock. Both were to prove very interesting and entertaining.

Early in the afternoon we pulled into a town called Quadrath, just east of the Erft Canal. We parked on the main street at the south end. While we waited for Danowski to get some information, Gene and I remained in the jeep. It was not long until we were making our first deal with a German civilian. We propositioned him for something to drink and he came back with a bottle of wine. We were witnessing and taking part in the absorption of the American army into the German populace. The only things that were going to slow up this process were the difference in language and the nonfraternization rule. It might be said that these two obstacles made the process more interesting and at times added an incentive. Both, of course, were eliminated in time by study and common sense.

We were going to live in German homes with German people for the next four months. How could you expect the cordial, good-natured American male to sneer at and turn down the hospitality of any country or nation, especially that of the German. Here we found towns and homes almost like our own, in many cases cleaner and neater. Here we were to find the kind of womanhood that would make a man feel like a man. Many American men and boys were to find the counterpart of their sweethearts, wives, and mothers in the German villages and cities. The German reaction to occupation might well be studied and copied by any nation that may some day experience a similar dilemma. Of course, much depends on the type of invader and also the ability of the invaded country to resist. The German civilian population had little to resist with since only the wealthy homes contained any amount or sufficient supply of small arms. However, they could have resisted us and no doubt our casualties would have been almost twice as great. Needless to say the war would have been prolonged another six months or so.

It may be said that our method of accepting the hospitality of our German civilians and returning kindness with kindness considerably aided our military effort to subdue the Nazi nation. If the German army had worked along similar lines, perhaps they would have conquered the Russians. Our armies, if forced to fight in the future, have a record of cordial and fair occupation that will prove as effective in aiding their advance as any armor-infantry column. Kindness to some people means weakness, but the German civilian had no doubt in his mind as we advanced with rifle in one hand and chocolate in the other. The American soldier could fight and be a good Joe, too.

We were soon moving again. Just before we made a left turn, a jeep coming in the opposite direction received a near-direct hit from a fairly large shell. From a block away it appeared that the jeep driver had been hit. We continued up a side street toward the area that we were assigned to. I was alert for any sniping shots by civilians or straggling Wehrmach soldaten.

Two blocks farther on we halted and started our job of finding suitable quarters for the company. This was the first time we encountered civilians. None of us could speak German and for the first time it appeared that we could not just move in and take any house we wanted, that is without any argument at least.

Due mainly to my failure to learn French in school, I assumed it would be impossible to ever learn the German language. However, I was to find it much easier than French and, of course, I was going to be a much more interested pupil with a much greater incentive. In Quadrath I made my wants known mostly by sign language. In a very short time I was to find myself using one or two words along with the signs. In obtaining a place for the outfit I would say, "American soldaton shlofen here," pointing to bed or room. The word for sleep could not be found in the "Pocket Guide to Germany" that was issued to us but it was a word that saw a lot of use. "Schlofen mit mere," became a standard and well-used phrase. The person addressed in this case was always a pretty fraulein. In Germany they say, "Ja Ja!"

We soon learned to say "essen" (eat), "schokolade" (chocolate), "Kaffee" (coffee), "wasser" (water), "eier" (eggs) "Uhr" (hour). Our German guide book said, "Always use 'please', (bit tah) when asking for something. We learned to say "bitte" and "danke" (thank you). A month or two later we began to put the words together. "Verstehen Sie English?" we learned to ask. "Nix versteche" we often had to say. Later when we asked the children or frauleins their names we soon learned the proper expression, "Wie heissen sie?"

The most used phrase during combat operations was, "Komen sie rans!" (come out). "Halt" was well understood by both armies.

Getting familiar with the people who lived in the house selected for company headquarters proved to be pleasant and interesting. The spokesman for the household was a young French slave worker. I was astonished to learn that he liked ii there and wanted to stay. The people he worked for were well-off. There seemed to be plenty of food, and leading me to the attic Pierre showed me a goodly number of fine bottles of wine and liquor. I opened a bottle and Pierre drank first. It was good stuff.

The best discovery was the warehouse and candle factory next to or adjoining the house. We needed candles more than any other nonissued commodity. Many times I had asked my friends and family to send me candles. None of these packages had ever arrived. Now I had my pick. There were Easter candles and Christmas candles, red ones and yellow ones, big and little ones. Every man in the outfit left Quadrath with at least one or two dozen candles in his pack. Our nights would be bright!

The rest of the company was not so fortunate. They came part way by truck but finished up with a long march, arriving in town several hours after us. I directed the platoons to their assigned positions, which did not require any defensive setup except, of course, the regular nightly guard.

My friend, Pierre, started me thinking. Why did he like it here in Germany? Why didn't he want to return immediately to his home in France? It was not long before I found the answers. Peirre had a German girlfriend. She was young like Pierre and very pretty. As we drove deeper into Germany we found that this fraternization between young male slave workers and German women was a common occurrence. It was becoming more and more apparent that German women liked men, regardless of their nationality.

These young male slave workers became privileged characters and straw bosses. They had the run of the factories, farms, and homes. Their women lovers protected them from the secret police and SS whenever they got into trouble The unlucky German male was at the front fighting and dying while foreigners lived in his home, ate the best food that Europe could offer and slept with his woman. Now I understood what "Berlin Sally" was driving at. She probably knew from first-hand experience what she was talking about when she warned us that some 4-F was going out with our wives and sweethearts!

Pierre also had at his disposal some very fine riding horses. I wanted to see them, being an old cavalry man myself. We had to go to the other end of the town and Pierre wanted his girlfriend to go with us. That was okay with me but it didn't look so good. And on the main street we ran into a lot of mechanized vehicles. I got scared when a cavalry major asked me where I was going. I gave some excuse about some German soldiers that wanted to give up. It didn't sound good at all to me, but he accepted the explanation.

We went to the tack room first in some low, small buildings across the street from the large barn. The rooms were bare, the saddles, bridles, etc. were either stolen or hidden. we crossed over to the barn and found some of the horses loose in the yard and some were out running around in the adjacent field, alarmed no doubt by the shelling and noise from the tanks and armored cars. They were fine animals with plenty of spirit. I had to be content to just watch them strut their stuff.

It was cold in Quadrath that night. Before I curled up on a couch in the dining room I had to accompany Danowski to battalion headquarters and that was another miserable two hours wasted sitting around waiting. To top it all we pulled out of town very late at night. It was a tough and weird march up over the high ridge the other side of Quadrath, weaving in and around huge slagpiles, pits and giant factory buildings Someone must have been watching us, too, because we came under mortar fire that hit the tail end of the column inflicting several casualties.

The next town, Oberraussen, was full of armored vehicles. We found some houses on the side of the town nearest Cologne in order to push off the next morning. It was some time before I finally rocked off to sleep in my cradle. It was a child's cradle, and I sure had to double up to get in.

The Letters of a Combat Rifleman

The next morning we were under shellfire, and they were dropping in at a very fast pace. It was just at this time that I was sent to contact the First platoon to obtain some very silly and unnecessary information. I don't recall now what the information was about. I was nervous and tired after a miserable and cold night and the prospects of going down that shell-blasted street made me shiver. At one point I ducked under a truck as I heard the shell coming. I made it to the platoon and back without getting hit.

We lined up in the street about an hour before we shoved off and this I didn't like either. Luckily the shelling had lifted. Just the same, I kept close by a tank that was standing nearby, ready to dive underneath.

We were heartened somewhat when a big column of prisoners were marched to the center of town just before we shoved off across the open fields toward Glessen, our next objective.

There was some confusion as we entered the open. After we had moved out about three hundred yards we spread out in a big skirmish line, the whole company abreast except Weapons platoon. Glessen was to the southeast at least a mile and a half away. The ground was almost level with just a slight rise and then a dip where the town was situated. In other words it was hardly possible to see Glessen. We were moving at a rather fast pace which is all right for riflemen but taxes the weapons platoon men with their heavy loads of machine guns, mortars and ammunition. We were half way out when ack-ack started to burst over our heads, too high to do any harm. The Germans had a surplus of antiaircraft guns, especially around Cologne. From now on they were to use them a lot as antipersonnel weapons.

To our right front a group of Jerries made off on the run toward Glessen. Danowski called up a machine gun section from Weapons and told them to set up their guns on the right flank and open up. The Jerries were too far off for us to see any results by the time the guns got going, but like all firing, it did bring some results. Ten or fifteen Wehmacht soldaten jumped up out of holes in front of us and came forward with their hands up. We let them pass through us toward the rear. I managed to get close enough to stop a half a dozen or so and asked each one I stopped, "Haben sie uhr?" I picked up three good wrist watches that would have only ended up on some MP's arm anyway. Danowski was too busy directing the company, which hadn't stopped its advance for one moment even during the machine gun fire, to notice that I was falling behind. As we neared the first buildings I was breathless and covered with sweat. My collection of souvenirs was beginning to weigh me down. To help matters some I discarded my entrenching tool, a shovel. I had been carrying it for five months and hadn't turned one spade full of sod. Besides, it made it very difficult with the spade hanging on the front of my belt to get in and out of the jeep or windows, etc. It didn't make sense to carry an entrenching tool on the back of your belt or pack, as it was impossible to reach a shovel or pick in such a position while you were lying on the ground.

The platoon advanced on into Glessen with little or no opposition while company headquarters remained at the outer rim of houses. There seemed to be some confusion and it was not long before big mortar shells started to drop around us.

Danowski, Reed and I finally got situated in a house near the top of the dip. We could see most of Glesson and in the distance to the southeast was a large town with some big buildings that looked like factories or hospitals. We were trying to spot the guns that were firing on us and after a few minutes I recognized some flashes near the large buildings. In the meantime, the German shells were landing on the lawn outside our house. This shelling was to keep up for several hours and it was here in Glessen that we suffered our only casualties between the Roer and the Rhine. George Reuitt, a Philadelphia boy, and another fellow in the same squad, were wounded when a mortar shell came in the window of the room they were standing in.

We were aided by tanks in taking Glessen and some of the other casualities from the shelling were sustained by the tankers. One particular tragic incident occurred at the southeast edge of the town when a shell hit a man standing near his tank. He was struck by shrapnel in the neck and didn't live very long after being hit. The fact that he had a twin brother in the same outfit seemed to point up the tragic death of this man. I recall the incident, too, because I heard a buddy of the dead man pleading with the medics to hurry and get the wounded man back to a hospital. The medics insisted he was already dead, that there was no need to move the man at all. Witnessing this scene I felt almost as bad as if the dead man was my own twin brother.

We counter-batteried the Germans, but they didn't stop shelling Glessen. Amid the bursting shells I had to run several messages around town and had to accompany Danowski to different locations. Finally we ended up in a group of farm buildings at the south side where we could see Dansweiler, just another twelve hundred yards to the southwest. More to the east was Brauweiler, a rather large town. Brauweiler was the location of the German guns that were shelling us. However, Dansweiler was the Third battalion's next objective. Colonel Clough, our battalion commander came into town just in back of us and set up headquarters on the main street. In a short time, Colonel Clough appeared at our end of the town to direct the advance into Dansweiler. We had some Mike company mortars set up near our location, and they poured the shells right back at the Jerries. It was a miracle that the Mike men did not get hit or have their guns damaged, as they did not dig any holes to work in.

Reed and I passed the time searching the buildings for something to eat. It was already about 3 P.M. and when you find you can relax a little, your stomach immediately goes on the offensive. Despite the numerous flocks of chickens and geese around the place, we couldn't find even one egg. So as usual we went on being hungry

The shelling was effecting Sugar Reed noticeably. He got down on the concrete floor of the dairy and didn't seem to want to get up again. I hugged the cement, too, when I thought one was coming in the door or through the window but at other times I sat on a stool and relaxed as best I could.

It wasn't long until we heard that King company was to mount tanks and take off for Dansweiler. This assault seemed to quiet the Jerries considerably, and we were able to watch the grand show from beginning to end. I never saw anything like it in my life, not even in the movies. If a similar attack were filmed by Hollywood it would no doubt be called phony and unreal. The tanks pulled out from among the buildings at the edge of Glessen and roared forth out across the very flat, open ground. There were only two objects that raised above the ground between Glessen and Dansweiler. They were two giant haystacks. Before our tanks had gathered speed they opened fire on these hay stacks with all their guns. It was a wonderful thrill to see the big 75 mm guns spit and belch and rock the tank a little as they sent their armor-piercing shells visibly through the air into the middle of the haystacks. Simultaneously the tankers opened up with their .50s and .30s. The tracers set the haystacks afire and that was the end of any possible enemy cover.

There appeared to be some resistance by infantry as we watched the armor-infantry team reach the edge of the town, but if there was any resistance it didn't amount to much.

Things quieted down in Glessen and company headquarters set up in some buildings on the main street near the center of town.

Reed, Effley, Bailey, and several other headquarters men, including me, found a nice clean home with plenty of sleeping accommodations and started to set up house. There were civilians moving in and out, but they soon took a powder. We went through their wardrobe of clothes and inspected everything carefully. The blackout curtains were drawn as darkness fell and soon there were lighted candles all over the place.

Hot chow was brought up and with it the mail. You can probably guess what I received in a package from home—a dozen candles!

We had a bed to sleep in, but as usual we got little sleep. About midnight we were alerted for movement. Assembling on the south edge of Glessen we pushed off down the road into Dansweiler. Coming into town we made a left turn and then faced in the general direction of the bigger town of Braweiler. Tanks were lined up in the street and our two columns straddled them and sat down on the pavements to wait for the order to push out.

It wasn't long until we took off, moving out along the road and then cutting to the right along a dirt road and across some fields. At the corner of a cemetery Danowski halted and ordered me to go back and bring up the tanks. The company had already reached Braweiler and there was no exchange of fire; hence it was safe for the tankers to advance in the darkness. Danowski went on in with the command section of headquarters.

I hurried across the fields and back into Dansweiler. Everything was quiet and each step that I took seemed to crack the silence like a rifle shot. It is surprising how much more frightening and lonely you can feel in combat when you are alone on the battlefield.

It was almost as bad if not worse as I took off in front of the tank column. The roar of the tank motors would certainly attract any close-by enemy if my footsteps didn't. I kept wondering, too, if the tank commander could see me in the dark and hoping that the driver wouldn't put on any burst of speed and run me down As I rounded the corner of the cemetery. I began to wonder whether or not I would hit the same section of town that the company had entered. I headed in the direction that company headquarters had moved and trusted to luck. We hit a street on the edge of the town and the tankers parked while I entered some of the nearby houses to try and locate our headquarters.

It took quite a while to find our command section and then there was a delay before we moved into action again. It was almost daylight when Captain Danowski, Reed, and I climbed aboard a tank and directed the column through town to set them in position and check the platoons. This was my first tank ride. There were to be many more. In the middle of Brauweiler was a tremendous prison. We later heard that it contained many Allied fliers.

We moved into the eastern end of Brauweiler, opposite a group of farm buildings known, I believe, as Ferlinersdorf. Company headquarters setup in a house in the most forward position. The platoons were to our left and rear. We got a fire started and warmed up some rations. There were no civilians in any of the surrounding houses, at least we didn't see any. In the short time we were in this location I managed to find my first camera. It was a rather large folding camera that used plates instead of film. I had to throw away my raincoat to make room for it in my pack. After all, the raincoat was worthless. Instead of shedding the rain it absorbed it and leaked like a sieve! The good raincoats no doubt went to the air corps.

About noon a patrol from the Second platoon made their way across the fields into the little settlement up ahead. We watched them through field glasses, hoping and praying that they would not be fired on. The patrol disappeared among the buildings and trees. It was not until we got in radio contact with them that we knew everything was okay.

Captain Danowski, Carl Zurcher and I then went forward, Carl carrying his 300 radio. The remainder of the Second platoon also moved up. As usual we finally set up in the building nearest Cologne. The weather was overcast but mild. If it were not for the mist and smoke we probably could have seen the spires of the Cologne cathedral.

It was a farm settlement and the house we occupied was connected with the barn and formed a huge square with several other buildings. There were civilians all over the place, but they soon collected in the kitchen and air raid shelter. Among the civilians were many slave workers both male and female. Some of the girls were soon occupying a bedroom on the second floor with some of the Second platooners. Captain Danowski walked right through the room apparently without noticing the four occupants in the bed.

The Letters of a Combat Rifleman

Besides entertainment, the slave workers also supplied some information. The Germans had been there the night before, they said. Also, the administrator had buried a lot of loot in one of the sheds. In short order, a GI had the head German digging up the loot. This pleased everybody, especially the Polish slave workers.

Always on the trail of pistols, etc., I soon found out that the administrator had an automatic pistol. When I questioned him, he had to admit the fact and then we went into the air raid shelter and he produced a French Ruby. This handgun is an inferior copy of the .32 Colt. I was not impressed by its appearance, but at least I had really liberated a pistol.

I went through the regular routine, informing the administrator that "Alles weapons, glasses and foto apparel were verboten!" The administrator was an honest man. He led me to the second floor and produced an almost new pair of eight by fifty German army field glasses. He explained they had been left there by an artillery officer.

Danowski and several other officers were busy most of the day observing to the front. In the afternoon we witnessed the First battalion moving out under a smoke screen. It was a good display of infantry deployed in attack formation since the ground was flat and there was no cover.

Units of our battalion also tried to move that afternoon but were hurled back under a concentrated barrage of ack-ack guns. Their objective had been Widdersdorf. A few shells landed in Ferlinersdorf but most of the day we remained in the buildings, and hence we were not bothered.

Hunger did bother us plenty. The hen house was locked, but we soon got the key. Our search was fruitless. Finally after some threats and a little detective work I got a crock of eggs from the air raid shelter, now crowded with Germans and slave workers.

The kitchen was crowded, too, with German women. They cooked my eggs. One fraulein hung her head and wept. Not for me but for the German soldier who had roared out of Ferlinersdorf on his motorcycle the night before and had promised to be back that evening. We kidded her because she felt that her lover would still keep his word.

Danowski had me check on the positions taken up by the Second platoon during the afternoon. Many of the men that I contacted were new to me as I had seldom visited the Second platoon. Three men in a house on the north side acted very cool and greeted me like an intruder. Perhaps it was because I showed too much interest in the .22 rifles and the shotguns that the civilians had surrendered to them. Perhaps, too, they wanted to protect their nice setup, a modern well-furnished house decorated with several nice looking frauliens. I had to stay a little longer than I wanted to as there were quite a few white phosphorous shells landing in the adjacent yards.

When darkness fell we were still in this advanced position with only radio contact with battalion and the rest of the company, including the remainder of the command section of our headquarters. Gene Bailey drove up under cover of darkness and we went for a ride. This was one time I really was lost. However, Gene and Danowski seemed to know where we were going, so I was not worried. There was a considerable amount of shelling going on however, and between that and the cold night air I was trembling all over. Cross roads were particularly scary spots since I figured they were probably zeroed in on them.

After a lot of winding around we pulled up to a large factory building. It was a vast and impressive place and apparently housed the attacking companies that had been thrown back in the attempt to take Widdersdorf. I got inside the building along with Bailey and Danowski and while the C.O. conferred with battalion, Gene and I talked over the situation with some men in a well-lighted blacked-out room. It wasn't long until we were back in our farmhouse again, Bailey returning to Brauweiler.

It was now about 11:30 P.M. and Carl Zurcher had been on the 300 all day. Carl was a young lad from Indiana, formerly with the A.S.T.P. He was very modest and seldom complained, both of these traits being very rare in the army. I never thought of it at the time but he had probably gone hungry all day, unless he had a K ration. I persuaded him to lie down and take a rest while I took over the radio for a few hours.

Chapter XIII
Taking Cologne and Paris

It wasn't long until I had another job assigned me by Danowski. He had to go back to a conference at one of the headquarters, probably battalion, and he wanted me to take over the job that he had been assigned earlier by battalion.

According to his orders I was to move up to a five-road crossing about two hundred yards to the northeast. At a certain time Item and King companies would approach this crossing and it was my job to contact the company commanders and see that they took the right road toward Widdersdorf. One section each of tanks and tank destroyers would also pass through.

I walked up to the crossing by myself as there was no one else to accompany me. Near the intersection I was challenged and I gave the password and advanced to find a two-man listening post. I believe the men were from Charley company. One man was inside a corrugated steel shed and the other outside. We talked quietly and I was awfully glad to have the company. It wasn't long, however, until they took off to the rear and left me there alone. I wasn't particularly afraid at night as long as I had a companion but on these occasions when I found myself all alone, I was a bundle of tensed-up nerves with my imagination running wild. I could see some shelling going on to the north and I figured my big cross roads would be next.

There were a myriad of stars in the sky but visibility along the ground was limited. Finally, I heard footsteps along the road that branched off to the northwest. It was a marching column I knew so I stood in the center of the crossing and waited.

I talked with the company commanders and pointed out the road running northeast into Widdersdorf. Item went up the left side and King company took the right side of the road. There was no hesitation or confusion as far as I could see. Everything went like clockwork and it was a good thing, because the intersection was a bad spot to park.

The night was silent again except for an occasional far off burst of artillery or mortars. Within ten minutes I heard the ruffled, almost idling noise of some big vehicles. They were moving slowly through the darkness and rather quietly for tank destroyers. Pretty soon the lead T.D. loomed out of the night and I was so close I had to look up at the man in the turret. I was recognized without any trouble and soon had the big-tracked vehicles started off down the right road.

In a couple of minutes the tankers followed and soon they were off in the attack. Another night attack was underway, and again we were lucky and successful. There was little resistance.

The next morning we were off down the same road in a jeep. Love company moved into Widdersdorf with the rest of the battalion. The only sign of a fight was a dead German soldier near the center of town.

Like every place that we moved into we started to set up house in Widdesdorf. Everyone would have a bed to sleep in if we stayed overnight. We even had some beer at the local tap room. We had a chance to write home and we got mail and hot chow. The air that evening was cool and spring like.

Perhaps the rested feeling, the nice weather and the good food had something to do with some of the exuberance shown by a couple of men in the Third platoon that night. They later were court-martialed for rape but were acquitted.

The next morning we were off on a long march into the suburbs of Cologne. This time there was no jeep, and I had to carry both my weapons, the Springfield '03 and the German carbine. We must have covered about eight miles by the time we reached the main street leading into Cologne from the west. On hand to greet us was a newsreel camera crew and we had our picture taken entering the famous city on the Rhine.

We set up on the western outskirts of the city where there were still some homes in fairly good shape. Most of the windows had been shattered even if the house had not received a direct hit.

At the end of our street was a giant barricade, bigger and stronger than any I had ever seen in the newspapers or newsreels. The Germans were going to defend Cologne street by street, but we must have hit them before they could organize their defenses.

The Germans in Cologne offered only scattered resistance. Our regiment with the 414th on our right attacked from the west. The Third armored division attacked from the north. The 414th and the Third armored did most of the fighting. Fox company of our regiment was the first infantry unit to reach the banks of the Rhine River. By March 7, we had complete control of what one correspondent described as, "the third largest rubble pile in Germany."

The Letters of a Combat Rifleman

During the next twelve days the 104th division actively defended the west banks of the Rhine River and organized a guard setup for Cologne and the nearby vicinities. Plans were made for the river crossing and we practiced with assault boats.

This period was a grand spree and rest opportunity for us battle-weary doughs. It was an opportunity to get cleaned up and for some lucky guys it was a chance to go on pass to Paris.

In Cologne we started to write letters home again. In my first letter since Merzenich, I explained to Jean and Billy, "I'm sorry I haven't written sooner but for a while now I have been on the move and have been pretty busy. The headlines for this date will tell you where I am. It has been pretty easy lately. The only thing is I need another good bath. It is almost two months since the last one. You will have plenty of back scrubbing to make up when I get home."

One of our first discoveries after entering Cologne was a big brewery with huge subterranean vaults, only a block from our house. After the long march we were plenty thirsty and so we lost no time in ordering a couple of male civilians to haul up a barrel of beer and tap it immediately. Later, individual barrels were hauled over to the platoon locations. Every squad in the company began holding open house. The standard greeting became, "Come on over to our house and have a drink."

The brewery was only the first step. We started to spread out. Bottles of all descriptions were rounded up and hauled back to the company area. The big majority was white wine, most of it bottled in the late thirties.

We drank toast after toast. We visited and drank with our friends and we had our friends call us. But with all the drinking, I do not recall seeing one man drunk. There were no shooting sprees and no cases of rape. Nobody got hurt and we all had a good time.

Extensive searches were made of all the surrounding houses. My prize loot was a big haul of "4711" perfume, powder, cologne and after shaving lotion. There were sets and individual bottles. It was good stuff and well packed. I had more than I could carry in my pack so I gave some to Gene Bailey and some of the other boys. I figured the stuff would make perfect gifts and now it looked like we would have time to send some things home.

There was little or no fraternization in Cologne. We still were reading the tab on front of our "Pocket Guide to Germany," which said, "Keep faith with the American soldiers who have died to eliminate the German war makers. Do not fraternize." I bumped into one old gentleman in the cellar of one of the better homes. We were crawling through a hole in the cellar wall that connected two houses when we came on him and his wife. They apparently did not know that the war was over for them because they were still living in the cellar when they had a beautiful, undamaged home above. It was a difficult conversation because he did not speak English and I still understood little German. I understood him to say that he was once a newspaper correspondent in Paris for a Cologne daily. When he worked on the Cologne paper he said that during the early years of Hitler they were free to write what they thought, but as Hitler and the Nazi party gained in favor and power they came under strict censorship. Party men were assigned to the paper and checked all copy. In Paris he had more freedom until France was overrun and occupied. Apparently, he had left Paris and returned home in front of the sweep of the Allied armies. As one newspaper man to another, I offered him a pack of cigarettes and left, not bothering to check his house.

In my letter on March 7, I mentioned the correspondent, "There is never a dull moment here. Things are quite different since I crossed the river (Roer) what with the civilians, etc. One fellow I talked to was a correspondent for one of the papers here and he worked in London and Paris. He told me of the setup concerning the policy of the paper and about the party men (Nazi) that moved in and did the editing."

There was little else in that letter except my longing to be home. I wrote, "Everything is easy enough now but I do wish and pray for the end of this war so I can return home to your loving arms, dear."

The next day we took off for the waterfront. It was a long march and the weather was clear and warm. I had to carry both my weapons again, which made it plenty tough going because I had a pack full of loot to boot.

The whole company set up in a German army warehouse that ran right up to the Rhine River. Our main job was to keep the civilians out of the warehouse. There was more food stored in the building than anything else. In one small section there were facilities for storing and repairing small arms. There were no small arms that we could locate, however. One big cabinet contained enough parts to make me a rich man back in the States. I didn't know this at the time and so I just selected a few handfuls of Luger parts and gave them to Fellmeier, our artificer to carry.

We found a dead civilian in one of the garages. He was covered with a piece of tarpaulin which I quickly dropped back in place as the sight of a dead civilian had a strange effect on me. I didn't want to pull up his sleeve to look for a watch or go through his pockets for souvenirs. I figured that he had been a victim of one of the air raids and that they had not got around to transporting him out to a cemetery for proper burial. It must have been an impossible task to bury all the victims of the air raids as the streets were nearly all blocked by huge piles of rubble. The main thoroughfares were cleared enough for one-way traffic but there were only foot paths through the side streets. The water houses were in pretty good shape.

The CP was on the first floor of a big house within the warehouse enclosure. Gene Bailey and I had a nice room with a stove all to ourselves. Gene never got much of a chance to use that room.

We had one guard detail in another section of the city and it was Gene's job to transport these men back and forth. I always accompanied Gene. That is except on this one trip when Gene did not come back. He took the relief up to the nearest approachable point to the winery that the guard was protecting and then waited at his jeep for the old guard.

This time the engineers did the damage, not the German engineers—our engineers. Gene's legs were almost torn off when a piece of trolley track came flying through the air and struck him. I never saw Gene after that. It was very hard for me to find the details of the accident. I wanted the details just like the brothers and sisters and mothers and fathers back home wanted the details of their lost or wounded loved ones. Gene was my best buddy. We worked together always. He was a good soldier. He never complained about the hardships or long hours of duty. He was always ready to go and always willing to help in any task. Gene was one of the old men in the company. He had served a long time and knew his job to perfection. Now he was lost to us. I was glad that he was going back but I wondered whether he would be all right again. I was sorry I missed the trip. Perhaps we would have both been sitting in the jeep or perhaps we would have walked up to the wine cellar to get a bottle. But one of us would have had to be with the jeep. Perhaps I would have gotten hit. Again my guardian angel had taken care of me. I could not help but feel that I had a friend in heaven.

When Gene took off without me that day I was out cooking up a deal for a Luger pistol. I believe it was one of the Third platoon boys that told me of the family of slave workers that could get me a Luger. They wanted food for their trouble. I could take care of that very easily as we were loaded down with huge cheeses, sardines and other fine foods. I tossed a lot of stuff out a side window where the Dutch slave worker was waiting. He carted it off home and we followed. The family was living in a dark, dreary cellar, like nearly all Cologne families. The wife set out some tea for us and we sat and talked. They told us their daughter had been taken across the river by the German people that they had worked for. I kept wondering about the Luger. Where was it and when would I get it?

Finally, Hans, the Dutchman, said that he would show me where the pistol was hidden. We took off through the buildings. That is we went from cellar to cellar as they were connected with big holes. About five houses away we came to a well-stocked cellar with things piled up to the ceiling. We started to search through the trunks and cabinets and boxes. We weren't having any luck and the noise that we made attracted someone upstairs.

A big German came babbling down the stairway. I motioned for Hans to hide as I didn't want him to get in trouble. I faced the German and gave out with the usual routine, holding my '03 ready.

"Vo ist das pistole? Alles waffens vertoben."

He got the drift of my broken German and produced the pistol. That was all I wanted. However, he insisted on going upstairs to get some more weapons. These other weapons turned out to be a bunch of ceremonial sabers. As I had already found some nicely engraved artillery officer's sabers back at the army warehouse, I told the big German to keep them as they had little or no military value.

The Luger was a DWM model, the best. It was in perfect condition in and out and there were two clips and a holster. Both clips were numbered, same as the gun. Believe it or not there was Winchester 9 mm Luger ammunition in the clips, each loaded with five rounds,. Hans told us the German was a Cologne policeman. As with most cops, it was apparent he very seldom fired his gun. But unlike most cops, he did keep it clean and in good condition, a national German trait.

I had one other experience near the water front while we were in the warehouse position. I was looking for targets across the river and accompanying Danowski on an inspection of some of the outpost positions. An officer approached me and asked, "Where did you get that rifle?" pointing to my '03 Springfield.

"It was issued to me back in Munsterbusch, Sir," I answered.

"Why I thought I collected all those Springfields. There were too many battle losses with them," the officer said. He continued to tell me that he was regimental supply officer and he ended up by saying, "I'm glad to see you carrying the '03, lots of luck."

It was now apparent that I was the only sniper in the regiment. The big battle loss on Springfields must have meant that the men threw them away when the going got rough or when the situation demanded the fire power of an M-1 or M-3 grease gun. I, of course, had had my first one stolen.

It was a lonely night that first night without Gene around. It had all happened so suddenly and at a time that seemed so safe. But that's how it was in the lines. Shells came in every day from the east bank of the river and no one knew whether or not the next one would have his number on it. But this constant enemy threat was of no more concern than the danger of another blunder on the part of our officers or supporting units.

I tried to forget my loneliness that night by writing to Jean and Bill: "There isn't much I can tell you now except that everything is just fine. I am okay and there is nothing to worry about. I'm missing you just as much as ever and I'm oh, so tired of this war. My only wish is to be home with you, safe in your loving arms. Then there would be no blackouts, no guard or security details and no races with death or noise of exploding shells. I love you, sweetheart."

"It is evening now and raining out again. We are having a cup of coffee. Darling, I wish I were having a cup of coffee with you in our kitchen—and then to bed."

Jean had mentioned in one of her recent letters that she wanted to have some of our meals by candlelight. I wrote in agreement, "I'm getting enough candlelight, but when you want to eat by candlelight we will."

I wrote again on the eleventh and mentioned the get-together with the Dutch couple, "This is quite a famous place where I am now. I was talking to

The Letters of a Combat Rifleman

a Dutch couple who live here—under force. They said two hundred thousand people were killed by air raids. Their children, age sixteen and eight, were evacuated by the Nazi across the river."

The German army warehouse was one place that should have been hit but wasn't. I don't remember seeing any big bomb hits and only a very few small or incendiary bomb hits. The whole place covered nearly a city block and it was in nearly one hundred percent operating condition. There were tons of excellent foods stored there. The barrels of cognac attracted the most attention. These were soon removed to a higher echelon.

We were eating regularly cooked meals and we were wining and dining on the best that Europe could offer. I mentioned this to Jean: "At present we are having a snack—toasted sardine sandwiches and wine. The Germans looted the sardines from Norway and the wine from France and Belgium. We get quite a kick out of 'liberating' this stuff.

There was no letter on the twelfth. That must have been the day we moved back to the west edge of Cologne, into the same area we occupied before. The CP set up in a bigger house. I was amazed to find a couple dozen bottles of fine wine in the cellar. We continued our high living. There was little or nothing to do except eat, drink and sleep. We wrote home and we received packages and mail. The mail service wasn't too good, however, even though we were standing still because I wrote in my next letter on the thirteenth, "Mail service hasn't been so good the last few days but I'm hoping for a letter from you tonight."

Perhaps the most important thing to happen to Love company in the way of good things was the awarding of a small number of Paris leaves. The number was small indeed. Four, I believe, the total was for our company. Sergeants Wyman and Delrogh were the first to go to Paris. They went well equipped and well heeled. I made a notation in my diary , "Loaned to Wyman and Delrogh, thirty-four hundred francs (Belgian). Max also took along one of my pistols to try to sell it to an air corps officer.

Those days in Cologne certainly run the extremes. We sang and laughed and talked of home and our return. Then there were moments of loneliness and longing and certain moments that made you want to scream and moan and fall on your face weeping.

My letter on the thirteenth started: "There isn't much I can say but I am glad to be able to tell you that I am feeling fine. Sometimes I feel a little downhearted, wondering when this war will ever be over. But I know it can not last much longer. You know how Americans are—always anxious to be moving. The only trouble is the American army is not like the American people. It is saddled by too many traditions. It is so un-American that I hate it and pray each day that this war will soon be over and I'll again be home with you, dear, and our Happy Chappy boy and we will be a family."

I don't remember what made me write the above paragraph. Perhaps it was premonition of what was going to happen on that black thirteenth.

Perhaps it was our marching back and forth from one end of Cologne to the other or perhaps Danowski or Thompson were after me again to put my sleeveless sweater under my shirt or have me shave off a couple of day's growth of whiskers. I needed a bath, that's for sure, because I wrote to Jean in the same letter, "It's been eight weeks now since I had a bath. I sure would like to get under a nice hot shower." But there were no showers in Cologne and no promise of showers.

My next two paragraphs sounded a lot better. I wrote, "Last night I had a wonderful experience. For the first time since I left our apartment in Baltimore I slept between sheets. It was also the first time in five months that I slept with my clothes off. Didn't have a thing on, not even my dog tags. It felt just like home but of course, there was one thing missing. I'll let you guess what was missing." I had found the clean sheets in the big house and I had a bed all to myself. It was a sort of warm up for the days or nights to come.

It was on the thirteenth that we had our assault-boat training. We went through with this training despite the fact that the Remagan bridge had been captured on March 7. For some reason or other I missed the daytime training period that was held on a lake in Cologne. Perhaps all of company headquarters missed the daylight session. I do not remember. Anyway, it was announced that we would have a night practice launching, entirely without lights.

First Sergeant Babcock ordered me to remain in the CP instead of going out for night practice with the assault boats. The reason I got the break was the fact that I pulled guard that night between 2000 and 2200. Someone had to stay on the wire to battalion headquarters.

Things were pretty quiet and routine in Cologne. That night I stood at the door once in a while and then would go into the hallway and listen to the radio. I was sitting there tilting back in a chair and taking it easy when the door was suddenly swung open and Sergeant Babcock almost fell on the floor as he lunged in. He staggered through the hallway like a drunken man. His rifle and equipment were gone and he had no field jacket or helmet.

"What's the matter, Sergeant?" I asked with alarm, helping him into the CP.

"The boat sank!" He choked and went on, "They can't find all the men. Ten of them are missing."

I was stunned. I could hardly talk. "What happened? Who's missing?" He took a drink of Scotch and I had one, too.

It all added up to the biggest tragedy that had ever struck Love company. It was terrible and unnecessary loss of life. Again the army had bungled. Again we were hit by our own side. Perhaps the main cause was "too much chicken."

As I heard the details, we began to speculate on the missing men. Old Tom Jennings showed up and he couldn't swim a stroke. Zurcher was safe, so apparently he didn't have his 300 radio strapped on his back. Delakas, Orrie Saylor, Hebish, and Valenzuela were safe. It was hard to think of all the names.

The Letters of a Combat Rifleman

It wasn't long, however, until we were able to establish at least the majority of the missing men. My best friend, Sugar Reed, was gone. And so was my good friend Louis Effley. They had left the CP laughing and joking, their M-3 grease guns hanging like anchors around their necks. They were both good swimmers and I couldn't help but think that the grease guns had helped to pull them under. Also they were in the front of the boat which plunged into the water, prow first, the outboard motor on the rear forcing it down under the surface.

The engineer on the outboard was a victim. We didn't know him, of course. Young Richard H. Bailey, a company runner, was drowned. And so was young Frederick J. Hubert, also a company runner. Eddie LaCavera, our supply sergeant was another key man that went down with the boat. And so was Omer E. Davidson and George W. Morang. A fellow named Davis was also lost. He was just a new man, having been with the company only a day or two. He was tall and good natured. He had been making his bed on the floor in the same room that I occupied. He was so new in the company his name was not carried in the division history, "Timberwolf Tracks." Instead of listing the men under "The Valiant Dead" the names of the drowned men appear under "Non-Battle Deaths" in the division history.

I wandered about the house that night in a daze. I entered Sugar's and Lou's room on the first floor by the door. Hubert had slept there, too. Now only Hebish was left—plus a lot of personal effects and equipment. I picked up Sugar's flashlight. It was a GI job and they were hard to get. I always wanted one but not that way. I could hardly hold back the tears. Gene Bailey had gone a few days ago. Now I had hardly a friend left. Since I was a father I thought a lot of Lou Effley. He was a father of two children. One was old enough to write. He had showed me her letter. I remembered how it had made me think of my Janey.

I went to my own room but that was empty and dark. That night I prayed. And since I was alone, I cried, too. I cried myself to sleep.

There was a tense, sad air about the company the next morning. I didn't know what to say to the men in the platoons. They didn't seem to know what to say to me.

Some of the details of the accident were discussed the night before but not in any official way. We knew there would be an investigation and soon it became apparent that the enlisted men in company headquarters were determined to see that it was no white wash. The boat was overloaded. It was made to carry eighteen men but twenty-four were put aboard. Lieutenant Thompson had ordered every man in headquarters to go out for the night training. This definitely was a "chicken" order since the supply section and the kitchen personnel would never cross a river with the assault section. One of the drowned men was a cook.

I couldn't get over the terrible, nightmarish thought of the sinking boat. In one minute we had lost more men than we had during the entire dash from the Roer to the Rhine. Even the news that I was one of the two men to make the next trip to Paris failed to change my thoughts or cheer me in the least.

But the trip to Paris was another "break." Just in time, perhaps, to prevent my "breaking." I had to get things ready and that helped me get the thought of the tragedy out of my head for a while.

But as the evening shadows fell again over the city it seemed like death itself was closing in with its black cloak to smother and suppress. Shells landed in our area and once again we realized that we had a common enemy.

My letter to Jean and Billy began: "I am so tired and lonesome tonight. It's not just because I didn't get a letter. You know I don't like to complain about hardships, but the terribleness of this war is sometimes hard to bear. When it gets serious they call it battle fatigue. We sometimes say, 'he blew his top.' It isn't any wonder men 'blow their top' when suffering, loneliness, hunger, and fear constantly beset them. (the house shook when I went to make that 'd' in 'wonder')

"But don't get me wrong, darling, I am safe. Just as safe as anyone here in Germany. I can't say what happened last night but it reminded me a lot of a night back in the early part of last July. As you know there are times that try men's fortitude's. You mustn't worry darling, as the incident would mean little to you. I'll tell you about it when I get home. It may not be fair to say this but the bungling on the home front is nothing in comparison with the bungling done by the army. After years as a war worker and service here and in the States, I think I know who is to blame for the prolonging of this war. I think I know who is mainly responsible for the needless waste or life—and, of course, material. In my opinion, it is the child-like actions and inefficiency of the army. The home front has never failed to produce the men, the money and the goods. It is time the army learned how to use them."

Our new location was a rather modern and not too badly damaged apartment house. Other troops had been there and we relieved them. They had their CP in the cellar. We moved to the upper floors.

There wasn't much doing in the way of security details. The broad Rhine made things comparatively safe. The amount of shelling was negligible. Our outposts were right down against the river. And some of them were extended by boat under cover of darkness to some of the piers that reached out into the river. There were no reports of targets and even though we exposed ourselves one day in a jeep we drew no direct fire from the east bank.

Wyman and Max returned from Paris the day before I left. They spoke in humorous and glowing terms of the good times they had had in that fair city. Since they were broke and Max had failed to sell my pistol, I had to borrow money in order to finance my trip. Syring, our mail clerk, loaned me five hundred francs, Eckert, the supply section jeep driver, loaned me twelve hundred and a young boy named Scott in the Third platoon loaned me fifteen hundred francs. I made the notation in my diary so that I would not forget.

The Letters of a Combat Rifleman

It must have been about noon on March 17 that I jeeped it to regiment headquarters near the center of Cologne where I joined a large group of men that was going back to Paris. Charley Brown, a Southern boy from our Second platoon was with me. Brown had been with the company all through the States and had been with them in the lines since Holland. He may have been wounded and hospitalized once. I do not remember. However, we did become close buddies during the next few days. Charley was single and he really took advantage of the status when he reached our destination.

We traveled by truck to a small Belgian town, arriving about six o'clock that evening. Brown and I took a walk. We had a drink and talked with the woman bartender. We were hungry, but there were no provisions for chowing. Finally we located an engineer outfit in the town and they were just finishing supper. Some of the other fellows making the trip had found the kitchen before us. Most of them were officers. The mess sergeant or man serving mistook Brown and me for officers and started to prepare us a platter. Looking at us closer he must have realized that we were not officers and finally he handed us a spam sandwich.

On the train it was all even-steven. We all tried to sleep on the crowded, hard, wooden benches or seats. It was a miserable trip. We arrived in Paris the next day before noon. When I stepped off the train I had over one hundred dollars in cash and a bottle of black and White Scotch that was worth half a hundred almost. I made a deal on the train with an officer. He must have been a rear echelon man because he gave me twenty-five dollars and the bottle of Scotch for the German binoculars that I had picked up on the outskirts of Cologne. I still had a P-38 and the big German plate camera to help finance my three days in Paris.

There isn't too much that I can say or remember about the next few days. We were bused over to a hotel and given individual rooms. There were French maids running about the place to see that everything was in shipshape. There was even heat in the building and we felt flushed.

My first trip was to the barber shop. This is after we had broken the seal on the Black and White bottle. I got the works in the barber shop. Even had a nice blonde manicure my fingernails. The toilet water and soap served to kill all other odors. There were no facilities that we could find to take a bath in the hotel so that had to wait. We did learn about a big quartermaster outfit in the city where we could shower and get clean clothes.

Well, between trying to locate that quartermaster outfit and visiting Pigalle I never did get to see even the Eifel tower, let alone the Arc de Triomph or the other great points of interest. Brown and I rode the metro for free but we never knew where we were going.

I couldn't make a trans-Atlantic telephone call so I sent Jean a cable. I wired: "DARLING I AM MISSING YOU VERY MUCH IT IS ALL VERY BEAUTIFUL BUT I WANT AMERICA AND YOU ALL MY LOVE"

I did manage to get around to the Studio Tronchet at 5, Rue Tronchet 8, in order to be photographed. I thought that it might be the last one and my son would want something to establish the fact the his daddy had been in the war.

R. Moreau, the photographer was a little alarmed when I pulled out the P-38 for one of the poses., But he didn't object. The picture turned out pretty good with my white sheepskin collar, newly washed and my helmet and combat infantry badge making it look like I was a real combat soldier. The grim look on my face made it a little too war-like and the people back home complained, set the pictures on the mantle piece for a while and then put them in mothballs.

The weather was beautiful and spring like. The boulevards were crowded with people including many beautiful mademoiselles. I had to stop and laugh whenever one went by on a bicycle, wearing high heels, fur coat and picture hat. It was perfect weather, too, to sit at the sidewalk cafes and sip white wine. It must have been all diluted stuff to boot because I didn't get feeling good until the third day.

I wrote only one letter to Jean while I was in Paris and that was just before we were scheduled to leave. There was a mailbox in the lobby of the hotel and they told us we could seal our letters and that they would not be censored. That was the only letter that I sent home that was "Opened by Army Examiner." It must have been a trick to see what we would write. I wrote to Jean and Billy, "Well, darlings, here I am safe and sound in Gay Paree. Sweetheart, Paris in the spring is really lovely. It is really a beautiful city. I wish so much that you could be here with me to see it. I would love to spend a honeymoon here with you, darling. Our reunion will be like a honeymoon.

"Most of the time I have spent in trying to find my way around to places like the quartermaster laundry, the showers, the PX and other stores. (and some cafes, too). I managed to get you some nice gifts. There is a pair of white gloves which were quite cheap for Paris, costing three hundred eighty-six francs which is about seven dollars and severity-five cents. In one shop they wanted thirteen hundred and seventy-five francs or twenty-seven dollars and fifty cents. They are size seven. I hope they fit. There is also a necklace for Helen and a beautiful yellow rose necklace for you. Both came from Germany.

"It was hard to get something for Billy but I sent a jigsaw type set. I also enclosed a book with pictures of animals in it that I picked up in Duren, Germany. I hope you like the nice powder set I mailed. I got that in Cologne.

"There are still many things I want to do in the remaining few hours. I want to send you a cable and that is first on my list. Darling, here I am in the midst of fashion and beauty but all I want is you. I miss you so and want you so. I don't mind saying now that I'll want to stay in bed with you for weeks to make up for the love I haven't been giving you. and there will be no "gifts." I'll give you a baby. Just as beautiful as the other two.

The Letters of a Combat Rifleman

"As I said, there are a million things I wan to write now, but I must close. I love you, my darling beloved wife. There will only ever by one Mrs. Charles Davis and that is you. Au revoir, sweetheart. I'll write you from the Cologne waterfront."

Chapter XIV
Remagan Bridgehead

Within less than forty-eight hours after I sat in my Paris hotel and wrote that letter, I found myself writing another letter to Jean in a dense forest several miles east of the Rhine River.

The trip home was fast. We left Paris in the evening and traveled over night by train to Belgium. The next afternoon we were back with our companies.

There were a lot of new faces in our company headquarters. The replacements were in good humor and did not seen to worry about the coming battle. Captain Danowski introduced me to the new men and referred to me as "the biggest looter in Love company." I don't think I warranted this introduction, but I didn't object. Danowski did have trouble locating me several times and it just so happened that at the particular times he wanted me and I wasn't around, I was out looking for something to eat or carry away.

The company was in a new location when we got back. They seemed to be along the northern river front section of Cologne, but I wasn't sure. We were due to move that night and our destination was the Remagan bridgehead.

"Old Tom" was now our jeep driver. He was an old man to be up there with the infantry. Tom and been with the company for quite some time and had been working with the supply section and the kitchen as a jeep driver and had also chauffeured us around on occasion. He was an old soldier and a good one. Old Tom was a quiet fellow and a rather big man. He looked like a combat soldier and he acted like a veteran. Danowski gave Tom and me an order to load down the jeep with sandbags. It had been all cleaned out and washed up during our garrison-like days in the city. We got hold of some burlap bags and filled them with dirt and covered the entire floor of the jeep. It was a precaution against severe results from mines.

About 0300 the next morning, we mounted up on trucks, wrapped up in plenty of blankets and started the fifty mile trip to the south. We were too chilled to be impressed much by the beauty of that section of the Rhine Valley as the sun heralded another beautiful spring day. We made the river crossing on a pontoon bridge as smoke generators partially obscured the river downstream. It must have been somewhere in the vicinity of Drackenfels, which is deeply steeped in Germany mythology, that we made the crossing. There were no tourist guides to announce the points of interest such as the castle of Siegfried, perched high on the cliffs and looking down upon another invading army.

We continued on by truck as the Remagan bridgehead was now greatly extended. We detrucked at Ittenbach according to the records. But it must have been near Ittenbach because I couldn't see any houses, let alone, a town.

We took cover on the reverse slope of a big hill in a pine forest that had been planted there as you would plant rows of corn. The trees were in straight lines and very close together. Our kitchen group was along, too, and they set up in the forest in a more open section where the trees grew normally instead of in rows.

The whole landscape in this section was big and beautiful and open. There were high points and low valleys, cultivated fields and deep, green forests, fast streams and winding roads. Looking down on one section we could see what looked like a portion of the Autobahn. Cub observation planes were using the broad cement highway as a landing strip.

I leaned back against a tree and wrote to Jean: "Well, here I am quite some distance southeast of where I said I would write my next letter. It is a beautiful spring day and the warm air and brilliant sunlight do not at all fit in with the sound effects. The strange contrasts make me feel as if this is a fairyland. Butterflies flutter by as planes roar overhead. The tall, black, forest trees stand silently and the radio on the trailer beside me is putting forth sweet music. They are playing, "As Time Goes By." And remember where it goes, "Woman needs man and man must have his mate—it's still the same old story of fight for love and glory, a case of do or die." Darling, I sure need you so much and now. I am fighting for love but not for glory. I'm fighting for you, darling, and for my Billy boy and for our other children and loved ones. Sometimes it is so hard to hate. Like this morning when I saw some German civilians fleeing with a few household belongings. One woman pushed a cart with a small child and a pile of clothes and other articles on it. Beside her, holding onto the cart, trotted a darling, little blonde girl of about five. Her doll bounded beside her little brother or sister. Her face was full of fear and wet with tears as the vehicles rushed by them. It is the terribleness of war being brought home to the Hun, and the little children must suffer with all the rest. We don't like it and we don't want it, but it must be.

"All this is worlds apart from Paris. But even there the people are near starvation among all the beauty and wealth of one of the greatest cities in the world.

"There are many other things I want to write about but that will have to wait a little as conditions are not so good now. I hope you got my cable and my letter and gifts from Paris.

"Until I get a better opportunity, good bye, darling. Remember, I love you, my darling, devoted wife. Please always love me and care for me."

That was the last letter for a while. Late that afternoon, Danowski ordered me to get ready to move. Before I left I joined Red White and a group of boys from the Third platoon. They were talking over old times and past encounters. Big Walter Boyd from Union, S.C. was back again from the hospital, just in time for the next big scrap. Everyone was in a good frame of mind. It must have been that we were combat veterans now and we were flushed with victory. From now on it should be easy. We weren't wondering who would be next but how many more days—or hours it would take to finish this war.

We jeeped it up to a group of farm buildings on the reverse side of a small hill. It was getting dark as we made our way forward on foot to the little town of Brungsburg. Danowski and I accompanied a First division man around to the different positions that we were going to take over at midnight. It wasn't a very big company that we were relieving and I remarked about it to some of the men in the CP. Company headquarters contained less than a dozen men. including the officer or officers. Some of them had been through twice as much combat as any man in our company. They said their battalion commander had the Silver Star with six oak leaf clusters. I can't recall now the number of awards in their company, but I believe they said there were ninety Bronze and Silver Star awards since Christmas. We didn't have half that number after seven months of combat.

It was a ghost-like town and pretty well beat up. Two tanks were backed into the rubble around the company headquarters building. They were covered with rubble as a camouflage since they were facing right toward the enemy. After contacting the unit on our left flank, we went back to the CP and waited for our company to come up.

Things were plenty crowded when our big outfit moved into town to relieve the First division boys. We had to divide company headquarters. I set up with the other group in a house up the road about fifty yards. I staggered around in the dark in what looked like a butcher shop, trying to rig up a blackout setup in one of the first floor rooms in the rear. The plate glass window was broken in the store and you could look right out toward the enemy. It was a moonlit night and the front of the building seemed to be in the brightest shaft of light.

After plenty of noise and effort, we had the room blacked out enough to light a candle. Then it was possible to find a place to sleep. The night passed quietly for headquarters.

The next morning, we had hot chow brought up before daylight and it was a good thing, too, because as soon as it became light we started to get direct fire. Direct fire is the worst type of fire to be under. There is never any warning. You never hear the shell coming, only the explosion after it hits, that is if you are not hit.

Every time someone exposed himself, a shell came flashing into our positions. We were all in houses. The outposts were drawn in from their foxholes just before daylight.

Danowski was plenty active all that day, moving back and forth between the platoons. I had to follow. The distance between each one or group of houses ranged from a few feet to about two hundred yards. As long as we moved real fast, the Heinies never had time to get lined on us. They fired a few late ones, but we managed to get about safely all day long. Most of the time we remained in a large farm settlement at the upper edge of the company sector. I think the bulk of the First platoon was located there.

Danowski and I went to an upper floor and searched the area to our front. There was a very gradual sloping ground of two or three hundred yards just in front of us. It was mostly cultivated fields. Then there was a wooded section and raising up to a dominating prominence was a huge slag pile. This is where we expected trouble. Without a doubt the gun that was shooting at us was located on that high ground or else the observer was located there. We had artillery F.O.'s in the house with us, but nobody was able to pick up the enemy gun despite the fact that it continued to blast at our small village all day long. Here was another example of effective use of available fire power. At least ninety percent of American gunners would never have attempted such brazen direct fire. And yet the Heinies sat there and fired all day long and were never spotted. They kept us pinned down, broke our communication wires and inflicted casualties. It was another example of how difficult it is to pick up an enemy position even though that position is actively being used. Here in this little town was another example of over emphasis in our training of camouflage. Our tanks were there facing right at the enemy and yet the enemy failed to pick them up. They were camouflaged, but they would never have passed the inspection of a training camp battalion commander, or any other training camp officer. Camouflage training is another waste of time. It can be put in a class with ju-jit-su, foxhole digging, bayonet training, aircraft identification, parades, close order drill and grenade throwing.

Another failure that day was our lack of support by units that were supposed to support us. This lack of support may have been our own fault. I do not know whether or not Danowski or the F.O.'s asked for it. But we could have employed an observation plane which might have helped. The planes were in back of us. We had seen them the day before. They would have had all day to pick that gun up and then perhaps we could have brought up a gun that could have fired directly back at the enemy position after it was located.

Without a doubt, the German gun was mounted on a panzer, and perhaps a big one, perhaps too big for any of our tanks or self-propelled guns to have even a fifty-fifty chance in a duel. So there we sat on that beautiful spring day—out gunned and out-maneuvered. The enemy had us dominated. He was in front of us in force and apparently determined to hold his ground.

Since we could not dominate the enemy's armed forces, we proceeded to dominate the civilian population. There were civilians in almost every house. Perhaps that is why the German guns did not shoot into the buildings.

It ii a long time between breakfast before daylight and supper after dark. Hence, we went to work on the natives. At the First platoon house, I got some fried potatoes and an egg. But that wasn't enough. Back at the CP sub station where I had slept the night before, a lot of civilians came up out of the cellar after daylight. And a lot of chickens came out of their coups and started to scratch around. We decided to put them both to good use, so we ordered one of the German women to kill a chicken, clean it and cook it for us. The fraulein refused, saying that Hitler had all the chickens counted and that the party wouldn't allow her to kill a chicken. Well, we had to laugh at that and that poor woman was the butt of all jokes, corny remarks and dirty stories for the rest of the day. By late in the afternoon, she began to look much younger and prettier and the remarks from both sides began to take on some double meanings. Faced by a battery of M-1s, the girl finally killed, cleaned and cooked the chicken of our choice. The domination of the civilian population would have certainly been carried much farther had we stayed there that night.

We soon learned, however, that we would have a chance to show our manly prowess by moving out under the cover of darkness and taking the enemy positions to our front.

Soon after dark we had hot chow. It seemed rather odd to walk right down the middle of the street that paralleled our positions just in front of the houses. There were few houses on the side of the street toward the enemy; hence, we were exposed practically all the time that we walked down the road. It was another bright moonlight night, too, and visibility was very good.

I ate my meal in the dark in the same room where it was served at the CP building. Then I got some seconds of bread and roast beef and made myself a big sandwich so that I would have something to eat the next day in case the kitchen crew couldn't get up to us. It seems funny now that I looked forward to the next day. Many of us were not going to be around for the next mealtime.

Joe V. Sykes, a very likable man in the Third platoon, and a fine soldier, had hardly time to digest his supper. Soon after he jumped into his foxhole outpost he was hit by shrapnel. An aid man rushed out, but it was no use. He was hit in the neck and soon died. Joe was the father of five children. I wondered to myself, "should the father of five children be up here fighting as a rifleman?"

The Letters of a Combat Rifleman

It was about 10 or 11 P.M. when we started to assemble on the road in front of our houses. Then we moved to a center position where the whole company stood together in the moonlight. I wondered what would happen if the enemy ever threw in some TOT fire. Or what would have happened if the enemy was just approaching our position in an attack?."

We were lucky again. We got moving without one shot being fired by the enemy. We moved out across the fields in single file. The First platoon was in the lead. Our command section was about in the middle of the column. It was a sneak attack and so we received no overhead fire. We were depending on surprise.

Soon we hit an open, plowed field. I felt sure that we would be seen crossing this. But if the enemy did see us they withheld their fire. On the other side of the plowed field was a gully and some undergrowth. We went out along the edge and we were now moving almost parallel to our front with a slight angle toward the enemy.

The movement became very slow and occasionally the column halted. It was hard to see the man in front of you in the woods and the trees and branches caught onto our weapons and packs and slowed us up.

Finally Danowski said, "Come on Davis, let's go and see what's holding them up." Tom took off like a big-assed bird and I stumbled and fought my way along the column just in back of him. Danowski was traveling light as usual. In contrast, I had a pack and two weapons on the outside and a pistol in my field jacket and one in the pack as well as all my other souvenirs, trophies, eating utensils and extra socks. My Springfield was slung over my shoulder and I had the Jerry carbine ready to fire.

We were not far from the head of the column when there was a burst of Heinie machine-gun fire, that dread, terrifically fast sputtering and then the even more dread rush of bullets. It was plunging fire. They were shooting down on us from the slag pile that must have been about one hundred fifty yards to our left. It was terribly accurate fire because the first burst hit one of our men. He started to moan and cry. I don't recall his name now, but I think he was a new man. Anyway, he lay there and died. I don't know whether or not he even received first aid although he must have because they had a good medic in the First platoon named Stephens. He was awarded the Silver Star, Bronze Star, and Purple Heart. The man that was hit was only ten or fifteen feet in front of us. The next burst fired by the Jerries had a much better chance of hitting us because everybody was flat on their face. I saw the bullets tear up the ground in front of me and the sparks from the tracers and bullets hitting stones made a fireworks display. But we were lucky this time and no one got touched. The point of impact was so small and concentrated for machine gun fire, it made it seem like that gun was only fifty yards away. The second burst that ripped up the ground would have cut a man in two. It must have sprayed dirt on the man just in front of Danowski.

In less than a minute, Danowski was back on his feet. I jumped up beside him and said, "We better get out of these woods." Danowski started to walk toward the edge of the woods without giving any orders to the company. I followed him. To reach the open we walked directly away from the enemy machine gun as we had only about ten yards to go in that direction to clear the woods. At the edge Danowski stopped. I came up and looked at the open moonlit field and immediately became suspicious of an object standing about thirty yards away. I studied this object while Danowski talked.

"Go back along the column and get the machine gun section from Mike company," Danowski ordered. The Mike men were attached to us for the assault. Also attached were the bazooka teams from our antitank company as the antitankers were unable to travel cross-country with their .57 mm guns.

Danowski continued, "I'll set one gun up at this road that runs through the woods up above here."

"And I'll set the other one up out there to the right were the woods projects out to a point," I suggested. In the meantime, I had finally determined that the object in the field was a farmer's roller. However, I kept my eye on it as I figured there might be a Jerry in back of it.

I went down along the edge of the woods a short distance and then cut in. I had no trouble in locating the Mike machine gunners which, of course, was a surprise. They were carrying light, air-cooled .30's and so it didn't take us long to get them in position.

I told the men on the gun in my position to wait until the other gun opened up and fired and stopped, and then for them to fire a couple of bursts. I also let them know that I was going to move a few yards to their left and open up with my German carbine between bursts by the machine gun. They knew the approximate position of the enemy gun as well as I did.

Danowski's gun opened up without delay and then the second one cut in. They were both loaded with tracer, as well as ball. This helped in determining whether or not they were hitting the top of the slag pile. It must have helped some, too, in demoralizing the enemy, because there was no reply to our fire. My German carbine worked perfectly. I used the one 30 round clip and then the spare one that I was carrying. That meant that I was out of ammunition and I didn't know when I would be able to get more. To lighten my load, I took the gun apart and threw the pieces into the woods.

While the Mike men stopped firing after a few minutes, they remained in position until we got the company out of the woods. The company came out into the same field that Danowski and I had entered when we left the woods. They took up a position along the near bank of the road that ran out of the woods and across the field, just about parallel to our front.

I am not sure what happened to our Third platoon, but it must have been at this point that they were detached and sent toward the slag pile to clear out that sore spot. I was separated from Danowski from time to time and so did not hear all the orders. When the company got lined up along the road bank, Danowski ordered the First platoon to send a patrol or squad up to a group of buildings about two hundred yards ahead. There were only open fields between our position and the buildings, with several fences running in both directions. The woods was now on our left and the slag pile was running perpendicular to our front about two hundred to our left.

Before the First platoon men got under way, Danowski ordered me to go over to the woods and get the machine gunners so that they could cover the forward movement. The First platoon men had a short fire fight with a few defenders who were killed, routed, or taken prisoner. There was only one causality on our side.

While we were lying along the road bank waiting to get the word to move forward again, we heard a tremendous rush of air overhead. It sounded like huge flocks of giant birds rushing by at hundreds of miles per hour. Of course, we soon realized it was a cascade of artillery shells—German artillery shells. We realized, too, that they were going well over our heads and that they would not land near us.

I turned my head and looked back over my right shoulder. The town we had just left suddenly exploded. It erupted as though it had been covered by one giant shell. It was the biggest demonstration of TOT fire that we had ever witnessed. For once, I was glad I was in a rifle company.

After the area up ahead had been cleared, we moved forward and jumped into the buildings. There was one dead German in full equipment lying in the courtyard of the house that I entered. There were several foxholes dug in front of the buildings. There was one of our men lying wounded on a table, but he wasn't receiving any attention. I saw to it that he was covered up and made as comfortable as possible.

There was quite a delay at this farm settlement, and I believe that perhaps that was the main reason for our heavy casualties. Part of company headquarters remained back on the road bank and the Third platoon, under Lieutenant McCabe, got so fouled up around the slag pile they had to go back to Brungsburg and start all over again. This was the cause of our delay at our new position as Captain Danowski did not want to move forward without the whole company.

The second section of company headquarters was left at the road I suppose, to maintain or try to maintain connection with the Third platoon and also guard our rear, or I should say, middle. They had the bazooka team from antitank company with them.

There was radio communication between company headquarters and the platoons via the 536 handy talkies. Hebish, Danowski or I carried the 536. Company headquarters also had two 300 walkie talkie radios and both the radios could contact battalion headquarters or each other. Zurcher operated his 300 in the forward position and a young lad, named Backus, I believe, just back from the hospital a few weeks, operated the other 300 with Lieutenant Thompson's group back on the road. But as usual, the radios weren't operating too well. In fact, Zurcher could not even get Lieutenant Thompson's group. Consequently, I had to go back and get the bazooka team that Danowski wanted brought forward. And, again, I found myself alone on the battlefield. It was only for a short time and just a short distance, but I got the creeps and chills nevertheless. I couldn't help but feel that some one was watching me from the woods, and possibly from the slag pile. This fear was more or less verified when I reached Sergeant Babcock and the other men still laying out there in that open field. Someone was taking pot shots at them from the woods. They told me the bazooka men were on the other side of the road. I crossed back again and looked and found them in a big, two-man foxhole. Both of them were sitting down in the bottom of the hole and that is where they probably would have remained had an armored vehicle come up that country road. When I told them the company commander wanted them to come forward, they started to give me an argument, saying that they had orders to stay with company headquarters. Our supporting elements were always referring back to some order that their own officers gave them instead of cooperating with us. In this case, the antitank officers probably thought that these men would be safer with company headquarters. They apparently didn't know that we often divided company headquarters up. Anyway, I finally got them to follow me up to the forward group.

It wasn't long until I got orders to go back and get the other 300 radio so that we could keep in proper touch with battalion. When I got down to the road position again, I found out that the Jerries were beginning to get the range. Backus, the 300 radio operator had been hit and so had two other men.

Zurcher soon contacted battalion with the other radio. They immediately ordered us to get moving, Danowski argued that he was waiting for the Third platoon. As I recall, Lieutenant Thompson had gone after the Third platoon.

About this time I found an opportunity to get up into the attic of the house nearest the woods in order to try and spot the Jerries that were shooting up our men out in the field. There were flashes like rifle shots every few minutes. I loaded up with some tracers and fired back at the flashes.

In the meantime battalion was still urging Danowski to move forward again. I couldn't blame Danowski for not wanting to move. We were strung out for a distance of at least a mile. Our position was due to our own mistakes. It was basic that you should travel in the open at night time. We had entered the woods and got fired on and stopped. It is basic, too, that you should not deploy. I learned that in the national guard. When you deploy you lose mobility and strength, and communication between units deteriorates. We were deployed all over the place. We certainly lacked mobility and strength; and our communications were in bad shape.

We started to worry about counterattack by armor when we brought up the bazooka team. As the minutes ticked by I became more and more worried for fear that the Jerries would draw up to our position with panzers and start blasting. That would have been slaughter. There were over one hundred men in three or four small buildings.

I crossed over into the barn where I found a section of the floor made of concrete. There was a concrete step near the hay mow and I got down in back of this as well as I could. There was a German prisoner cowering there, too, and in the darkness I reached over and grabbed his wrist. We might both have been killed the next minute. But that didn't stop me from transferring his watch to my right wrist. I had one on my left wrist.

Danowski couldn't hold out any longer against battalion's order to move out and so we started to move forward. Again, we went single file; and again ran in the same direction as the slag pile, perpendicular to our original front. We were now a good distance past the slag pile, however, and so we did not have to worry about someone on higher ground. But again the column got slowed down to a crawl and finally stopped. And again Danowski and I went foreword. It was tough going. I never did reach the front of the column and I never found out the reason we stopped.

It was starting to get light and then we received some shellfire via the direct route. There was a lot of German machine pistol shots zipping through the trees down below us. It was about this time that Danowski ordered the forward observer to call for some fire to be placed one hundred yards in front of us. The Germans weren't exactly in front of us because we were stretched out on a diagonal so that actually the enemy was more on our right side than at our front as they were attempting to retake the farm settlement that we had just left, and that was only one or two hundred yards to our right rear. Unknown to me at the time, the Third platoon had managed to get forward to the farm settlement, minus, of course, a few killed, wounded, and lost. They ran into some trouble at the slag pile.

Our artillery fire started to come over and it landed just in the right place. It couldn't have been better. Then the artillery F.O. reported that another company had just called for fire to be brought in thirty or forty yards. That was it. The upper part of the column was hit first and hard. There were cries for the medics all along our position. Luckily, the tail end of the column was where we got hit last. Most of the company headquarters men started to dig in, including the artillery F.O. and his two assistants. We had some weapons platoon men near us, too, since they were at the end of the column.

Danowski ordered the artillery lieutenant to call back and get the fire lifted immediately. I was laying there in a fold in the ground only about twenty-five feet from the radio when Danowski gave the order. I looked at my watch and figured that I would lie flat on my face for twenty minutes. I still recalled our experience at Lucherburg when they were throwing in the timed fire stuff. It was lucky for me that day that we didn't get timed fired. It was lucky for the company because there probably wouldn't have been anyone left. It was bad enough with just a few tree bursts.

I didn't see what happened during the next fifteen or twenty minutes. The shells continued to come down upon us for at least ten minutes. When I looked up, Danowski was still walking around. The artillery men were huddled above their partially dug holes. Some headquarters and Weapons men were still digging. The first man that I noticed hit was laying only about ten feet away. I didn't notice him right away. He was lying on his back.

I stood up eventually and looked around. I stared at the artillery men. I walked closer. They were dead. A shell had landed in the middle of a group of four men, the three artillery men and one man from our Weapons platoon. They were close together—too close together. There was the shell mark in the middle of the group. some men said later that they were killed by a tree burst. A tree burst would have probably hit me, too. The shell fragments must have caught them all in the stomach and chest. The artillery officer's binoculars were lying there out of their case. I didn't want them. And I didn't want his good wrist watch.

Danowski approached and said he was going back. I didn't understand. Finally it dawned on me. Danowski was hit, too. There were a lot of other walking wounded that filed past me. There were still some cries for medics There were a lot of litter cases.

The man near me was still alive. But he was too weak to call for help. He was bleeding from the nose and he had that death pallor. I remembered my training—make a wounded man comfortable—protect him from shock. I picked up the field jackets of the dead men and covered the wounded boy. He was one of the bazooka men from our antitank company. I knelt down beside him and asked, "Are you warm?"

His answer was, "No." There were no more field jackets around so I dropped my cartridge belt and took off my own jacket. I knelt down and put the jacket over his head, leaving it open just enough so that he could get some air. After a minute I raised the jacket and asked the man if he felt better with the jacket about his head and neck. This time his answer was, "Yes." I tucked the jacket back around his head and that same time I said, "I'll get the first litter that comes up for you."

It wasn't long until the medics were on the job with litters. I saw the first one and I shouted and waved my hands for them to come my way. There were other cases that needed the litter just as bad, maybe even worse, but I was sure that the bazooka man needed immediate attention. And I had promised him the first litter. He got it, and I felt relieved.

I never saw that man again. Like a lot of others, I often wonder how he made out, if perhaps he survived.

There were still rifle shots whistling about the trees every once in a while so I went to the edge of a cliff that looked down on a sort of pit or opening. It was full of small trees and underbrush. It was from this direction that we received some of the direct fire. At least the shells were hitting just on the edge of the side of the cliff. and I figured the gun must be shooting form below; otherwise, they would have hit directly into us instead of just at the edge. The dead artillery men were only a few yards away. I crawled to the edge and looked down. There was an American Sherman standing there. Two tankers were leaning against the side of their vehicle smoking cigarettes and soaking up the warm sunlight. I shouted to them to warn them of the German riflemen that were in the woods below us and also to let them know that we were in position above them. I couldn't help but think that they were the ones that had been firing at us.

Love company was now an immobile, leaderless, scattered bunch of men. We all dug foxholes. I had to borrow an entrenching tool. Someone found some straw and we lined our holes and sat back and rested in the spring sunlight. The digging turned out to be a waste of time. The enemy was pushed back by other units and we received no more shellfire.

I started to feel hungry after the excitement wore away. It must have been after 12 noon when I unwrapped my big roast beef sandwich and finished it off.

Later in the day one of the men in the Weapons platoon became agitated over the dead buddies. I worried about the wounded ones but I couldn't see any point in getting stirred up over the dead men. There was nothing we could do to help them. However, this young blonde fellow, who was to crack up later on, insisted on removing the bodies off the hill. There was a big path that led down to the farm settlement. The litter bearers had come up that way. The blonde boy got a litter and several men helped him remove one of the dead weapons men. On the next trip he picked on me to help with the man who lay with the artillery men. I didn't have to help him, but I felt like a heel when I said something about the idea being foolish. It was a hard point to argue and since the dead man was a good friend of his. I understood a little how he felt.

The men hesitated when it came to picking up the body to lay it on the stretcher. This is when I finally decided to help and get the job finished. I turned the dead man over and lifted his head and shoulders. Another fellow pitched in and we got him on the litter. My fingers were matted with blood. It was a gruesome ordeal, but it didn't affect me physically.

The news that hurt me most that day was the story of the death of Howard "Red" White. Somehow or other the story of Red's death reached us on the hill. When I went down with the Weapons men I inquired about Red. They showed me where he lay. Someone had taken his grease gun. Otherwise, the body had not been touched. I stood there and stared at Red. I couldn't see his face. He was covered with rubble for the most part and he lay face down in the debris. Another one of my best comrades was gone. He had died, I felt, because of too many mistakes.

The death of "Red" White (Howard J.) and the severely wounding of Captain Thomas Danowski was a tremendous loss to Love Company. Our two best men were gone. The 10 men killed and the 31 wounded by our own artillery was another tragic loss that seemed to always haunt us. Who would be the next victims?

Espinoza told me the story. A German tank had drawn up near the building. Espinoza got in back of the manure pile. We had two tanks up there by that time but they refused to move from in back of the buildings. The German panzer fired. The first round took the top off the manure pile and almost buried Espinoza. It hit the doorway of the nearest house. Red was standing in the doorway. We lost the best soldier in the company. But it took an 88 to get him.

Walter Boyd, just back from the hospital, was another casualty. Big Walt and his hearty chuckle was another great loss to the Third platoon.

In the late afternoon, what was left of Love company came down off the wooded hill. There had been forty-one casualties. Thirty-one from our own artillery fire. About twelve men were dead. A squad leader in the Second platoon arrived back from Paris and found his entire squad dead or wounded.

We were reorganized and best of all we got some hot chow. The kitchen men piled our plates high with food. They seemed to want to make up for the hot breakfast we had missed. There was more than enough to go around. I sat down and leaned against a tree, my meat pan between my legs. As I raised my spoon with the first mouthful, I noticed the dried blood still on my hand. It didn't effect me at all. I was hungry. A meal never tasted better. With some good, hot food under our belts we would be ready to attack the next position. And perhaps at the next mealtime, we would be among the missing.

About dusk we were off down a country road, headed in the direction of the retreating enemy. Lieutenant Thompson was now our company commander. Lieutenant McCabe was executive officer. The two socialites were working together.

It was only a mile or two to the next town. There were antiaircraft shells bursting above the trees in the distance as we came into the small town of Griesenbeck.

As was standard procedure, I grabbed a bed in the house assigned to company headquarters. We blacked out the windows and lit candles. Lieutenant Thompson soon made an appearance, looked around and said, "Davis, I'm sleeping on that bed," pointing to the one I had my pack and rifle on.

There wasn't anything I could do. I had to sleep on the floor.

I had already laid down to go to sleep when Thompson ordered me to get my rifle and accompany him on an inspection of the platoon defense setups. "I want to make sure they are on the alert," he said.

We walked down the street together. We first noticed a man standing in a doorway. Thompson called from the middle of the road, "Is that the Third platoon?"

"Yeah, this is the Third platoon," the guard replied.

"Don't yeah me," Thompson spoke back sharply. "Yes, Sir."

The Letters of a Combat Rifleman

The guard didn't speak. I was dumbfounded. I knew that Thompson was strict and caste conscious, but I never dreamed he would carry it that far. It was night time and how could the guard distinguish rank in the dark? Thompson should have called the man down for not challenging us, not for failing to say, "Yes, Sir," The army sure taught rank and position. They failed to drive home the more important subjects of weapons training and tactics. Our officers made plenty of blunders in the field at the expense of human life, but they never erred in upholding the caste system, lodged so firmly in their minds by West Point teachers, that it came forth naturally, mechanically and almost unconsciously, as though they had drilled for years.

At that moment I decided to get out of company headquarters at the first possible chance.

The next morning offered my first opportunity to rid myself of my social and military superiors. I said to the Lieutenant:

"Sir, I would like to transfer to the second platoon." Thompson must have been a little surprised. He asked me to sit down and explain my reason for wanting to transfer.

"Well, Sir," I began, "I can't seem to get a rating in company headquarters. And the Second platoon has had a lot of casualties and could use some more men."

Thompson looked at me and asked, "What's the matter, Davis, don't you like me?"

That was a hard question to answer. But without hesitating, I said, "No, it's not that, Lieutenant. I just want to get ahead and I don't seem to be getting anywhere in company headquarters."

"Well," Thompson answered, "I'll give you twenty-four hours to think it over. If you still feel the same tomorrow, you come to me and tell me and I'll let you transfer over."

That was good enough for me. I knew what my decision would be in twenty-four hours. Thompson talked about working together, the same as I had worked with Danowski. He asked me to stay in company headquarters. But he knew why I wanted to make the change. And he probably knew what my answer would be on the morrow, too.

We stayed in Griesenback until later that afternoon. It gave me a chance to speak to Sergeant Wyman, leader of the second platoon. Sergeant Wyman called me a fool for wanting to transfer. I appreciated the advice but it didn't quite make sense. And yet I had to agree with Wyman.

Then I went to Max Delrogh, leader of the Third platoon. Max was different. He was glad to hear that I wanted to transfer to his platoon. He needed men and he offered me a good job. His platoon guide would not cooperate fully with him so he offered me the position. I told Max the details about my transfer attempt and assured him that I would be working with the Third platoon as soon as possible.

After this good offer from Max, I decided to get in touch again that day with Thompson and ask for an immediate transfer. I told him of the job I was offered and he reluctantly agreed to let me go over to the Third platoon. It was a move I was never to regret. As a matter of fact, it probably saved my life.

When we loaded on trucks that afternoon to keep up with the speeding Third armored division, I was the last man to get on the Third platoon truck. I had taken over my new job as platoon guide.

The trucks didn't take us very far, maybe ten or fifteen miles. For the first time I began to experience some of the hardships of the platoon riflemen. Company headquarters got into a house and barn near Geisenhausen. The platoons were assigned big holes in an adjacent field. We had straw to sleep on, and also sleeping bags, so it wasn't too rough. I found one advantage as a platoon guide—I didn't have to take my turn on the guard schedule.

The next morning we wearily crawled out of the ground and stretched our chilled bones. The weather was still clear and spring like.

We stayed in Geisenhausen most of that day. I found a chance to write to Jean:

"I have not been writing every day because I have been very busy since I returned from Paris. Today I received some of your letters from March 2 and 3 and I know you must have been worried because I wasn't writing.

"I am glad to say that I am in perfect health and that everything is all right.

"The house plan you enclosed was a dream and I know we will have something just like it as soon as possible after the war.

"Yesterday, I received the Christmas box Florence (my sister) sent and it certainly contained some wonderful goodies. This morning we had two fried eggs and they are serving steak now."

Before we had dinner, Tom, the CO's jeep driver, got the best news that a doughboy could possibly wish for. They were orders for Tom to return home to the States, immediately. Tom's life was saved—by a matter of hours, almost. Eckert took over Tom's job on the jeep.

We took another truck ride that afternoon. There were not many signs of combat along the roads. But we must have stopped just short of the firing line. We dug holes on the side of a sloping hill. On the crest of a hill just ahead an ammunition truck was hit by shellfire. It sent up a big fireworks display.

We dug our hole big enough to get all of our Third platoon headquarters into a sleeping position. Max was there directing the construction and excavation and doing as much or more work than the rest of us. Harry Osajnak from Brooklyn who was now acting platoon sergeant was a member of our little group. Allan Wilson, our platoon runner, completed the unit. Allan was from Perry, Oklahoma.

In the search for pieces of lumber for the roof, I crossed the road at the bottom of the grade and went on up to a cabin in the woods on the other side. There were bullets whistling through the treetops so I got out of there quickly. We finished our roof with pine boughs and then covered it all over with dirt so that we would have some protection from shellfire.

Our kitchen set up in the nearby pine woods and served hot chow, and soon afterwards, we crawled into our fart sacks.

We didn't even have a chance to fall asleep. They got us up and we climbed back on the trucks. This time we ended up at another field where there were already plenty of holes dug in the ground. Some were open and some covered. Schmidt, one of our squad leaders, and a few other men as well as myself decided we didn't like the idea of crawling into another hole as if we were playing groundhog.

We crossed the road to a burning house. A small barn at the rear was still in good shape as the fire had not yet reached that section. In front of the house was a burned-out German tank and in the orchard at the rear was a German 88 that had been partially destroyed.

The floor space was limited so that we could not all get a position. Two men pulled some hay out into the orchard and went to sleep on the ground. I got a spot inside but had to lie next to a dead goat. At 5 A.M. someone woke me up. It was a good thing, too, as the whole place was on fire and in another few minutes we probably would have all been enveloped in flames. It was almost daylight as we lay down again under the apple tree.

After breakfast, we were back again on trucks and we made a trip through Alterkirken, following up the armored units and the 414th regiment. The 414th boys were mounted on the Third armored tanks.

Outside of Kotzenroth we detrucked and moved into the town ready to battle any defender. There was no opposition, even though at the time we were spearheading the armored outfits.

We set up a defensive position. The Third platoon sent out a patrol and we established an outpost on a high hill on the north side of the town.

While Max and I were placing the men at the outpost, we sighted two uniformed men below us on a road coming into town. They were more than six hundred yards away so I fired over their heads in order to attract their attention. We waved for them to come across the fields toward us. They came on the run.

They were young men, but their uniforms were not German. Also they had no helmets so we knew they were not enemy soldiers. When they reached us it was not hard to determine their Italian nationality. Max, however, demanded identification. Satisfied that they had been POWs, Max relieved them of several hundred German marks and told them to take off for Italy. "You won't need the marks, anymore," Max told them.

Back in town the company found a barber shop and also the barber. I felt a little nervous in the barber's chair. It was something like the first time an enemy civilian offered me a drink.

During the afternoon several big columns of armored vehicles passed through our small town. There were two small boys living in the house we occupied. They were probably about three or four years old. Two days later I told Jean about them in a letter:

"The many situations and experiences I have been through would take hours to tell. In one place I stopped, there were two small towheaded youngsters, the smaller one about Billy's age. I had a lot of fun teaching him to give the V sin with his fingers to all the passing vehicles. He had quite a time holding the two fingers up and the other two down with his chubby little thumb. But he learned fast and was soon rewarded when a GI threw him a bag of candy. If those little ones are brought up like their American brothers, I think the world could live in peace forever. It is our responsibility to see that Billy doesn't have to come over here twenty years from now to fight the next generation."

After a good hot meal we took off down the country road on a long march to Weifeld, arriving after dark. Late that same night we moved again. This time we went by truck to Niederdresselndorf, another small town situated among green hills. It was a nice setup. There were no damaged houses. The bedroom in the platoon CP house was nicely furnished. There were twin beds with silk covered mattresses and fine bed clothes. It seemed almost a shame to lie down on these beds with our muddy combat shoes and dirty, soiled woolen olive drabs. It was a bit crowded, too, because Max, Harry, Wilson and I had to squeeze into two single beds.

At breakfast the next morning, we met the German frau and her young son whose home we were occupying. Like nearly all Germans they were nice and polite to their conquerors. The boy was very bashful and did not want to accept our offer of chewing gum and chocolate.

We had time to examine some strange houses at the end of our street that morning. They were apparently used for some sort of party activity. We arrived at the conclusion that it was either some kind of training school or else they brought the unmarried mothers-to-be there for seclusion. There were no civilians in any of the buildings that we could question.

It was before noon that we loaded up again and took off in the fast drive across Germany. So far we had been lucky. But our tourist-like trip couldn't last forever.

CHAPTER XV
Road Block at Eibelshausen

It wasn't a very long trip this time. Maybe another ten or fifteen miles, maybe more. Perhaps we went east. Maybe we moved north or south or even west. We never knew where we were going and I doubt if anyone was ever certain, including the column leader.

In most cases our company commander was at the head of the column in a jeep. Sometimes we had units attached such as tanks or TDs. We nearly always traveled just as a company, with units attached. It was very seldom, if ever, that we moved by tanks and trucks in battalion strength. It was assumed, no doubt, that a rifle company could take care of itself. Of course, while we were moving along one road, King company and Item were no doubt moving along almost parallel routes. We never knew or at least the platoons were never told what units were on our left or right or what outfits were up ahead or in back of us. In this fast, fluid situation there were times when nobody had even a remote idea of the location of individual units, especially rifle companies, traveling fast and independently on the flanks of armored thrusts.

We didn't know the overall picture either, but now it seems apparent that we were on the north flank of the armored spearhead that was attempting to close the Ruhr pocket. Our best source of information was the army newspaper, *Stars and Stripes*. But we were moving too fast for their circulation department and it was seldom that we ever got to see a copy. When we did, the news knew more about what we were doing than we did ourselves. I finally got the full dope when Eisenhower and the other generals started to publish their books about the crusade in Europe.

We detrucked in a bad position. It was on the side of a very long sloping hill. There was a small town at the bottom. Beyond the town were more hills and valleys with more small towns nestling on the flat areas. The enemy was on the distant hills. Lucky for us, he was not there in strength. We would have been slaughtered if the Jerries would have had some 88's set up in force. Our trucks pulled into the field on the left side of the road and proceeded to park as though they were moving into a motor pool back in the States.

Luckily we got into the town without being fired upon. The Germans were in bad shape when they couldn't take advantage of a situation like that.

We walked to the other side of the town and halted. There were other troops in the town. We sat on the side of the road or on the house steps and talked to the other GIs. They didn't know anymore about the situation than we did.

We moved out at a fast clip. The German observation was good, too, because we had only gone about two hundred yards in the open when some big stuff started to come in. It was placed right along the road that we were traveling and just at the correct range. But no shells burst real close to any of us. The shrapnel tore through our ranks but we were properly spaced and there were no casualties. When the first one hit, quite a few men hit the ground in our platoon as the bursts were near the end of the column where we were. Max and I hollered for the men to get up and keep moving. They got up immediately and started to move very fast. We cut off to the right side of the road and then we were out of range.

A cub plane circled to our left in an apparent attempt to spot the gun that had been firing on us. He was suddenly fired upon by some light antiaircraft guns which forced him to dive and take off like a P-51. American Shermans raced down a road to our right and crossed our front and passed along a high road to our left.

We raced through two villages in the valley at a fast clip. There was no more opposition. After covering about five miles we stopped at a small town called Eiershaussen.

It was still quite early in the afternoon. We flushed the town amid a lot of confusion. A couple of Frenchmen caused most of the trouble. They were already packed up and ready to leave for France. The German women didn't like the idea of their slaves leaving for their homeland. Most of the women were crying lover's tears. Here was another minor tragedy of the war. The frauliens weren't the youngest and prettiest ones we ever saw so we couldn't blame the Frenchies for wanting to take off immediately. Dorothy Dix and Pec Westmore would have been of more help than us doughboys.

The platoons were stretched across the front of the town in a defensive setup. Wires were run out from company headquarters. The platoons were in order from left to right, first, second and third.

Max got a call to report to company headquarters. I went along. It was a very big house with plenty of rooms. I said hello to the few remaining men in headquarters that I knew. Hebish was still there doing the communication sergeant's job. Carl Zurcher was on the 300 radio. Orrie Saylor, my York, Pennsylvania buddy was still around. And Val, the big Indian, was still on the job.

We went to the CP on the second floor. Thompson gave us orders to put out an outpost to our front. There would be one or two from each platoon. It looked as if we were going to stay for the night.

While we were talking to the CO, the First platoon brought in a prisoner,. He had walked into our lines and surrendered. He could speak fairly good English, claiming that he formerly lived in Chicago. Getting to the point, he said there was a German army payroll outfit in the woods up ahead and that they wanted to surrender—along with their five hundred thousand dollar payroll. There were two other men, the prisoner explained, and a wagon with a team of horses.

Thompson started to give the Heinie a hard time. He told the prisoner that he didn't want any horse and wagon and that they must enter our lines at exactly 5:25 to 5:30, or they would be shot.

The prisoner explained that three men couldn't carry half a million dollars worth of marks, that they would have to use the horses and wagon to haul it in. Thompson was adamant. The prisoner shrugged his shoulder and repeated his argument. Finally, Thompson agreed to let the prisoner haul the money.

Max and I must have both got the same idea at the same time. We took off as soon as we learned the route and time the Germans were going to bring in the payroll. I had noticed that the prisoner was wearing a good Swiss watch and I figured that a payroll outfit would undoubtedly have sidearms as defense weapons. The half million dollars' worth of good money was an added incentive.

Max notified the squad leaders of the defensive setup and then we personally took the first two men out into the orchard in back of the house and placed them in position. We then explained to the outpost men that we were going out in the fields to our front and move up toward the Second platoon area and contact their outpost.

It was almost dark as we took off. We gave them the password and said that we would come back in the same way in about half an hour. We cut out fairly deep in order that the Second platoon outposts would not see us and then we cut sharp to our left and broke into a trot as we realized that there was little time left in order to arrive on the road in time to intercept the Germans.

In the semi-darkness we stumbled into holes and ditches. There was another fellow with us. I can't recall his name now. We all had to laugh at the idea of our no-man's-land payroll holdup even though we had trouble catching our breath, due to the long run.

It was a longer distance to the road leading into town in the First platoon area than we figured. In the darkness ahead of us we heard the sound of an approaching wagon. We ran as fast as we could. But the payroll, pistols and Swiss watch galloped safely passed us. We stood and panted. Our bold hold-up attempt in no-man's-land had failed. But it was fun; we needed some excitement to fill in the dull periods. My guardian angel was working over time. Had we succeeded, who knows what sort of person I might have become.

The next morning, we hit the trail again. This time the First platoon was mounted on tanks. We were in trucks at the tail end of the column and I, as platoon guide, was in the last truck. Sandwiched in between was a section of .57 mm guns manned by our antitank company. With all that stuff they must have figured they were sending us on a dangerous mission.

They pretty well had things figured out right. We went for a long, long ride. We passed through many towns. We ate our lunch of K rations while moving. I took a couple of bites from a D bar.

At 3 P.M. we raced through a town at top speed. It was slightly down grade and we must have been doing about sixty miles per hour. It seemed strange that the natives were all scurrying for cover. Many were still running toward their houses as our last truck sped through the town.

About six hundred yards the other side of the town our truck ground to a stop. We could see the entire column stretched out in front of us due to the sloping ground. The tanks were stopped near a railroad overpass just short of the next town that nestled in the valley between two ranges of high ground. Someone shouted, "Piss call!" We jumped off the truck to relieve ourselves.

The truck driver must have been paying more attention to the situation than we were. He pulled into the driveway of a house along side of the road at the right and started to turn his truck around. It was just at this point that the enemy struck.

There was a quick fast burst of machine gun fire. This was followed by three rapid shots from an 88. Our last three tanks at the head of the column were the victims. Apparently, they could not depress the gun enough to get the first two that were close up against the blown railroad bridge that acted as their road block.

There was a slight hesitation and then the fourth shot whizzed just inches above the top of the cab of our tuck. We were just pulling out in first gear. The black driver slammed on the brakes, stopped the truck and jumped out of the cab and took off. The whole back of the truck unloaded almost as fast as the cab section. I was the last one off despite the fact that I was sitting by the tailgate. I stopped to get my pack from under the seat and it got tangled up in the mess of stuff on the floor. I was glad later that I took time to retrieve my pack.

For some reason or other the Heinies stopped firing. Perhaps one of our 57 mm gun crews helped save the day. They gave us the best support we ever received. While we were trying to take off they unhitched their gun from the truck. Swung it around and started to throw twice as many rounds of AP stuff back at the Germans. I don't believe they could see a target, but they directed their fire straight down the road into the near end of town up ahead. That was the best gun crew I ever saw in action. They had a gun and they used it. Their action, no doubt, saved many lives. They took a chance but it paid off.

On the left side of the road was a large saw mill and another house. The whole company and what tankers were left, got under cover among the saw mill buildings. Two .57 mm gun crews managed to wheel their guns back by hand into a position between two of the buildings. All the tanks were abandoned as well as all the trucks.

Max and I began to place the Third platoon men in a defensive setup to cover our rear and the left flank. Everyone was very nervous. We placed a BAR man in back of a concrete culvert to cover the road to our rear and he was shaking so he couldn't hold the automatic rifle. The lone house was on the highest ground that we occupied. We placed a squad there. There was still higher ground to our left and also to our right and rear. We had open fields of fire in almost every direction.

As we set up our defense we heard the details of the activity at the head of the column. We were told that Thompson, leading the column in a jeep, swung around and told the tank commander that he was going up a dirt road that paralleled the railroad to the right and see if he couldn't find a way to get around the fallen bridge. Zurcher, who had been operating his 300 radio on the jeep, jumped of to relieve himself. Eckert and Lieutenant Thompson started off up the side road by themselves. They were just out of sight when the Jerry machine gun cut loose, Eckert and Thompson were among the missing. Seven tankers were killed. Miraculously, the First platoon men that were sitting on the outside of the five tanks were untouched. Our company was still complete except for our CO and one jeep driver, Eckert.

While getting the defenses organized, I noticed an object on the crest of the hill to our left front. It appeared to be a vehicle of some sort, perhaps a tank. But after studying it a little I decided it was just the contour of the land.

A little later someone else started to study this object and without hesitation started to shout about a tank coming at us. I wanted to dive under a pile of lumber like most of the fellows were doing but I decided it would be better to get one of the 57 mm guns into position. Most of the gun crew had taken off, but we managed to swing the gun around to face the oncoming tank. It was then that I finally realized that the "tank" was the same outline I had been studying about five or ten minutes previously. I felt pretty cheap when I realized how excited I had been and how I had cursed that gun crew. I almost felt as though I had started the false alarm.

With things quieted down and our nerves a little less taut, we began to make plans for a forward movement. This organization was handled primarily by Max Delrogh and I gave him my best assistance. We assembled the remaining officers together and started to formulate a plan of attack.

Second Lieutenant McCabe was the only State side officer left so he automatically became company commander. As our new leader, he had nothing to offer. Max and I planned mainly with Lieutenant Smart, the First platoon leader who had won his commission in the lines.

Our plan was for the First and Second platoons with Weapons to move out to the right where there was a gully and some cover from a few trees and undergrowth. The Third platoon would delay about five minutes and pull out in a skirmish line across the open fields to our front and left front. The town was to our right front so we would have to bear in that direction as we moved forward. The artillery FO was ordered to prepare a concentration of big stuff on the town itself. He went aloft to a sort of tower on one of the lumber buildings and laid in a few sighting rounds.

The attack got snafued at the start. We moved out on time, but the other platoons delayed. As a result we were out there in the open, moving toward the town while the other platoons were still back in the buildings. That left us open to a concentrated fire from all the Jerry weapons up ahead. But for some reason or other, the Jerries withheld their fire.

The whole platoon was in a skirmish line. We did not use any scouts. As platoon guide, I walked about ten yards in back of the center part of the line.

After moving half of the fifteen hundred yards we had to go to reach the first house, we realized our prepared artillery fire had not started to come in. So we slowed down until we were almost standing still. The men did stop when I first yelled to Max and asked him "What about the artillery fire?" We got them moving again but at a snail's pace. We slowed down until we were almost standing still. These were anxious moments for our small force.

Some Jerry ack-ack guns opened up on us, and we stepped it up a little. I began to worry about the Jerry mortars and their direct fire big guns. I began to think that perhaps they were withholding their fire until we got in real close.

Then, just at the moment when we were sweating out the most ticklish predicament we were ever in, there came a rush of big stuff over our heads. It was just in the nick of time. There was HE and WP and some proximity fuse jobs. It was terrific! What a show! The town rocked and caught on fire.

In another minute we were up to the railroad embankment. The squad on the left went up and over. The other men went down the right side of the embankment. At this point the Jerry infantry cut loose with rifle and machine gun fire.

The squad on the left side of the tracks hit the ground. As platoon guide, I was walking near the crest of the embankment and I signaled and called for the men to get up and keep moving.

They jumped and started shooting at the nearest houses, now only about one hundred yards away. Patton, the bazooka man, used up three full magazines with his carbine. Juan Garcia, a reliable BAR man, cut lose with more fire power.

The Letters of a Combat Rifleman

I forgot what a target I made standing on the tracks until some close ones started to crack around my ears. At the same time, a Jerry machine gun opened up from the middle of the town and sent a stream of tracers up at an angle to clear the tops of the house. At our range they were just about going over our heads.

I hit the prone position and emptied five rounds of my '03 at the nearest house and then loaded some tracers and fired over the houses at the Jerry machine gun. By this time, the men on the right were inside the town. They told me later they were surprised to see tracers going over their heads toward the enemy.

It was about this time that there was another rush of big stuff but in the opposite direction. The TOT fire landed on our line of departure. And, again, I was glad I was in a forward element.

Max had given Wilson orders to contact company headquarters on the 536 and let them know that we were in the first houses and that it was safe for the tankers and antitankers to move forward. Wilson was standing near me but just a little forward and at the bottom of the railroad embankment as I came off the top and started to catch up with the other men. He was having difficulty making contact, even though we were only about one thousand yards from the CP. I took the set from Wilson and started the proper call procedure.

"Hello, One Love Three, Hello, One Love Three, Over," I called. There was a faint message. It sounded like Delakas on the other end.

"Hello, One Love Three, Hello, One Love Three, Message for you, Over," I almost shouted into the mouthpiece.

This time there was some response. Delakas answered, "Hello, One Love Three, Hello, One Love Three, Send your message, Over."

Without resort to any code, I told Delakas we were in the first houses and that it was all right for the tankers to come and get their tanks. I also requested that the antitank men come forward with their guns.

Wilson and I then went forward toward the town. We entered the first house and found two men there. They did not know where Max or the rest of the men were except that they had moved farther on into the town. I told Wilson to stay with the two men, and I started out over an open piece of ground toward the next house.

A high wire fence had me stopped for a while. It's an awful sensation to be standing out in the open trying to figure out your next move. I found an opening and entered the house. It was getting late and inside it was dark enough to cause me to stumble around from room to room. In the gloom I was calling out, "Max, where are you . Yo, Max!" There was no answer.

I looked out a second story window in the back and there was Lieutenant Smart and the other platoons just coming into town. Naturally, I let them know that we had been in town a long time. But I had to admit that I didn't know where the rest of the platoon was located. Even I didn't want to claim that they were already to the middle of the town.

That's exactly where Max and the rest of the boys were at the time. They didn't even wait to contact the other platoons. They just moved right on in until they were at a main corner where there were several buildings burning. At this point they got a little mixed up and started to call the Jerries., mistaking them no doubt for men from the other platoons. Luckily, there had been no casualties so far.

I finally made contact. The other platoons remained just where they entered the town. The Third platoon was spearheading. We were in a dangerous spot and it was difficult from squad to squad because the light from the fires silhouetted a man as he crossed back and forth across the street or from building to building. It was very tough moving about inside the house, too, because we had moved in in the dark and we didn't know the floor plans.

Max kept asking me to contact company headquarters, still back at the lumber mill. I tried every solution I could think of except climbing up on the roof. I leaned out of second and third story windows until I almost lost my balance. Then I tried going down in the courtyard but that didn't work either. I got some faint reception and I knew I was talking to Delakas. Finally, I understood him to say that he wanted to know who was calling.

I identified myself by name and repeated the request for "tin can opener." It was all in vain. If the CP did receive my message, than the antitankers refused to budge. The tankers also remained stationary.

Max and I finally ended up in the cellar of our house where the civilians had a couple of candles burning. It was a bad spot because the light shone through the cellar door that opened onto the street at the corner of the house. With some difficulty we made the civilians understand that we wanted the light blacked out better.

I broke open my pack and started to look for something to eat. There was still a small can of smoked turkey that my sister, Florence, had sent to me in her Christmas package. It was a very small can, but as hungry as I was, I couldn't eat it all. I left the remains sitting on the cellar steps.

The 536 radio was still open. The antenna was extended and consequently, I had to hold it on an angle so that it would not scrape against the rafters. We were getting a lot of static, which for a 536 is pretty good because most of the time you get nothing at all.

At intervals, I tried again to contact our CP. To make things more difficult, a couple of small children who had been sleeping in the back of the cellar were awakened. They started to scream and holler and I couldn't blame them. And there wasn't anything that we could do to quiet them. We offered them chocolate, gum and candy but they wouldn't shut up. I often wondered since then if those little tots will ever get over that nightmare. In that remote country village, they were no doubt unfamiliar with scenes of warfare. Strange, bearded and steel-helmeted men carrying all sorts of strange weapons and weird contraptions and speaking a foreign language, must have made them think they had been transported in there dreams to a nightmarish hell.

The Letters of a Combat Rifleman

We began to wonder ourselves when we suddenly started to receive a message in clear unmistakable tones. The broadcaster had a slight German accent. He started to tell us that we were sitting on a keg of powder, that we should get out of town and right away.

The mysterious voice continued, "At ten minutes of ten the whole town will explode." We glanced at our watches. It was about ten to ten already.

The announcer then started to count the seconds. Each count, of course, giving the number of seconds that were left before we would be knocked sky high. "Nine, eight, seven, six, five—." We looked around at each other in amazement, and with a little amusement, too, because we knew the town wasn't going to blow up.

"Four, three, two, one!" Then there was silence again. That was the end of the message. The fires outside burned a little bright, but there was no explosion. It was all a Nazi hoax. The reception had been so good we figured the hoaxer may have been in the next building or at least in the next block. We speculated that the Jerries had captured Lieutenant Thompson, Eckert and the jeep and, of course, the 300 radio and perhaps a 536. They were on the right channel and they must have known they were on the right channel. But we never found the answer.

A little later Max got a message by runner that he was to report back to the edge of town for a meeting. Max and I entered the same house that I had entered earlier when I had been looking for the platoon. At the meeting, held in the dark on the first floor, it was announced by Lieutenant McCabe that battalion had radioed an order to keep moving and to take the remainder of the town immediately.

When we were stopped at the lumber yard, we moved out in the attack on our own initiative, not on an order from battalion. We probably would have proceeded again of our own accord after a plan had been worked out. Perhaps we would have stayed put for the night. Anyway, we did not like the order from battalion. Quite a discussion took placer there in the dark. After it was finally decided to carry out battalion's order without an argument, plans were made for the next movement.

The Third platoon was finished spearheading. At least I thought we were the last rifle platoon to start up the street. There was a column of men on each side. We went very slowly through the darkness, picking our way along the sides of the houses, around front steps and along fences.

Our course took us straight ahead along one of the main streets on the south side of the town. We covered the whole length of the town from southwest to southeast without incident. At the other edge of the town our street formed an apex with a main road that led out of town to the southeast. The railroad also came out at the point. There were no houses along the roads near the apex except one that was located right at the point. The rear door opened on our street and the front door opened on the street to our left.

I was only about twenty-five yards from the house when there was a burst of automatic fire. It was one of our guns, not a fast German machine pistol. Nevertheless, we all hit the ground. I crossed over the road and got down between the steel rails.

Then, less than a half minute later, there was a big burst of flame that lit up the entire area. There was a tremendous explosion followed by another quick blast. A big motor started up but coughed out immediately. I saw it happen but I couldn't figure out what it was that did the firing. The big ball of fire was less than twenty-five yards away and it was just to our left front and on the other road. Of course, in the darkness we did not know there was another road leading into the one we were on. That is the men in the rear of the column did not know.

I decided to get my head up a little higher than the steel rail I was in back of so I could get an idea of what was going on. There was another flash and another blast. I didn't duck and so was able to see the outline of a tank on the other road. But the flash was so close to the tank and passed so quickly that I thought that the tank was firing at our men in the house in front of me or else at our men up ahead at the front of the column.

After a third tremendous flash and blast the tank started to burn. Then, in a few minutes we got the news. I never found out who located the tank or how the whole episode started, but Sergeant Harold Eugene Schmidt, our best squad leader, fired the burst of automatic slugs at a Jerry and sprawled him out on the street in front of the house. The Jerry must have run outside first because there had been a lot of noise like someone trying to run through a house full of furniture in the dark, just a second before Schmidt fired.

This happened as Patton, our bazooka man, was getting into position to fire on the Royal Tiger tank. Luke went through the house and out onto the street on the other side. It must have taken plenty of guts. He knelt in the middle of the road, only twenty yards from the rear of the tank, and fired three rounds. After the first round, the Jerries tried to start the motor but it coughed out right away. Luke went back to the front of the house and got another round from the assistant bazooka man. This second one was a dud so Luke fetched another rocket. The third one finished the job. There was a rush of hob nailed boots on the hard road and the surviving members of the crew made it safely to a house on the north side of the road about twenty-five yards away. They left four of their comrades inside of the panzer, dead. The whole action had been carried out by four or five men, all Third platooners. Again, Max directed the proceedings. This time I was in the background shaking from cold and fear. Luke Patton was later awarded the Silver Star for his fine work.

We moved into the houses in back of us and it now became apparent that we had moved from one side of the town to the other and we were finished for the night. But as things turned out I never did get to sleep.

We first began to hear stories about different civilians saying that they had seen an American officer taken prisoner that afternoon. According to the civilians, this officer was wounded while driving a jeep.

The Letters of a Combat Rifleman

There was a lot of moving about in the house where we set up the platoon CP. Some men were trying to sleep while others were looking for a place to lay down and some, even though it was about 3 A.M. were breaking open K rations to grab something to eat. I was sitting on the floor leaning against the wall and listening to some of the chatter and discussion about Thompson being the wounded American officer when a shell crashed through the corner of our house and tore into the house across the street.

No one appeared at all alarmed. Someone immediately came up with the solution to the latest enemy threat. It was the burning Royal Tiger outside that had fired the round through the house. The big 88 was pointing right at us, and there must have been a loaded round in the chamber.

Information continued to come in from the civilians. We heard that the American officer and some enlisted men were being held prisoners in the same house that the German tankers had fled to after the panzer had been hit. We checked the scene from the upper stories and it was then that Max gave me the order to organize a patrol to raid the house and effect the rescue of the GIs held prisoners. Max didn't want to point the finger, so he said, "Either you or Schwartz." Schwartz and I decided we would both go. We selected Garcia, a good, dependable BAR man, and another good soldier named Johnson, to accompany us. Johnson carried his M-1 rifle and Schwartz, a squad leader, had his grease gun slung across his chest. To add more fire power, I borrowed Osajnak's Thompson submachine gun. To make sure we had some supporting fire in case we ran into trouble, I stationed another BAR man in a rear second story window to give us cover.

We assembled between two houses on our street where we stood looking at each other like doomed sheep. Finally, I said, "Let's go!" I took off down along a high wooden fence that partitioned the plots of ground in back of the houses. We headed toward the other street where the Royal Tiger was sitting, and we came out almost opposite the house we were headed for. The street was up on a high embankment and as I ran up the slope I fell forward near the roadbed at the top and waited for the other men so that we could all make the rush together. With only a slight hesitation, we dashed diagonally across the road and into the front door, passing an American ambulance parked in front of the house.

The four of us took separate rooms on the first floor and rushed into clear them out. They were empty. I went to the top of the cellar stairs and shouted, "Kommen raus!" I called several times but there was no answer. Just as we were about to toss down a grenade someone called out in English.

There was quite a conglomeration of men at the bottom of the stairs. The German tankers were there, three of them. But the GIs were already in charge despite the fact that they were supposed to be prisoners. One GI had taken a Luger from one of the Jerry armored men and he was now holding the Jerries prisoner. There were also several other Germans, including two aid men who had been attending the American wounded.

There were eight wounded Americans who had been unloaded the day before from the American ambulance parked in front of the house. The wounded men were being driven to the rear, after becoming casualties while participating in an armored spearhead thrust that was many miles in front of Eibelshaussen, the town we now occupied.

The wounded American officer turned out to be a captain from the Third Armored Division. He was sitting up in a corner despite the many compresses he had wrapped around him. We never liberated a person that appeared as grateful and happy as that captain. He had reason to be glad, of course, because this was his third liberation. He had been a German prisoner three times.

The captain had quite a story to tell. There wasn't much we could do to get the men out of there at the present so we stood there and listened. In the meantime, daylight had put in an appearance outside.

The captain told us that the Third Armored Division had sent a column of ninety vehicles through Eibelshaussen at 5 A.M. the previous day. The captain was going through later in the day to deliver a secret code message to the armored spearhead. He was riding alone in a jeep. The Jerry outfit that was in town when the big armored column went through or that came in afterwards, opened up on this one-man invasion.

The Royal Tiger fired almost point blank and hit the captain's jeep on the right front wheel. The captain was wounded and taken prisoner. His captors wanted to shoot him right then and there but he could speak pretty good German and he was able to persuade them to have his wounds dressed and forget about the "mercy" killing.

His jeep was only about twenty-five yards down the street from the house where we found the captain. They carried him in and a German aid man put on the compresses. At this time they had not bothered to search him. Finally he worked out a plan to get rid of the message. First, he told his captors he was cold and he asked them to put him next to the stove. They obliged and then he asked for a drink of water so that he could have an opportunity to throw the message in the fire. The Jerry aid man, the only one in the room at the time, went out to get him the water. The captain promptly threw the message in the fire and thus insured the security of his comrades in the armored spearhead up ahead.

When we finished with the greetings and story telling, we rounded up all the Jerries and marched them up to the first floor. We promised the wounded GIs that we would have another ambulance there to pick them up just as soon as the town was cleared.

Back at the platoon they were getting ready to move out and clear the rest of the town. Our efforts on the north side brought in a couple of prisoners and some souvenirs such as Lugers and Finnish hunting knives. Max presented me with one of the beautiful knives that an old frau turned in as a waffen.

The Letters of a Combat Rifleman

I made a mistake, perhaps. when I opened up with my '03 and some tracers at what appeared to be an entrance to a cave, high up on a hillside toward the east. Anyway, Max blamed the return mortar fire on my plinking. But I think the shells came in too soon to be a reply. Perhaps the Jerry observer was up on the high ground, but I think that he saw our searching parties and decided to drop a few shells in on us. However, all the shells landed around Max and me. We ducked into a house and hugged the kitchen floor. The natives were screaming and hollering and running around the rooms like frightened chickens. The shells were pretty big and they were shaking the house so we kept shouting at the civilians until they took cover in the cellar.

Back at the platoon CP we started a big roundup of food. The civilian owners of the houses were not in a very cooperative mood and so we gave them a hard time. After we got finished frying eggs and potatoes and eating K rations, the place looked like a cyclone had hit it.

And while we were sitting there eating, a German Jeep drove into town, thinking, perhaps, that the place was still in German hands. A couple of boys grabbed up M-1s and fired right through the kitchen windows. It was a nice bit of shooting. The driver was hit in the leg and that stopped the Volkswagen. We were a trigger-happy bunch now and that is what pays off in combat.

We finally got the news about Eckert and Thompson. They were both lying dead back on the road they had turned into. The jeep was still there with everything in tact, including the radio. Thompson's body was in the ditch next to the jeep and Eckert's body was still behind the wheel.

Again, I had escaped sudden death. My guardian angel was guiding me safely. I couldn't help but think, too, that I if I had been on the .50 caliber machine gun I might have saved Thompson and Eckert. But more than likely, I would have been the third victim.

It was about this time, too, that we learned that all the packs that had been left on the trucks back at the lumber mill had been thoroughly looted. The boys in my platoon were completely cleaned out except for a few K rations.

After some picture taking at the Royal Tiger and the knocked out jeep, I tried on some Lufwaffe uniforms and had my picture snapped in them. Luke Patton and I swapped places snapping the camera shutter. I made a nice shot of Luke standing in front of the knocked out tank, holding his bazooka.

Luke hated the Germans, and he was naturally suspicious of them. He explained the setup at our house where there were two young German men lying in bed in the basement. According to his explanation, the two men were really drunk and not sick as the woman in the house claimed. Luke's theory sounded logical, and we were just going to go down into the cellar and order the two men out of bed, when we got orders to move out right away.

CHAPTER XVI
Martial or Marital

It looked as if we were going to start for the next town on foot. However, we halted at the northeast edge of the town and waited on the side of the road. As we sat there large groups of civilians were streaming back along the road into town. They said they had been in a cave on the outskirts.

Finally, we were ordered to move into the houses. The Third platoon selected a modern home and the whole outfit moved in. It was very crowded but there were enough beds for nearly all the men. We had to sleep two men in a single bed because a bunch of reinforcements came up and some were assigned to our platoon.

When we first got the news about the new men, we decided to clean up the front entrance to our house. A couple of GIs must have been hit there because the cement steps and the small uncovered stone porch was littered with two GI helmets and other equipment and smeared with pools and streaks of fresh, dried blood. Down the street a little way in front of the Weapons platoon CP lay the body of a GI. Nobody bothered to move it. He looked too peaceful to disturb.

We put an outpost up on one of the hills and spent a peaceful, uneventful night.

The next day I found time to write to Jean: "Just a few lines to let you know I am just fine. Time is very short these days.

"I hope you will get your Paris gloves in time to wear with your new spring suit and hat that Jewel made for you. I know I would not be disappointed in your appearance. I can't wait until I see you looking so beautiful all dressed up in your new outfit.

The Letters of a Combat Rifleman

"I don't know if I misunderstood your February 2 letter or not. Anyway it didn't sound so good. You seemed disgusted with the whole situation. You said that you heard that soldiers did not want any martial relations after the war. I can assure you that is true. We have had enough martial relations to last a lifetime and then some. But let's skip the whole matter and if you are not writing, I certainly would like to hear from you, darling. Remember, nobody said anything about marital relations. That's the kind I like.

"Things are pretty quiet at the moment. The kitchen stove is going, the clock on the wall is ticking, the sun is shining and everything is all right with the world. But remember, I said, 'at the moment.'

"Just after the word kitchen, the platoon leader called me and I busted in on a party with a bottle of cognac. On the table we have a bottle of 1943 Lorcher Roder Eiesling. You figure that one. Anyway, it is a white wine. But these moments are rare and far between. Last night I went to bed at nine and got up about nine. In the past I have been lucky to get three hours a night. But we are all praying for the end.

"Well, that's all darling. I love you very, very much. You are my love and my wife and the only woman in the world for me. Keep loving me and keep praying and keep writing.

We stayed in Eibelshaussen most of that day. We wrote letters home, rested up and got plenty to eat and drink. Little time was spent in searching or exploring. Some of the fellows walked up to the slave labor camp on the road leading out of town. Some of us went up on the hill where there was another camp and a big stone building that formerly was an SS headquarters. A guard on the door refused to let anyone enter as they wanted to keep all the records intact. We contented ourselves by teasing the big black German police dog that was in a large pen in front of the building. He was the most vicious looking dog I ever saw. I could just imagine what happened to the slave workers who tried to escape. I tried to line him up in my sights several times but he wouldn't keep still and I was afraid of hitting one of the steel bars and getting a ricochet.

We took off in the afternoon after a couple of long armored columns passed through us again. We stopped before dark and set up in another small German village just at dusk. Nothing happened during the night except that one of our tanks accidentally ran over some of our own mines that were placed on the road for the night.

We were off early the next day on a long tank ride. I found the tanks were easier to ride due to the fact that the tread followed every contour of the road. It did not bounce down into a hole or rut in the road like a truck. The tanks traveled at fifty and sixty miles per hour just like the trucks and jeeps, which made it pretty cold on the outside. We overcame this discomfort by wrapping up in big quilts and blankets that we were always able to requisition from the civilians.

The tankers had only on request—"Watch for Jerries in holes along the road." A Jerry with a bazooka or panzer faust could put us out of commission with one shot.

In a letter to Jean a few days before, I gave a description of our cross-country travels: "This morning we are having beautiful spring weather just as we have had for over a week now. The scenery of this section of Germany sure fits in with the weather. I have passed through country the likes of which I have never seen before. There are tall pine forests, deep glens and dark-colored rivers and streams. Adding color are the cultivated fields and small towns. But for all the beauty I'll still take America, first, last, and always.

CHAPTER XVII
Hartz Mountains

On our tank ride we passed through similar country, finally ending up the day near Medebach. We did not know it at the time, but division had information that the Jerries would attempt to break out of the Ruhr pocket through our lines in this area. Our regiment, echeloned to the left rear of the Third armored division and the 414th and 413th infantry regiments, was to receive the main enemy thrust. But during the days that we were tied up near Medebach, the other units continued there advances to seal the pocket at Paderborn. As an example of this wide open, fluid situation, our regiment was extended over a forty-mile front. Due to the threat of an enemy breakout attempt, this front was reduced to twenty miles.

With our arrival in the Medebach area on April 1, the regiment was able to contract to a seventeen-mile front. Later twelve. Also, on this date the Krauts started their drive with units of three divisions and all the armor they could muster, but our First battalion, located in Medebach, repelled the enemy tanks and infantry, and within two hours the fire was over.

This information we learned later when the division history was published. We entered a quiet town about six miles from Medebach, had a hot supper, and went to bed.

At 0600 the next morning, companies C and I repelled another strong attack on Medebach. It was then that the big boys decided this growing enemy threat should be eliminated. Little Love company was selected to do the job.

It was misty, wet and cold that day we walked up the paved road toward Medebach. I had two rifles again. One was a beautiful German-made sporter.

I wanted to pack it up and send it home. But as soon as I realized we were going to walk instead of ride trucks and tanks, I decided to get rid of my prize.

First I took out the bolt and tossed it in a small creek that we passed over just near the edge of the town. Then I lifted the beautiful sporter up over my head, grasping the front of the barrel in both hands in order to break the finely-grained walnut stock. But just then a tanker, sitting along the road, shouted, "Hey, let me have that rifle." He got it and I sure realized what a joy it is to give. I didn't want to break up that fine piece anymore than I would want to shoot my best friend. It no doubt found a good home as the tanker went back down the road to the creek to find the bolt.

Out of town the road took a course through rolling hills covered with pine trees and some open fields where sheep grazed. At one spot a man dressed in civilian clothes hurried across one of the fields on our left. He carried a staff like a sheep herder. However, there happened to be no sheep on that side of the road and he seemed to be moving in too great of a hurry to suit me. I brought up my Springfield and intended to stop him with a warning shot but Max said, "Nix." The mysterious figure disappeared quickly among the tall pines about five hundred yards away.

Just up the road another one hundred yards we entered the woods on the right side and had orders to go through it parallel to the road and in an extended skirmish line to the right. The other platoons deployed also, some on the left side of the road.

It was easy going through the pine woods, but the pace was awfully fast, especially out on the extreme right flank where I was. We didn't go very far, perhaps a mile at the most. Coming out on the road again, we saw that the other platoons had captured a few enemy soldaten. They were poor excuses for soldiers. Most of them were very old men. But these old fellows were giving the fuel and food and communication routs plenty of hot spots. Noncombatant convoys were being ambushed with regularity.

The main enemy band had no doubt escaped our search. And I had a feeling that the man with the long, flowing garments had a lot to do with their elusiveness.

We boarded trucks at this point and pulled up the road the remaining miles to Medebach. At the time we did not know the name of the town and we knew nothing about the general situation. Medebach seemed like a peaceful town. It was rural-like and not over six or eight city blocks long. As soon as we entered the town we detrucked.

In short order we got into some of the buildings and the boys started to break open some of their rations since it was already mid afternoon. The house we entered had a small barn attached and we were able to get some fresh milk from the pretty young milkmaid. The warm kitchen and the chance to get a bite to eat helped a lot, since it was misty and cold outside.

It wasn't more than half an hour and we got orders to fall out in the street. While we were standing near the trucks waiting for the order to mount up again, some big mortar shells started to drop in on us. Since we were still on the far edge of the town away from the enemy, it was apparent that the Jerries had a good observation, or intelligence, or both. Most of the shells were dropping right in around us.

I became very nervous when the shells started coming in and no one bothered to issue any orders about moving out or getting back in the buildings.

After more than five minutes delay the head of the company started down the main street toward the center of Medebach. I don't remember that we had suffered any casualties up to this point, but there may have been some men hit in the other platoons.

Lieutenant McCabe was shaken up by a shell that burst very close, but I don't believe he was wounded. We had a new company commander. His name was Darcey. He was transferred over from Mike company.

We hugged the buildings and doorways as the column started and stopped its way through town to the other end. As quickly as possible, we got into some buildings when we found out that we were stopping for orders. The shells were continuing to come in.

There were plenty of GIs in the houses we jumped into. They started to give us the first idea of the terrific attacks that were made against Medebach. They pointed out some of the battered Jerry and GI vehicles.

The house we were in was a nice, big modern home. almost every room was crowded with GIs. Charley company was maintaining an O.P. in one of the upper floors.

Coming down from the O.P. I noticed a man lying near the foot of the banister. He was slouched over in a half sitting position and appeared to be dazed and exhausted. When I saw his face, I recognized the young, blonde fellow from our Weapons platoon who had insisted on removing his dead comrades from the hill near Brungsburg. He refused to get up. It was another case or combat fatigue. I never saw him after that.

We soon got the information that our platoon was going to move out in the attack mounted on our two remaining tanks. I finally offered to lead some of the men up the road on foot. Max turned this offer down.

Somehow or other we got all the men on the two tanks. When about fifteen men try to cling to a Sherman tank, you can hardly see the tank. I hung on for dear life and thanked the dear Lord when we stopped at a road junction about four hundred yards outside of Medebach. The road we came up was tree-lined and there were fields on both sides. Beyond the fields loomed the ominous pine forest.

We dismounted and jumped into the only house at the road junction. It was a building, something like a highway inn. We set up in the beer parlor and waited for new orders. Nobody seemed to know just what the score was. We knew we had to go father up the road, but we didn't know how far. I figured the Jerries would let us know when to stop.

There was a badly wounded civilian lying on some tables in the beer parlor. He said he was a Dutchman. Nobody attempted to help him or give him first aid.

Max and I continued to work on the problem of transporting our platoon up the road. When a section of heavy machine guns from Mike company pulled up with two jeeps, we thought we had a solution. However, the lieutenant in charge, the same fellow that worked his way in the chow line twice in Lucherberg before some of the enlisted men were fed, refused to help us. He said he had too many men on the jeeps already.

There was nothing left to do except load up again onto the two tanks just as we did before. I was just about ready to lose my grasp on the tank on the last short ride when we stopped at the road junction. I began to wonder what would happen on the next jaunt, especially if the road became rough or we went forward for any distance. So, again, I offered to lead some of the men on foot but Max declined the offer.

Fifteen minutes after we stopped we were back loading up on our two panzers. It was beginning to get dark as we pulled out with a roar toward the mist-shrouded landscape in the distance. Visibility was less than two hundred yards as we slowed to a stop about eight hundred yards farther up the road. Why we stopped I don't know. I didn't know either, where the rest of the company was located. They must have walked up the road ahead of us or in back of us because I soon learned that they were in the field to our left.

We deployed along either side of the road in order to protect the tanks. That was our job for the night. We didn't know it at the time but just about fifty yards ahead was a very big house, level with the road but set back in the hillside about one hundred feet. A mountain-like hill rose very abruptly right from the right side of the road. It was covered with rocks and trees and for all practical purposes it was too steep to climb. We had little to worry about from that side. On the left side of the road was an open field that ended about seventy-five yards away where the woods took over. There was a ditch on the right side of the road but none on the left. That was the layout we were to occupy all night long. We didn't know it at the time, of course. We only knew that we were moving along a road and that we stopped. We could see the mountain to our right and the open field with the woods beyond to our left. We couldn't see any other troops of any kind and we couldn't see what was up the road ahead of us.

We didn't have to be told that the enemy was close. We knew that. We didn't have to be told to get off the tanks when they stopped. That was second nature. It was routine by now to immediately set up a defense as soon as we became immobile.

The first enemy to strike was the weather. The mist turned into drizzle. It continued until early the next morning. There was no shelter for anyone in the Third platoon. Max tried sleeping on the road near the tail end of the lead tank during the night but that didn't appeal to me. I stood on my feet for nearly the full stretch of the darkness.

The Letters of a Combat Rifleman

It wasn't long until my clothes were drenched. The worse sensation was feeling the cold water run down the inside of my arms, starting near the shoulder and finally getting soaked up again where the elbow or wrist contacted the clothing. To top it all off, it was very cold that night.

Some of the hair-raising events of the night were to help at least in keeping my mind off my physical discomfort. The Jerries started things a poppin' shortly after total darkness set in. They opened with a terrific bang. An 88 mounted on a Royal Tiger supplied the bangs. To make things worse, they pulled their panzer right up in front of the First and Weapons platoons, dug in out in the field and started to blast away at a range of about seventy-five yards. The panzer stood on slightly higher ground just to our left front and at the most, only two hundred yards away from our tanks. It was plunging fire, directly into the platoons in the field. Boy, did the dirt fly out in that field! Our boys just wormed their way a little deeper into the ditch along the road. Max and I stood near the tanks and watched. Our first though, naturally, was to fight back. We figured the two Shermans were our best bet. But we didn't reckon with the Sherman crews. When we asked them to fire back at the Jerry panzer, we got the usual reply.

"We are out gunned. we couldn't penetrate his front armor. We know where he is but it's no use," the tank commander explained. It was the same old story. Our Shermans were good transportation for riflemen. When we got pinned down by enemy tank fire, we might just as well have had a couple of trucks.

While placing the men in our platoon in a defensive setup, Max and I found out about the house up the road and also about the disposition of the other platoons. We became plenty worried when the tank switched its fire and threw several rounds into the big house. The top floor was set on fire. Max suggested that we go up and see if anyone was hit and if there were any medics present.

Entering at the front door we immediately began to step on bodies. Loud snores told us that these men had not been bothered by the shelling. It didn't even wake them up. It was the same situation throughout the whole building, at least on the first floor. No one bothered to go upstairs to fight the fire and we didn't bother to investigate the upper floors. It was difficult enough trying to move about the ground floor. It was pitch dark and apparently nobody bothered to try to black out any of the rooms. With some difficulty, we picked our way around the sleeping forms and asked in each room if there were anybody that was hurt.

All of the Jerry shots must have gone high. It would have been slaughter if the shells would have landed on the first floor. With the light from the fires, the Jerries should have lined up on the lower floors and fired at least another half dozen rounds.

There was plenty of distention in the company that night. The rumors told about the Second platoon being in a house. Lieutenant McCabe saw to that. Although Max and I moved from the tanks to the house to the platoons in the field, we never saw Lieutenant McCabe or our new C.O., Lieutenant Darsey, during the entire night. The tall Texan spent part of the nigh in a ditch. I don't know what ditch because I didn't see him. But he must have been in hiding somewhere. It certainly is strange that the company commander did not come around to check on our position at least once during the hours of darkness.

When the Third platoon boys heard about some of the other men being under cover for the night, they griped plenty and asked for temporary breaks so that they could get warmed up a little and perhaps dried out. As I recall, Max did allow two or three men at a time to go up to the house and catch an hour's sleep.

We were certain there were First platoon men in the house because we talked to some of them. The Second platoon must have all been there, too, or else they were in another house to the rear somewhere. However, the majority of the First and Weapons platoons stuck it out in the rain, mud and shellfire out in that open field.

The Jerries didn't keep up their big fire very long. They next started to shoot small flares directly into our front. This didn't seem to bother us much because most of the flares landed on the ground between our lines. Max and I were crossing the road from the house to enter the field to contact the platoons when a flare lit up the area. We got down and remained motionless and apparently we were never spotted. It seems a miracle that they did not spot our two Shermans. Perhaps they did. Anyway, it wasn't long until they opened up with some machine gun fire, using plenty of tracers.

It was about this time or perhaps a little before that we got a request from the hungry lieutenant from Mike. It seems that he was down the road about fifty yards in back of us with his two or three jeeps. His men were safely in the ditch along the side of the road. He must not have been able to get any of them up on their feet, because he asked Max to loan him some men so that he could push the jeeps up the road and park them right in back of the tanks. He felt that he would be safer if he moved forward with us. Naturally, he didn't want to turn the motors over. Personally, I think he would have been safer back down the road. And also, his group filled in as a rearguard in that position.

This situation griped us plenty. It was only a couple of hours ago that this officer refused to let any of our men ride on his jeeps because he had too many men on them already. Now, he could not find enough men to push them fifty yards over a smooth, flat, macadam road.

Like good little riflemen, we went back down the road and pushed the jeeps up to the rear of the tanks. As I recall, we didn't even give the Mike officer an argument. It was useless to argue, we had found out by this time, with your supporting units. You always lost anyway. Combat riflemen were the fall guys in this war. They were the dumb, uneducated suckers. They were the strong backs with the weak minds. They weren't handicapped enough. They had to fight within a fight. It's no wonder some of them cracked up. I don't know how I kept myself going.

When the tracers started to fly, the tank commander almost took off, too. Man, he really became excited.

"They're trying to locate us by bouncing tracers off our sides," he moaned to Max. "We gotta do something."

It was almost amusing. I would have laughed right in his face if it weren't for the fact that we were standing right next to his tank with the possibility that we all might be blown to kingdom come at any minute.

Now he wanted to do something. It was all right for our men to get slaughtered out there in the field. But as soon as his tanks were threatened, that was different.

He came up with the wildest, most fantastic solution to our situation that one could imagine. Our generals and ordinance experts probably won't believe it, but this is what the tank commander proposed: He would get in the lead tank alone and fire one round at the Jerry tank and then jump out and get in the ditch. Well, at least he picked on himself and not some PFC. Next, he proposed that when the Jerry panzer opened up on the lead tank our second Sherman would then start shooting. It was a brave plan, I must admit, because if one shell wouldn't penetrate the Jerry Tiger, then five or ten fired from two different tanks would probably bounce off, too. It was a smart plan in that at least we would go down fighting. If he waited for the Jerries to locate the tanks with tracers, then we wouldn't even get a shot in.

The tank commander soon admitted the futility of this first suggestion, and without waiting to take a deep breath, he proposed that at the same time we try to work two bazooka teams forward so that they could fire on the tank, too. This suggestion didn't make any more sense than the first one. The Jerry tank was no doubt surrounded by infantry just as our two tanks were. On that dark, rainy night you would have to get within at least fifty feet before you could see any sort of outline of an object.

Nevertheless, we agreed to the plan. It was arranged that the bazooka teams start moving forward at 10:50 P.M. and the lead tank would fire its lone round at the same time.

Max and I had one bazooka team. We could not find another bazooka in the whole company. Finally, we went to the hungry Mike. He almost died shaking. After we informed him that we didn't want a bazooka team, just a bazooka, he became very cooperative. A rocket launcher, with rockets, was fetched off of one of the jeeps immediately.

It was perhaps a waste of breath but we begged the lieutenant to give us supporting fire, if necessary, with the heavy .30 caliber machine guns that he had mounted on the jeeps. He refused, of course. I think we finally persuaded him to mount a couple in the ditch so that they could be used, if necessary. We knew the gunners would never get out of the ditch if things started to get hot.

It took, quite a bit of time to make all these arrangements. Max was running the whole show. We were out in the field with the two bazooka teams and Max was checking his watch. It was about 10:49. There was just one minute to go.

At this moment, we heard some very sweet music. The Jerry tank turned over its smooth, quiet working motors. They revved up a little and we could tell that it was turning around. What a relief! Especially for those four men in the bazooka teams. The tankers, no doubt, breathed a lot easier, too.

That ended the excitement for the night. Miraculously, we had suffered no casualties. The Jerries, despite the fact that they dominated us and did about ninety-nine percent of the firing suffered at least two dead. They may have had more casualties since they also received some well-placed WP shells in their area. The two Jerries were stopped cold as they came down along the fence just off the road and about fifty yards in front of our tanks. Two were taken prisoners as they came up the road in back of us.

King and Item companies were on our right but we did not know this. They attacked about the same time we did that afternoon but met great resistance and lost two tanks.

CHAPTER XVIII
The Ruhr Pocket

I feared the coming dawn although I wanted to see daylight in order to get moving again and get warmed up. If it had been another ten degrees colder, I probably would have ended up with trench foot and pneumonia. As it was, I developed a bad cold the next day.

The mists slowly lifted to reveal a new day and the entire panorama of the small battle site. The very broad tracks in the soggy field traced the exact movement and position of the Royal Tiger that had faced us. It must have been a Tiger to make such wide, shallow tracks and move so quietly. I couldn't help but think how our small, mobile Sherman would have mired down had they tried to negotiate off the road in that same field. The generals that designed the Sherman were satisfied, and so was Patton. But what about the poor GIs that had to operate and depend on them!

It had stopped raining but the clouds were racing low and fast. It was damp and we were chilled to the bone.

It was a ticklish and perhaps foolhardy position, standing there in the open as the light revealed our entire setup. The Jerries could have remained in the fringe of the nearby trees and waited until we all got up on our feet and then cut loose with heavy machine gun and other small arms fire. I stood ready to dive in a ditch at the very first sight or sound of any trouble. The men in the field stood up and stretched and walked about to bring back the circulation. We were able to get underway forward again without receiving any fire at all.

The Third platoon supplied the first effort in our new movement forward. Sergeants Schmidt and Delrogh moved up the road to a forked junction where they removed some mines so that our tanks could move forward. They also disconnected the charges wired to the trees on either side of the road. These had been set to blast the trees across our path. A lone Jerry was killed at his charger. Max and Smitty received the Silver Star for this action, I believe.

At the fork in the road we came in contact with Item and King companies. Item advanced forward on the left of the road while King moved on the right. Our Third platoon went up the middle with the tanks. Some TDs also moved up the road in back of us.

The road turned to the left at this point and we didn't go more than one yard when the Jerry infantry in the woods on the left side of the road opened up on Item. The company commander was badly wounded. I can't recall his name now, but he was a nice fellow and a good leader. There were other casualties but we were not hit.

Up the road another three hundred yards was a big house on the right. Beyond the house the woods closed in right up against the road. We made for the big house. Most of the way I kept in the ditch, and crouched low. The tanks and TDs were in a bad position there on the open road. It soon became apparent that the Jerries had pulled their armor pretty far back. That was a lucky break for us, a very stupid one on their part since they could have used their panzers to good effect and without danger from air attack because of the bad weather. Any kind of self-propelled 88 could have stood off the road in the woods to our right or left front and knocked out every tank and TD on that road. It would then have been very simple to open up on us doughboys with the panzer covering the German riflemen.

We moved up the center and got into the big house without a single casualty. Like typical American doughboys, we quickly got the fire going and started to dry out our field jackets, and some of the fellows dropped K ration cans on top of the hot stove. Being frail American capitalists, it was only natural, too, that the whole three companies tried to get into that lone house. Well, anyway, it became rather crowded, and as usual, everybody was glad to stop in the movement forward in order to catch a little rest and get something to eat. We hadn't received a meal now for more than twenty-four hours.

One of the TDs pulled up in front of the door and started to cut loose with everything it had. The big gun was booming shells into the trees on the left side of the road and the .50 caliber machine gun was throwing tracers and AP stuff straight up the road ahead. Another tank or TD stood just behind it and also joined in with a tremendous burst of firepower. It was a great show. Our armor sure could display a lot of fire power as long as there was no competition. It seems that in our race across Germany, our fire power increased and decreased in proportion to the fall and rise of the enemy fire power. When we got the Jerries running, our tankers sure could dust their tails and keep them going.

The Letters of a Combat Rifleman

Finally, we had to call a halt to the terrific display. It seems that they were getting a little behind or I should say that Item company and our other two platoons were getting too far ahead. Anyway, the armor boys were hitting into our ranks. The first tank or TD was stopped easily enough. But it was quite a job to get the second one stopped. It must have been that the first vehicle was a TD and the second a tank. I don't remember now. Anyway, the lead panzer couldn't communicate with the second one, and consequently it took some time to stop the flow of steel and lead. I almost shouted myself hoarse trying to tell the armored boys to stop. Despite the fact that the second vehicle was only about twenty yards away from the house, it was impossible to make the men hear us. And we felt that it was suicide to walk out of the house so that is why we kept telling the lead vehicle to communicate via radio with the second one and order the fire to be lifted. A lot of shouting and arm waving finally stopped the trigger-happy gunners.

It wasn't long, perhaps half an hour, until we got orders to move forward and contact our other two platoons that were now in the woods up ahead. I took two men and we dashed out the front door and ran for the woods about twenty-five yards up the road. We moved cautiously through the trees looking for the tail end of the other platoons. Two Mexican boys, Espinoza and Durand, were with me. They were to extend to the rear and the three of us were to act as connecting files, keeping in touch with the other platoons and also with our platoon that was to move forward along the road to cover the tanks.

We moved forward a considerable distance before we caught up with the company. They were rather bunched up in some places and seemed to be extended in a column of platoons. It was hard to tell the formation there in the woods.

Within a few minutes after I made contact, we started to receive a mortar barrage. As usual, it was a very accurate fire, falling right down on us. And as usual, everybody hit the ground. They should have kept going on right away because the fire wasn't that concentrated. Immediately after the first shells burst, there were cries of "Medic! Medic!"

There's nothing that chills your blood more than to hear the anguished cry of the wounded, alternating with the whine and burst of big shells, I hit and hugged the ground just like the rest, especially since the majority of the bursts were in front of me. Lying there on the forest floor, I thanked God that I wasn't a line company medic. I raised my head just enough to see two of them moving toward the wounded. Stevens was probably one of them. He was always on the job. It seemed to me that they were moving from perhaps a safe spot right into the midst of the bursting shells. It took a lot of guts. They were unarmed and they moved about while the fire was heaviest. They exposed themselves while we crawled like snakes into folds and crevices in the ground. That's the last job I would want, combat medic.

I had sent back word that we were in contact with the company. Durand didn't seem to be worrying about maintaining this contact. He was right up beside me and when the shells started to land, he began a rather comical "predictions of things to come," predictions that proved to be one hundred percent accurate.

The shells were landing on both sides of the road, but not very far inside the woods. The Jerries were smart, and they apparently had us pegged for the exact range. Durand would say, "The next one is going to land on this side." Then he would dash across the road and hit the deck just on the other side. For some reason or other I followed him. Every time he was right. We went back and forth across that road about five times, working our way forward on each run. The Jerries were smart but Durand outsmarted them.

During this shelling, I lost contact with everybody including Durand. I must have misinterpreted one of his predictions and zigged when he zagged. Anyway, I moved forward until I saw the houses up the road about one hundred yards. It appeared that there were some GIs already in the first house on the right side of the road. I came out of the woods and started at a trot and went right on past the first house and on up to the next one on the left. A big Jerry greeted me on the steps. He was spread flat on his face with more blood spilling around his body than flowed through his veins. There were plenty of GIs already in this house, and it soon became apparent that there were more in the houses up the road. It was just a little settlement, not more than half a dozen houses at the most. The one I entered was a big place. It must have been a sort of highway inn because there was a beer hall on the first floor as well as living quarters.

My clothes were still slightly wet from the previous night and so I got near the stove that the fellows had already started. After taking off the chill and warming my feet, I started to look around. The place was pretty well messed up. It looked as though it had been hit with at least one big shell, which caused a heavy dust to settle over everything. Plenty of Jerry equipment littered the floor and tables in the beer hall.

I surprised the boys and myself, too, when I opened a closet in what appeared to be the living room and liberated a beautiful camera. I don't recall the name now but it was a wonderful piece of foto apparel. It took 120 film and also plates. It was designed also to take very close up pictures of insects, etc., and it was apparent that it had a very fine Germany lens. It was in almost new condition and enclosed in a nice carrying case.

I carried this camera right on in to the last town that we took and then because I thought we were going to still keep moving forward in the attack, I decided to get rid of it. It was with some difficulty that I persuaded one of our truck drivers to accept it as a gift. It was no doubt worth at least one hundred dollars.

In short order our entire platoon along with one of the tanks pulled up, that is everybody except Espinoza and Durand. Our connecting files had now become our "missing links." I told the story about Durand to Max and concluded saying, "Perhaps the Jerries crossed him up and laid in two straight on the same side of the road." anyway, I became worried and considered it a good possibility that they had been hit. But it was too late now. We couldn't go back to look for wounded. And anyway, there were medics still working back there in the woods and they no doubt would make a good search to pick up all the dead and wounded.

In a few minutes Max got a message to report to the company CP located up the road another one hundred yards. I went along, too.

The CO gave us the unwelcome news of an immediate movement forward again. We heard the plan and then went back to alert the men. It was tough news but we didn't complain too much. My feet were dragging and it was difficult for me to keep my eyes open. I was hungry, but the ever-present danger kept my mind on other things.

We filed out on the road and the company moved forward in two columns. We covered at least a mile of rough road. Then we went up a big, long hill, cut into the woods to the right side of the road and then moved forward in a big skirmish line, the Third platoon the deepest in the woods.

The going got tougher in the woods. We alternately moved forward and halted. At the halts I wanted to lie down and fall asleep. The hill sloped up to our right, and we had to walk on an angle to keep our balance.

It was even more difficult for me because I moved back and forth along our platoon trying to keep the men in place and hustling along the stragglers. Bursting shells at intervals reminded us that the enemy was aware of our presence. We looked ahead for the forms of riflemen between the trees.

It was just like hunting in Pennsylvania except everybody had their safety off. I wasn't worrying so much about a line of Jerry riflemen and machine gunners suddenly opening up on us. It was the dreaded thud of big stuff dropping just in front of us and off to the sides. We couldn't even see the bursts. I was weary and gripped with the fear of sudden death. It was so impersonal. It came with a sudden, terribly quick rush of air, unseen but leaving its terrible mark in earth and flesh. Where would the next one land? Would it have my name on it? These were some of the questions going through my mind as I winced at each booming thud.

We went a good distance. It was all wooded territory. We couldn't even see the road that we figured was still on our left. We didn't know where we were going or even if we were continuing in the same direction. We didn't even know our objective, but we looked ahead for an opening in the trees that might indicate a town or road.

The pace increased and we seemed to swing around in a big left turn. It seems that we swung to the right of Kustelberg, made the turn, and then raced into the right side of the small town.

I was on the extreme right end of the platoon when we made our swing and some of the men on our end of the line came out into a partially cut-over section of the woods. Fifty yards to our right there was a dirt road, and beyond were open fields.

The pace continued to increase and then the line of skirmishers really cracked the whip. I was gasping for breathe. A lot of shells started to land in the open field on the other side of the road. I was getting farther and farther behind. Then the first houses appeared about two hundred yards up ahead. I ran toward the road so that I could make better time. It was like running toward your own grave, but I figured I could make better time on the road and it should take me only half a minute to get into the first house. It was immaterial that the houses might be full of Germans. It was imperative that we get into a house, any house.

My open road run placed me in town in front of the entire platoon. Breathing hard was Max, right on my heels, and in front of all the other men who were by no means lagging. Max shouted: " Get into that house," pointing to the first one on my right. We both started for the front door but stopped dead in our tracks when two Jerries broke from a house to our left. I threw the '03 to my shoulder and opened up. Max cut loose, too. A terrific barrage of shots from in back of me made me turn in apprehension. Almost every man in the platoon had his rifle up in the firing position. It was a shower of .30 caliber ball ammunition that went hurtling toward those two hapless Germans.

I dropped to one knee as a safety measure and fired another couple of shots at the fleeing Germans who had now been joined by several of their comrades. In fact, there seemed to be Germans springing out of all the houses in front of us.

It should have been like knocking down pins in a ten foot bowling alley, but everyone of those Germans kept running until they had all disappeared among the buildings up ahead. Some, no doubt, had been hit. But none were stopped as far as I could see. The ranges varied between fifty and one hundred yards.

Here was a case of plenty of shots per minute but no hits. It was a good example of poor marksmanship. We lacked sufficient training, but it seems that perhaps the main cause of our misses in this case was the physical exertion course we had just run. You can't hold 'em and squeeze 'em when you have been living on a starvation diet plus working long hours on end.

Here was a good example, too, of how easy it is to pass through a hail of shots and still come out untouched. Perhaps those same men had successfully passed through similar volleys in Russia, Italy, and France.

With still a couple of rounds left, I moved forward and off to the right side of the road where I knelt in back of a pile of lumber and started to put shots into the windows of the houses on the other side of the small village. The town was laid out in a U-shape, with a broad meadow forming the inside section of the U. I fired across this meadow at the houses on the other side, as it seemed that we could possibly have caused a lot of casualties at that short range of less than two hundred yards.

The Letters of a Combat Rifleman

It was at this point that I discovered the disadvantage of my scoped, Springfield '03. Between the time that I ejected the last empty case and loaded the last of the five rounds in the magazine by hand, (I had no five round clips) all the running Jerries had disappeared and things in general had quieted down. Regardless, I fired another few rounds into the windows of the houses across the meadow. It was just a precautionary measure. I figured it would keep any Jerries over there inside of the houses with their heads below the window sills. Besides protecting us from flanking fire, it also discouraged the Jerries from running out the back doors and out across the fields toward the road that led out of town on the opposite side.

The whole platoon worked its way forward through the town. As usual, the third platoon was spearheading. According to one account in the division history, L company followed the TDs into town after K company had made it safe. Perhaps the main part of Love company followed the TDs into Kustelberg, but it was the third platoon of Love company that rolled back the resistance and made the town secure. We found it the same, from one tip of the U all the way around to the other tip. We immediately set up defense positions on the other side of the town and I do not recall seeing any GIs except the men in our platoon.

Max, Wilson, Osajnak, and I set up headquarters near the base of the U and on the side toward the retreating enemy. Very few were able to make their escape from the town, however, because we moved in too quickly. We must have rounded up almost one hundred Jerry soldaten, including some rather high officers. Later we heard that we had broken up a whole regiment. We caught most of its leaders in Kustelberg including the CO and the ranking medical officers. The top ranking medic was clean and well dressed. He didn't escape even though he had a very modern civilian automobile. Being a doctor as well as a high ranking officer, he was doubly put out and insolent when I questioned him and ordered him to put his hands over his head. He was smart enough to get rid of his watch and the keys to the car before he was searched. In fact, with all the prisoners that we took in Kustelberg, I still came out empty handed as far as souvenirs were concerned.

We weren't yet settled in the big house that we picked for our headquarters, when a young lieutenant from Item or King company came in and said he was taking the house over as his headquarters. Max, of course, was cooperative and we started to put our packs on and picked up the rest of our gear and moved over to a house closer to the enemy. This movement interrupted our search for food and souvenirs, and before we could resume that search, a direct fire 88 put a permanent end to all but imperative movement.

Max and I continued to move about as we checked each squad and defense setup. As we reached each new doorway, the 88 would boom. With the direct fire aspect, we never knew the shell was coming until it hit the house or the street outside. It was all high explosive stuff, and it burst on contact. A few rounds of AP or a couple of duds would have caused plenty of casualties. As it happened, we had only a few men wounded. Squad Leader Schwartz, the Brooklyn fire-power artist, received a shrapnel wound in the hand or arm when one of the shells hit a window frame and burst inside as well as outside.

In the meantime, an enemy soldier walked across the fields into our position and surrendered. He claimed he had several comrades down the road a piece, and that they all wanted to give up. This was routine. We let him go and he promised to come back with the other war-weary Jerries. They never showed up. Perhaps it was a gag. Perhaps he came in just to get an idea of our strength, and to see if we had any armor in back of the houses. Perhaps his comrades got cold feet. It was worth the chance we took because we had nothing to worry about in regards to an enemy counterattack. We were confident and cocky, now. I always felt that if and when the Jerries attacked us in daylight, they would be cut down like wheat in front of a binder. Perhaps that is why they invariably attacked under cover of darkness. They knew better than we did that that was the best way to get in close without suffering a lot of casualties. But the defending force in a night-time skirmish still has the advantage as long as they stay put and don't lose their heads because a few enemy soldiers are in back of them as well as on both sides and to the front. We were now beyond the panic point.

Darkness settled down and then we got word of hot chow. And it was hot and there was plenty of it, too. My meat pan dripped gravy and fruit juice as I slowly picked my way back to our house where we had a blacked-out room and candles. We were on the first floor, as usual, and the few civilians that were still in town were in the cellars. That was a meal that we really enjoyed. It was one of the good things about the American army. We didn't have a meal for almost two days. The enemy sat there in front of us and to a great extent above us, since they had higher ground. They would look through their gun barrels and watch us. And yet we sat there in a lighted room and enjoyed a good American meal of roast beef, gravy, mashed potatoes, peas, sliced pineapple, and coffee. And miracles of miracles it was hot. Our mess sergeant, Staff Sergeant Chester M. Kivilosz from Chicago, Illinois, should have received the Medal of Honor instead of the Bronze star.

The night passed almost uneventful. There was no enemy activity. But we made up for that. They must have alerted us for movement about 2 or 3 A.M. Other units came into town and took over our positions. In the darkness, I saw some still darker forms. They were black infantry troops. They were good soldiers. They volunteered to fight in the infantry and that's more than a lot of white boys did. In fact, most of the white troops that were transferred to infantry units during the Battle of the Bulge made the switch under orders. They were forced into the infantry. A fighter pilot squadron leader based in England told me that he didn't want to pick the two men that were requisitioned from his outfit for service in the infantry at the time of the Bulge. This major's superior officer suggested that he select two men that he wanted to get rid of or in other words, the two worst soldiers in the unit. The major, according to his story, turned this suggestion down on the grounds that the infantry needed good men, not a bunch of gold brickers. He finally found a way out by holding a lottery. He was amazed, he said, to see the same boys that left their outfit for France, return in less than a week wearing the Purple Heart. These incidents pointed up to the men in the rear the quickness and suddenness of death and injury in real front line units. The men must have spent several days in making their way forward. Once they reached the real front lines, it was sometimes only a matter of hours until they felt the sting of enemy steel. And then they didn't live in fame and go down in flame—they lived in filth and went down in mud and blood. No wonder there were so few volunteers. No wonder the threat of infantry duty kept the rear echelon boys right in line. Transfer to the infantry hung over their heads like the hangman's noose. Those dark skinned doughboys might have looked plenty scared but they had plenty of what it takes to make a good American soldier.

There were plenty of outfits that pulled into little Kustelberg early that morning. The vehicles of the Seventh Armored Division were parked everywhere so that it was difficult for our outfit to get lined up on the road for the march to the rear. At dawn, the armored men were to smash at what was supposed to be a reeling, defeated enemy. The reports that came back later that day told of bitter resistance and long casualty lists. It was a credit to the German leadership and organization the way they always managed to place another unit in your path despite previous heavy losses. Every time our hopes rose they were again dashed on the rocks of despair. It seemed the war would never end.

We dragged our weary bodies down the country road away from the enemy. We had done our part. We stopped the counterattacks and got the enemy on the run. Reaching the small group of houses where we had stopped momentarily the day before, we fell out along the road as the columns of tanks and armored cars rolled by incessantly. It was daylight now, but the air was cold and damp. Everything was wet. We borrowed some gasoline to start a big fire. It was such a big fire we had no difficulty burning the wet wood that we tossed into the flames.

Finally, we went on back to the big house where we had guarded the tanks on the road. There we had a hot breakfast. We saw some of the big plane transports flying very low through the rain clouds on their way to supply the armored spearheads up ahead.

After breakfast, we climbed on trucks and headed toward a quiet sector. As we rode past the big roadhouse at the road junction, we saw the Dutchman still lying on the table where we had left him almost two days ago.

Usseln, I believe, was the name of the town we drove to. It was peaceful and fully intact. Nestling down among the high, steep hills it seemed to be in a world all its own. It was just what we needed to rest up for a few days.

The enemy couldn't have been very far. We did maintain a couple of OPs while we were in Usseln. But we had nothing to do except sleep, eat, and write letters home. Of course, we had wires out and we had to keep someone on the phone twenty-four hours a day.

Sitting at the field phone on the night of April 6, 1945, I wrote to Jean: "Here I sit in the middle of the night with nothing to do but my duty which is easy enough compared to some nights. Someone just called and complained about somebody flashing lights. Maybe someone drunk. Who knows. Anyway, I am so awfully tired of this war I don't know what to do. Perhaps it's because I have a cold, but I do need your loving and tender care. Even a doctor needs a doctor."

Reflecting back on our fight at Medebach and Kustelberg, I continued to write: "Sometimes we think the war is nearly over but always something terrible happens that makes us think differently. Anyway, the weather hasn't been balmy as I wrote about in my last letter. Also, Albert (my brother) wrote and told me that Roland Breen, my nephew's best friend, had died. (Actually, Roland had been killed during the crossing of the Roer River but I couldn't say that in my letter.) You know what that means. He said Vic (my sister) cried for a couple of days. Roland was like another son to Vic and Frank. I don't feel so good about it either, and yet such things are almost routine here. I wanted to go see Roland when I was in Cologne but never got the chance. (He was stationed north of us with the 29th Division). I'm sorry I didn't now. They want the details but they are hard to get and hard to give out. I realize how it must be for people back in the States but ces't la guerre. And la guerre certainly is everything that Sherman said it was."

I went on to write almost three pages, finally ending with: "The candlelight, late hour and cold in the head are making things a little blurred. But before closing, I want to tell you I love you so very, very much. Just you, darling. And I pray each night for our quick reunion. Heaps of hugs and kisses to my Happy Chappy boy. Write often, honey. Good night."

The next day I wrote my first letter home using division stationary. The big, gray Timberwolf on a green background was in the upper left-hand corner of the letterhead. Across the top middle was 104th INFANTRY DIVISION. My unit was no longer a military secret to the folks back home. The line in green caps at the bottom of the page boasted, "Nothing in hell can stop the Timberwolves."

We were really beginning to sweat out the finish now. I thought more and more about the end of the war. It did seem to be just around the corner. I kept wondering if my guardian angel would see me through to the very end. I began to write about this in my letters to Jean. On April 7, I wrote: "I received some of your recent letters the day before yesterday and I am very happy over that. However, the war still isn't over and so I'm still sweating out the finish. Pray God it will be soon.

THE LETTERS OF A COMBAT RIFLEMAN

"The weather here has been wet and raw and that is one reason I have a cold. Today, however, the sun is out and it sure feels wonderful. The path to Berlin may still be long and hard, but I'm hoping and praying. He certainly has been watching over me and I feel that our Jane is helping Him."

Jean had mentioned in one of her letters an incident where a marine ran out of a theater during the showing of a war picture. I answered her questions and doubts by writing: "That marine in the movies must have been a battle fatigue victim. I don't want to see pictures or talk about the war when I get home, but after being able to stomach the real thing, I don't believe a picture will bother me."

I had foot trouble, as well as a cold in the head, so I decided to visit the aid station while it was convenient. I had an ingrown toenail which the medics fixed up just right.

Lieutenant McCabe was the only other man that I saw on the sick list. He had been pretty well shaken up by the shell concussion, but they refused to evacuate him. He appeared to be in as good condition as the next GI and I was pleased that they turned him down.

It was that day or the next that we jockeyed out of our rest town mounted on Sherman tanks and trucks. The Third platoon was assigned the tanks again.

It was a beautiful spring day and we enjoyed our ride through the countryside, stopping again at another small village. We stayed overnight and the next day after breakfast, we mounted up again on our steel steeds and swirled away down the tree-lined roads toward more adventure and sight-seeing.

Our combat duties had now turned into a sort of Cook's tour. We were weaving our way across Germany. We lived in small towns, and stayed overnight in large cities. We walked through the dense forests and crossed the cultivated fields. We lived with the natives, and began to learn to speak their language. The ever-present possibility of a shot or shell ripping into our vehicles added a zest and tingling uncertainty that no Cooks tour ever possessed. Luckily f or us, from now on there was to be more and more sight-seeing and less adventure.

I don't mean to say that the killing and destruction was over with entirely. I was still to lose some of my best buddies in the month of fighting that remained.

We were entering a new phase of the Battle of Germany. The Ruhr pocket had been sealed when our advanced tank-infantry teams met up with the Second Armored division of the Ninth Army at Lippstadt, near the big city of Paderborn, heavily defended by SS troops.

Over three hundred thirty-five thousand German troops were now encircled in our trap. Our forward elements had raced two hundred miles in eight days to forge this ring of armor and infantry.

Beyond Paderborn flowed three important rivers: the Wesser, Saale, and the Moulde. The Saale and Mulde Rivers flowed into the Elbe River below Mageeburge. All these rivers faced us running in a general north-south direction. However, none were to offer any great obstacle in our forward movement. We were to stop at the Moulde River and contact was made there with the Russians about two weeks previous to VE day.

But let me get back to the little town of Doseberg that we pulled out of in bright spring sunlight. Captain Darsey, the big Texan, had come around to the platoon and introduced himself before we left. We now were being officially led by our sixth company commander.

Our dust-raising column entered a small shoe factory town just before lunch time. The only trouble we had here was keeping the civilians out of the shoe factory. it seems that they had been making shoes for about five years and yet were not allowed to buy any of their own products. One of the boys in our platoon finally had to fire a burst from his tommy gun in order to force the crowd to scatter.

Max, our stout five-by-five leader, was naturally working all the angles. He propositioned the young girl in the house we were staying at, offering her a swell new pair of shoes if she would, "schlaufen mit his soldaten." Max wasn't interested himself, he was trying to get one of us fixed up. For once, Max failed. It proved, too, that there were good German women. Well, at least it proved that they were not all mercenary.

While Max was trying to peddle the shoes, I opened up a good box of chocolates that I had received in the mail from my brother, Bill, in Pittsburgh. They were super and I let the German civilians in the house see them and also sample them. I wanted to impress them with the goodness and abundance of America. They were impressed and pleased.

We had a hot dinner at the shoe factory town, took some pictures in the bright sunlight with some of the native girls. Then we mounted up again on our steel steeds and took off down the tree-lined dusty roads toward the east.

It was a long ride. We were not uncomfortable. There was plenty of room on our tank. At various halts along the way, I pulled out my box of chocolates and passed them around to my buddies and also to the boys in the tank.

W didn't see many towns. It was mostly big forests and farmland. As we ascended from high ground to cross the Weser River, we saw our only casualty—a dead American infantryman lying in the woods only about ten feet from the road.

It was almost dark as we moved northward after we crossed the pontoon bridge. As darkness closed in tight, we dismounted and stood around in the cold evening air.

Darkness—and the dreaded hours of uncertainty engulfed us physically and mentally. Where were we? Where were we going? Where would we sleep? Would we be able to get into houses for the night? These were the questions we asked ourselves as we waited. The chill and dampness of a cold spring night moved in about us. Perhaps the one question uppermost in a lot of minds was, will we eat a hot supper? The answer was no. We didn't eat at all.

We didn't wait around too long, maybe an hour, maybe less. The orders were to set up a defense for the night. Regretfully, we pulled away from the few houses along the road and went back into the fields and woods. I was a squad leader now. The change was made just after Schwartz was wounded. I took over his Third squad.

It was dark, pitch dark, as we took up our positions. My squad was part way up the side of a hill that was wooded at the top. I split the men into two outposts with an interval of about fifty yards. The squad was very small so we had only three men in one position and four in the other. Max told me to contact the First platoon on our left and so I went up toward the wooded section along with one of the other men. It was plenty scary since there was the possibility of being fired on by both the enemy and also by the First platoon. However, they must have been expecting us because we made contact without any trouble.

Well, we spent a typical doughboy's night in the open. We shivered and shook with coldness and fear. We had our infantry sleeping bags along but we may as well have carried an extra pair of socks. When we weren't on watch, we crawled in the bags and hoped that we wouldn't get stuck there if the enemy started coming through the underbrush. The only thing it didn't do was rain. At least we had one thing to be thankful for.

The rising sun melted the mists and thawed our bloodstreams. We were first-class Americanish soldaten again, ready and almost willing to press the attack. Of course, first we wanted to eat, as Americans are in the habit of doing. It so happened that our leaders were not thinking about American habits that morning. They ate, no doubt, but they pushed us off up to the road on an empty stomach.

Then the going got tough. They formed us into skirmish lines that extended off into the woods. There were steep inclines, gullies and too many fences. I got dog tired and I guess all the men were puffing and dripping sweat. The officers stood down on the road and kept shouting for us to keep in a straight line, guide right and guide left. If there was any enemy in that section of the woods, we gave them ample time to clear out.

Over a period of about six hours we chased about in a big wooded area, constantly on the alert. The enemy must have been around according to the way we worked and watched and waited. But we didn't see one solitary soldier.

Early in the afternoon, we assembled some tanks and trucks, and we left the big forest and entered another small village. King company was there when we entered.

We took over the other side of the small town in the direction of the fleeing enemy. But we weren't interested in the enemy as we pulled into this sunlit German country hamlet. We wanted to eat. It had been about twenty-four hours now since we had a meal, and we had been working hard enough to eat six meals in that time. Of course, there were a couple of times when we had an opportunity to build a fire and make some coffee with our soluble K ration unit, and the little bit of water that we had in our canteens. But we needed some solid, warm food to satisfy our appetites.

Our prayers were answered when we discovered that the deserted German army truck column in the middle of the town was carrying rations. They were German army rations, of course, but they must have been for some general or high echelon officer. There were barrels and big two-gallon bottles of cognac, all types of bologna, cheeses and other foods. My squad took over a house near the center of town, got the women working and we soon had all we wanted to eat and more than we could drink.

It wasn't long until we were moved to another house so that we would be in a position for the next attack. We were told that we would move toward Heisebeck within a short time. The Third platoon was assigned the job of going into town on the flank while the other platoons were to enter via the road, mounted on tanks.

After receiving this information, I ordered all drinking in my squad to stop. It wasn't necessary to tell most of the men. I could see that Duran was feeling his oats. It seemed it took only two or three drinks to make Duran half drunk. He had a bottle of cognac, just like a lot of the other fellows. I didn't take it away from him but I guess now that I should have.

When I got back to the squad after making a reconnaissance from a hay loft, Durand was pretty well under the weather. He was just about able to move out with us as we started across the fields toward Heisebeck, only eight hundred yards away across more or less flat, open ground.

Heisebeck was taken without a shot being fired by the Third platoon. We rounded up a couple of prisoners and immediately started to organize a defensive setup for the night. There were rumors of a counterattack.

The civilians were cooperative and we had the burgemeister walk through the streets announcing that all "foto apparel, waffens and glasses" were verboten, they must be turned in to the Americans. So, we acquired another lot of junk.Most of it was divided up on an equal basis. A lot of the stuff was destroyed or tossed in nearby streams. It was the pattern we followed throughout the rest of Germany. We were always looking for good pistols. and cameras. As we picked up better items, we traded, sold, gave away or threw away the things we didn't want or couldn't carry. I dreamed of a Leica camera. I didn't know then that there were different model Leicas or that there were other German cameras just as good. My friend, Bill Moore, whom I had hunted and fished with in Canada, had a Leica, and I knew it was a good camera, one of the best. So my search centered on a Leica, any Leica. No Leicas turned up in little Heisebeck.

Durand, in the meantime, wasn't cooperating with the civilians. He started to break their flower pots and in general made a lot of noise so that he had quite a few of the women and children in a state of nervous tension. We tried to quiet him down, but he just wouldn't listen.

After we changed houses, I tried to get Durand to lie down and go to sleep so that he could take his turn on the outpost that we were setting up on the road out of town. Durand wouldn't listen. Finally, we decided to lock him in a bedroom where he couldn't bother anyone. He took a swing at me but missed. I pushed him and he fell flat on his back, looking up rather startled. I was even surprised myself because Durand was a big man.

I now forget the subsequent details. It was just a little while later that the First Sergeant sent down an armed guard and Durand was disarmed and placed under arrest. The war was over for Durand. We were to see him from time to time with regimental headquarters. He was under arrest but they naturally couldn't lock him up. His trial would have to wait until the fight was finished.

CHAPTER XIX
Duderstat-Nordhausen-Halle

We stayed overnight in Heisebeck. There was no counterattack. Things were quiet after Durand was taken away. The next day I found time to write to Jean. From the tone of my letter, it was apparent that I still considered death as a possibility.

I wrote, "How are my loved ones? I have no special news but I know you would be interested to hear that I am okay, My cold is getting better, too.

"I'm hoping and praying the war will be over real soon now. Let's hope by the time you get this letter the Germans are thoroughly spanked. And may I soon be on my way home to America and you two darlings.

"But if I am still called to join our Janey, I know you will be well taken care of. Billy will have a loving and good mother and you, darling, will have a good brave son to help and protect you and take care of you. You will not have anything to worry about. give Billy a big hug and kiss for me. I love you, darling, now and forever. As ever, Your loving husband, Charles."

There were no more letters home for a while. About 10 P.M., we were alerted and moved to an assembly point near company headquarters where we mounted up on trucks. It wasn't a very long ride. We entered another small country village, stumbled around in the dark looking for a place to sleep for the night and finally settled down with just one guard on the front door.

The big house we took over was crowded with civilians. I went around the upper floors with the old man that was the head of the family. Pointing to the largest bedroom I told him, "American soldaten shlaufen here." Then the old man started to jabber about "soo feel kinder" and "frauleins." Finally, after seeing so many sleeping forms in the beds, I decided to take over the

The Letters of a Combat Rifleman

first floor rooms. There were one or two couches and we had our sleeping bags along to spread on the floor beneath us. We spent another quiet night.

It was another beautiful spring day that greeted us after breakfast the next morning. We had a chance to wash up a little and I took some color pictures of some of the little girls in their native costumes. The several big girls in the house did not become friendly with us. It seems that someone stole some of their money during the night. Before noon there was another column of trucks and tanks drawn up in the narrow twisting village street. The Third platoon was assigned the tanks. We waved to our German acquaintances as we rumbled away.

The countryside was beautiful. There was nothing to disturb the spring tranquillity except the dust that we churned up on the side roads. We hit some of the main highways and about noontime, we passed through Gottingen, which looked like a small city. There were plenty of civilians on the streets and there seemed to be a holiday atmosphere about the place. Our column slowed up but didn't stop in Gottingen. We raced on eastward, entering another small city called Duderstadt. It was just like a parade except for the shouting we did. Some of the frauleins answered us and nearly all the population waved. Of course, a lot of GIs made vulgar remarks on these occasions but luckily, the Germans didn't know what they were saying.

We remained in Duderstadt almost twenty-four hours. We met many Canadian and American POWs for the first time. They told of their experiences of marching back and forth across Germany. These road marches seemed to depend on how the different fronts were faring. If the Russians were making a sweep to the west, the Jerries marched their POWs westward. If our American columns were moving fast, the Jerries turned the POWs around and marched them toward the east again. All the POWs were in poor physical condition. Their clothes looked like they were too big for them. It was apparent that they had all lost plenty of weight.

The sight of our buddies and the story of their suffering didn't make us feel any too good toward the civilian population. "Doc" Gavitt, Mike Susskind and I went on a camera shopping spree. We hit the shops first on the business street, but they had already been looted. So we started out and gave some of the better homes a working over. Mike was good at German and "Doc" knew his French real well. Our search wasn't very successful. We got an armful of cameras, but there were no Leicas or any other top quality photo equipment.

We destroyed a half dozen cheap cameras, mostly the box type and took the rest back to the company. We discovered that other things were turned up in Duderstadt. The boys had a very large barrel of cognac tied to the rear of the tank we were riding on. There was a spigot on the barrel so that we could have a drink any time we felt like one.

It is hard to recall all the details as we sped eastward beyond Duderstadt, which we left the next day, mounted on trucks and tanks. We flushed villages quite regularly but with little or no fighting. There wasn't much time to write home. The incoming mail could not keep up with our forward movement. The enemy was on the run. There were just a few more good fights remaining in the Wehrmach.

In one day, the Timberwolf division extended their gains forty miles eastward into the Reich. Every available vehicle including Jerry equipment aided in the fast advance.

Nordhausen, a once beautiful city near the southern foothills of the Harz Mountains was one place the Nazis decided to fight. It was crushed by an air-armor attack.

We pulled into the devastated ruins and found some houses that were still habitable. A defense setup was arranged with the tankers as evening approached.

Nordhausen proved to be an interesting and well-stocked little city. The next day we remained in Nordhausen as the armored spearhead paused briefly while provisions were made to contact the retreating army in the Harz Mountains.

We started out early to explore the town. My prize was a good camera. I told Jean about it my letter dated April 13, 1945:

"We have beaucoup cameras now, and I am taking plenty of pictures. I have a good Kodak Retina II that I got from an SS trooper. It takes 35 mm film and I have several rolls of color."

The SS trooper was a young Belgian who confessed to us that he was a member of the SS. Like a silly boy, he took us to his room and brought out two good cameras that we immediately confiscated. I won the Kodak Retina on a coin toss.

We also learned or heard that the town was noted for making good liquor. They said they had been making liquor in Nordhausen for more than five hundred years. We unearthed some good stuff. We celebrated the occasion that evening by lighting candles and sitting around a large table drinking toasts. We drank shots of fifty-year old cognac and chased it down with Lansom champagne.

We ended up out in the street with our rifles. It all started when somebody found a good .22 German rifle and some ammunition and we started to plink at the signs and glass insulators on the telephone poles. The one .22 rifle wasn't enough and that is when the fellows started shooting with their M-1s. Miraculously nobody got hurt. Max finally called the whole thing off however, when a German woman pushing a baby carriage. came down the middle of the street just as one of the fellows cut loose with a BAR. The woman screamed as though she was going to be shot on the spot. And she didn't stop until she had raced passed us and turned the next street corner.

We received some reinforcements in Nordhausen, but my squad lost two men when we pulled out of town about 1100 that night. Juan Garcia, my assistant squad leader, and a big chap named Johnson, failed to show up.

They joined us a couple of days later, claiming they were still asleep in the house when we left.

We entered a small town late that night and bedded down. The next morning I found time to write to Jean:

"I love you. I love you. Do you like that for a start, darling? Everything is just fine here but that does not mean that I am not missing you. I want to come home to you more and more each day.

"I have no news except that I can say the war is moving fast. I am very close to Berlin and hope to be there soon. We are going so fast we have not been getting mail."

The war had less than a month to go now, and our fighting would be over in less than two weeks. So the pressure to make the finish line was mounting. I kept wondering if I would get through safely. As usual, I mentioned the subject to Jean:

"We are all sweating out the finish now, and all hoping and praying to get back alive. But even after that, it is likely that I will have to go immediately to the South Pacific."

For Billy's benefit, I wrote, "There is a most intelligent-looking cat sitting here at the table. He is eating breakfast with the frau and her daughter. I know Billy would certainly like him for a playmate.

"These small towns are so crowded with refugees from the bombed areas that we have to occupy many houses along with the civilians. The bomb damage in Nordhausen was terrific, and the city was bombed only twice. One civilian said twenty thousand people were killed. The mayor wanted to call it an open city but the SS leader wanted to defend. But they have no defense against our bombers. The Luftwaffe is kaput.

"I hope by this time you have received the gifts I sent from Paris. And also the pictures. Keep writing and keep loving me."

My return address on the envelope was the only announcement I made of my promotion. The abreviation Sgt. now replaced Pvt.

Oberrobligen, I believe, was the name of the town we woke in that beautiful spring morning. The trees were beginning to bud. It was warm enough to work without our field jackets on.

We had a job assigned to us early. We organized a small task force of several jeeps, making sure we had plenty of fire power.

My friend, Orrie Saylor, now driving a jeep for company headquarters, was in the column. Orrie and I worked together. We put the windshield down and mounted a light A-6 machine gun on the hood.

We had two towns to check. They were just small villages. The first one produced about twenty disillusioned Wehrmacht "supermen." The civilians brought them out of the cellars and we took them prisoners without firing a shot.

Orrie and I entered the next town on a different road than the rest of the column. The idea was to meet in the center of town. Just as we reached the first row of houses, I pressed the trigger on the A-6 and fired a burst. Orrie was so surprised he nearly jumped out of his seat.

We mounted the A-6 on the ground and questioned some of the people that were making their way toward the West. Most of them were slave workers fleeing the fighting area. We weren't successful in getting information concerning German troop movements. It began to appear that there was no organized resistance in front of us.

We relaxed a while in one of the German houses and accepted their hospitality and then formed up with the column and headed back to our base. A German truck transported the prisoners while the jeeps were loaded down with cameras, sabres, knives and pistols of all descriptions. Orrie and I collected our share without walking away from our jeep. Back at headquarters, we divided up the stuff with the other men including a section of fellows from Mike company.

We pulled out in force that afternoon, resuming our uninterrupted advance to the east. The only important happening was an addition of two good recruits to the Third platoon. Otherwise, we pulled up to the west bank of the Saale River at Halle on April 15 without any other outstanding event.

It was an event to enlist our two new recruits. They were Yugoslavian slave workers. While in the process of flushing a small town, Mike and Al approached us and asked that they might join our outfit. Harry Osajnak acted as interpreter. Max didn't have too much difficulty conversing with them either because they were well acquainted with the German language since they had been in Germany several years.

Max's answer was, "Yes, you can join us." I was surprised but pleased. Why shouldn't we enlist all the help we could get. This was a war of all Europe against the Nazi. And Mike and Al had good reason to make war, if not better reasons than we had ourselves. Mike claimed that the Nazi had killed his father and mother, made his wife a slave worker and had taken away his children. His family was completely wiped out or scattered.

Mike and Al were assigned to my squad. I wanted to talk to them and ask them plenty of questions, but we had a difficult time understanding one another. It was with reluctance that I limited our conversations to a few words in German and some hand and arm signs and signals.

Max had no trouble in getting uniforms for Mile and Al, but we were unable to find helmets for them. They were more interested in the M-1 rifles we issued them than they were in anything else. It wasn't long until they could field strip the rifles and clean them without any help. Mike wanted to know where and how his rifle shot and so we let him practice all he wanted. He proved to be a good shooter, mainly, no doubt, because he was interested and wanted to learn. Mike and Al were determined to get even with the ex-captors.

Halle, the largest city in Germany that was spared the terror of Allied bombing attacks, was our next big objective. The 414th regiment made the main assault against strong resistance.

The Letters of a Combat Rifleman

It must have been April 14 that we pulled up toward the west bank of the Saale River, flushing towns on the way up to relieve units of a 414th task force.

It was dark as we moved forward. We had no information concerning our objective or mission. Each town presented another problem. Maybe we would meet resistance, maybe we wouldn't. We hadn't suffered any casualties for quite a while, but we never knew when or where the next explosion would take place. There were still organized German forces in front of us. We would catch up with them sooner or later.

It was tiring work. We walked, rode trucks, tanks, and TDs. We waited along roads, standing quietly in the cool spring night air, always hoping that a burst of artillery or mortar fire would not probe our area. It was a sort of unpleasant dream.

We entered one town about midnight. The men sought places to relax and still be ready for the next order. I was restless, going about to different rooms in the building we occupied. It looked like a restaurant in the dark. I couldn't find a good place to lie down. There were no security precautions taken that I remember. Outside were several tank destroyers that we had been riding. The crews more than likely remained with their vehicles.

Before anyone had time to fall asleep, Max gave me orders to go up the street with my squad until we came to the edge of the town where we were to flush the houses and set up positions to check any enemy that might come down the road.

Like all combat and especially night operations, the whole movement was indefinite and its outcome unpredictable. Just picture yourself in a strange little town, with visibility limited to about fifty feet. You don't even know it's a little town. You receive orders to move to the end of the street. Where is the end? You start out. It may be one block. It may be eight miles. How can you tell where one town ends and the next begins? Many queer thoughts run through your head.

I assembled my squad. It was still a small group. Not many replacements were able to catch up to us. A boy named Rowe was now my assistant squad leader. Garcia had been busted. Rowe looked like a kid, but he wasn't. He was blonde and light complexioned. Rowe was married and he may have had some kids. I don't remember. When he came up he held a buck sergeant's rating, that is how he happened to be my assistant. I had no complaints. Rowe was a good soldier.

And like all good American soldiers, Rowe and the others wanted to know what was up. It aggravated me a little. I slipped up sometimes on this small but all important detail. I was always brief with my briefing. Perhaps it was because I had become tired and cynical. After all, it was the same old story—just move forward, take the next town or keep going until you're stopped. There was always a plan, but the plans never worked out as they were planned, so what difference did it make? Sure, we were going up the street. To the end of the street, of course. We were to secure the houses at the edge of the town. Then we would wait for further orders. It was fairly definite. But why did the men have to know this? They were just going to follow me, anyway.

But they had to know. They were American soldiers. They didn't want to be led like sheep to the slaughter. I had liked Lieutenant Thompson because he was thorough in his explanation of details concerning an attack. That was about the only thing I liked about him. I should have realized that the men I was leading were just like me. They wanted to know where they were going and why. I had almost reached the point where I was willing to just walk eastward, ever eastward without asking any questions, stopping only long enough to eat and sleep. I had almost reached that point. But like an American soldier, I never did. I shouldn't have expected my men to be any different. I should have explained more willingly and more thoroughly. No doubt many times long explanations of attack plans to American troops never came within a mile of similarity with what actually happened. But it set the stage and it gave the men an idea of what might have happened. And most of all, since they were Americans, it gave them their chance to approve or disapprove. If it sounded okay, they kept their mouths shut. If the idea was screwy, they sounded off.

Our plan worked out that night. We started off in single file, walking close together and making very little noise. I led the way with my '03 in the ready position, the safety off.

Max never said anything about the Y fork in the road. I hesitated a little and then took off on the road to the right. We hadn't gone very far, maybe a block, when a man jumped up in front of me and started to run down the street. I couldn't see him. I only heard him. Max hadn't told me what to do in a case like this. I fired from the hip. The first round was a tracer. It must have just whizzed past the man's head. He hit the street and started to scream and shout and kick. At first I thought he had been hit, but then the fiery ball had kept right on a straight, uninterrupted path down the street and out of sight up the road.

He was on his feet, hands in the air and shaking all over when I reached him. He was a civilian. At least he was dressed in civilian clothes. I did give him a chance. I shouted, "Halt," once before I fired. "What was he doing on the street," I tried to ask him. He didn't understand me and I couldn't understand his babbling.

Suddenly, there was a lot of noise from behind a fence next to the house on the left side of the road. Without warning, I fired two rounds into the fence. All was quiet.

That was the end of our shooting for the night. We took over several houses. They were filled with people, all civilians. We didn't get any information out of them. We didn't have time to become acquainted or even to sit down and rest. Within a short time we were back on the TDs and racing for another town.

The Letters of a Combat Rifleman

The next place was sort of big. There were trolley tracks and large buildings. We got into a bakery shop and waited. In less than an hour we were on the move again, this time on foot. Eventually, we ended up in another big building.

I was exhausted. It must have been about 4 A.M. when we got our outposts set up and had completed the taking over of the 414th positions. The rooms we occupied were crowded, but I found a place on the floor and went to sleep.

Good-natured Max, with his never-ending energy, probably never went to sleep. He told me what happened when I finally awoke and got back on my feet.

As daylight revealed our position, we found ourselves on the bank of the Saale River. We were in the large city of Halle. The building we occupied was a hospital. All the staff and patients had fled.

Max studied the opposite bank with his tired, squinting eyes. He had a habit of squinting so that it appeared as though he had some weakness of the eyes. But there was no weakness about the gray matter behind those squinters.

A big concrete bridge, half in the water, was the first thing visible as the morning mist lifted. And there on a rampart on the far side Max spied a German officer, standing fully erect and searching our area with field glasses.

Good-hearted Max didn't want to wake me—that was his argument. He grabbed my '03 and bowled over the not-too smart "superman." He continued to take pot shots at the other Jerries in the rampart. They were manning a machine gun.

Max showed me the scene when I got up. There was still some shooting left for me. I watched and waited. Pretty soon one of the machine gunners took off from the bridge. He made a beeline for a big truck-like vehicle about twenty-five yards away. I fired. He lay spread-eagled under the truck after plunging headfirst. It is doubtful that I hit him. Some of his buddies had escaped successfully the same way before I arrived on the scene. Altogether, about four men made it to the truck and then from the truck to a row of buildings, their run from the truck to the houses being more or less protected by the upper part of the bridge. The distance from our position to the truck was about three hundred yards.

I didn't take time to eat that morning. During the course of the day I shot at more targets than I had seen in the last two or three months. Also, the kitchen didn't get up to our position until later in the day.

Our firing position, high up in the top floors of the hospital, didn't remain a secret very long. We did so much firing I don't see how the enemy could help but spot us. Our advantage was in height. We were on the sixth floor. The enemy's answering shots all went into the ceilings of the rooms that we occupied. They were shooting up at us at almost a forty-five degree angle.

However, despite this return fire, we never located the positions occupied by the enemy riflemen. At least we were never sure that we knew their positions. They were just as smart or smarter than we were and kept back from the windows and openings.

With field glasses, we were able to pick up some military telephone wires and we followed them to a big mansion not far from the water's edge and just a little to our right front. I gave the windows and doors a going-over with 30 caliber slugs.

There was plenty of shooting all along our front. It was give and take. The Jerries were using machine guns occasionally and we were using some mortar fire.

It wasn't long until I got a call from Weapons platoon. "Jerries running from building to building," was the report. I went over and sure enough the boys were having lots of fun plinking at the daring Germans. The range here must have been five hundred yards; hence, the results weren't good, especially since the targets were moving plenty fast. The Jerries were all moving to our left or northward. The buildings they used for shields were marked with red crosses and big POW signs. That didn't slow up our firing any. The Jerries apparently were trying to get forward to positions where they could stem the advance of the 414th boys who were coming down the east bank of the river. It was our duty to do everything in our power to stop them, slow them up and harass their movements. It was tough on the POWs to be caught in such a spot.

At the greater range in the Weapons platoon area it seems that the boys felt safe. There must have been more than five of us standing on a balcony in plain view of the enemy when a burst of fire hit the building. We didn't get any direct hits but felt the sting of flying particles of stone. One of the men received a slight cut on the face.

Backing off the balcony, I started to find a position on the top floor but not in an exposed position. It certainly was beginning to be a gentleman's war. I asked the occupants of the apartment to go down to the cellar or one of the lower floors so that they wouldn't be bothered by the noise. Then I opened one of the curtained windows so that I wouldn't shoot through the glass or cause other damage. The first couple of shots in this neat, undamaged apartment seemed awfully loud and out of place. It was different from shooting out of deserted, windowless, and damaged buildings and houses. It almost seemed as if I were shooting out of my own bedroom back home. Just imagine the noise and vibration you would cause if you went upstairs in your own home in town or country and started shooting a .30 caliber gun out the window.

In less than an hour, the rat race was over. I had to look for new targets. It was then that I noticed that the mortar fire had disturbed some wild animals on the rocky hills the other side of the hospital-like buildings that were marked POW. The area was quite rocky and hilly. The animals appeared to be of the deer family. Finally, I decided it was an outdoor zoo, with the animals living in natural surroundings. There were other species of deer, sheep, etc. The range was more than one thousand yards, perhaps twelve hundred. The mortar shells had them all running back and forth in their compounds and the exploding shells must have caused plenty of damage.

We had one casualty that required hospital attention while we were on the banks of the Saale River. Bogus, a southern soldier, got shot in the derriere, accidentally. Our side was still ahead in scoring self-inflicted casualties. The accident was caused by some bum handling of a .32 automatic pistol by a fellow soldier.

Back in the hospital after a hot dinner, I heard the noise of an advancing force coming from our left. There was quite a fire fight going on between the defenders of Haale and the advancing 414th infantry.

To aid our boys fighting down the opposite bank of the river, I now climbed to the highest point in the hospital. I went up a ladder into the loft where I found I could shoot under the eaves. The one drawback was the sand that completely covered the floor, put there, no doubt, to smother incendiary bombs. Every time I fired, the muzzle blast raised a terrific cloud of dust, dirt, and sand. I had to shoot in a prone position in order to get under the eaves and this really made the sand fly.

I spotted my target in the zoo area. The range was at least one thousand yards. A soldier ran from behind a large stone wall, kneeled in the middle of the roadway as though he were going to fire a bazooka. The distance was so great I could not tell whether the man was American or German, even through my rifle scope. I had no binoculars with me at the time. A spotting scope would have come in handy.

I waited for him to fire. There was a big cloud of smoke and then I knew he was legal game. Our bazookas made no big cloud of smoke. I squeezed off a shot, holding high. The Jerry darted in back of a wall.

I chambered a new round and waited. In less than a minute, the target reappeared. Again, the bazooka man knelt in the middle of the road and aimed his rocket launcher in the same direction. I held and squeezed and touched another shot off before the German could fire his weapon. It must have come very close. The Jerry darted behind the wall without launching a rocket. He never reappeared. The Third Armored tanks were safe in the zoo area.

We pulled out of our positions along the Saale that night, making a long march to the north where we crossed a pontoon bridge. We covered another few miles in what seemed to be a southeasterly direction from the Saale River. Finally, the column halted in a small town and after we had flushed the houses, we picked a spot to catch a few hours' sleep. The Third platoon took over- several houses and nearly everyone had a bed to sleep in. Allan Wilson, our Oklahoma runner, slept on the first floor of our house along with a pregnant woman. Allan was the only one we felt we could trust.

After breakfast the next morning, we took off on foot, again. We covered plenty of ground that day and flushed several towns. Our new Yugo recruits proved to be very valuable men as our movements had to be coordinated with other units and we had to be sure we were going in the right direction and moving toward the assigned town or objective. Mike and Al were up at the head of the column guiding. When in doubt, they conversed easily with the civilians in order to get information.

We halted in one farm village long enough to drop our equipment and grab something to eat. Then we were off again to the next town. Captain Darsey was leading the column.

Spickendorf is where we halted, I believe. The date was April 16. Death stalked the tree-lined road to Spickendorf that day, hand in hand with fate.

We took over the town without any trouble. My squad was assigned to a squalid farm building on the edge of town. Our kitchen was up with us but they were slow getting started. In the meantime, we could think of nothing better than one of the nice plump chickens that scurried around our feet, gracing the dining room table. I told Sam Swavely and Frank Cuilla to get working on the idea. The man of the house wouldn't cooperate. Naturally, he didn't want to kill one of his own chickens. So I told the boys to go up the road a bit and get a couple of chickens from one of the other houses. They produced the chickens but I don't think they bothered to leave the backyard. Anyway, the old man refused to kill the birds. Finally, I got tired of arguing and planted a GI boot on his rear. He was plenty mad, but he finally killed the chickens and then the frau dressed them.

In the meantime, the old fellow wanted to see my commandant. I obliged him and we both went up the street looking for Max. I don't know or remember what Max said but the farmer seemed satisfied after his complaint was aired. Maybe Max said Eisenhower would pay him for the chickens.

It was during this dispute with the German that I heard a long burst of .50 caliber machine gun fire. It sounded as if it was up in the air and not far away. It was the death knoll of my York, Pennsylvania buddy, Orrie Salor. Captain Darsey forgot or thought he had forgotten his musette bag. He sent Orrie back to the last town to check and see if it was back there. My big, silent Indian friend, Valenzuela accompanied Orrie in the jeep as was customary. A P-51 caught them, along the tree-lined road, and Orrie was killed. Val was very seriously wounded. I never saw him again. The jeep was hardly touched. I had now only a couple of friends left in company headquarters. Who would be next? Would I start down the home stretch, only to be cut down perhaps by someone on my side? For some reason or other, I didn't enjoy my chicken dinner that night.

We checked out of Spickendorf that day as the sun started to wipe away the mists and announce the beginning of another warm spring day. Checking the house to make sure we didn't forget any items of equipment, I found two grenades and some other stuff laying on the kitchen table. Rushing out the door, I found our tank already pulling away. The war was now moving almost too fast for me. I threw my equipment aboard and mounted on the run.

The Letters of a Combat Rifleman

We passed a hospital full of wounded Jerries. White flags were everywhere.

Cautiously, we crossed a section of the Autobahn and then we swept down the overpass into the town of Brehna. There was no resistance. It was a fairly large town and there was a double track rail line running through the southeast part.

We set up headquarters near the railroad station, assigned a guard there and settled down to wait for further orders. We stayed in Brehna for at least two days.

We were surprised to find that we had telephone connections with the towns in front of us. Mike and Max had some fun by contacting the burgemeisters of the surrounding towns and ordering them to surrender, explaining that it was no use for them to hold out any longer against our panzers.

I found plenty of time to write to Jean. My letter dated April 17 contained seven pages.

It began, "Things are still happening here in Germany, but I am glad to say, darling, that I am okay. Also that a few days ago I got some letters from you that were only about a week old and that is very marvelous considering how deep in Germany I am. In fact, we are going so fast that we are beginning to eat off the land, taking towns with electricity, finding Russian money and liberating thousands of POWs, Poles, Russians, French, etc. I'll enclose a Russian bill that I 'liberated.' It is five rubles and is the real McCoy."

Bill had enclosed a small felt chicken from his Easter basket in one of the letters. I pressed it under the leather chin strap that crossed the front of my steel helmet. It was a talisman from my son. I thanked him in my letter.

"Many thanks to my Billy boy for sending me his rooster. I was very, very proud of it and wore it on my helmet. However, I lost it while riding on a tank."

The weather, of course, was mentioned: "The weather has been chilly, especially at night but it has been generally clear and spring like. I have been taking pictures. I have four cameras, all very excellent and worth an average of one hundred dollars each. However, we are not allowed to send cameras home. I'll be sure to get one good one home at least. I am taking 35 mm color film now with a Kodak Retina II."

We were allowed to mention any town that was fifty or more miles away so I told Jean about the POWs in Duderstat.

"We rescued quite a few American and English prisoners in Duderstat and I had my picture taken with an English captain who was captured at Tobruk and an English private. A Canadian prisoner captured at Dieppe joined our company and is in the First platoon. We took another town and two Yugoslavians joined us and they are in my squad. They are excellent soldiers and are only happy when we are attacking. They are good guides, interpreters and interrogators. Mike, whose father, mother, and children were killed by the Nazis, is listening to a German broadcast and has a big smile on his face. The news must be good. The end is in sight, thank God. But there are always sudden happenings which remind us that there still is a real war on. And we are all sweating out the finish."

At the end of one paragraph I said, "Also (I'm enclosing) a railroad ticket to Berlin. It's no good to me because I'll have to walk and ride panzers to get there." I was to hear about this item later on.

My closing paragraphs reassured Jean of my love and contained some advice for Billy:

Before I forget I must say, dearest, I love you, oh, so very, very much. I need you just as you say, to take care of me in every way. And to be my companion and my lover as only you know how.

"I'll close now and write tomorrow if it is at all possible. Darling, I'll write every day that I have time. Just keep loving and trusting me and caring for me and keep writing. Give my love to my Happy Chappy boy. He is the best little boy in the world. Tell him to always be good and brave."

Brehna was quiet. I don't believe an enemy shell ever landed in the town. But, there were plenty of happenings to keep us busy and interested.

There was plenty of talk about our next attack. Delitzsch was the name of the town that entered every conversation. At Delitzsch there was a concentration of Hitler youth, werewolves and fanatic SS. The combination Delitzsch and SS was heard more and more. We wondered—were we to keep hitting hard spots? Was I to die or get hit when the war was already won? We enjoyed ourselves in Brehna but we feared the future. We knew that more of us had to die. We wondered who?

The evening after I wrote to Jean I got a call to report to company headquarters. The executive officer wanted to see me. I'm not sure of his name now. He was young and big and arrogant. He always appeared to be acting or be putting on a false front in military bearing.

"What town are we in, Sergeant Davis?" he asked swelling his chest and getting red around the neck as though he were going through a voice developing exercise.

I couldn't say a thing. I wanted to say, "I know what town we are in. The name is right on the tip of my tongue but I can't remember it. It begins with a "B." I wanted to get the answer to that question more than I wanted the answer to any question. The lieutenant was testing me I was sure. As a squad leader, I should know the name of the town we had just taken. Finally, I had to admit failure.

"I don't know, Sir."

That was the right answer. I couldn't have given a better one because the lieutenant immediately produced the railroad ticket from Brehna to Berlin that I had enclosed in my letter to Jean.

The lieutenant executive officer started to rake me over the coals. He threatened to bust me, court martial me and a couple of other things. There was a lot of talk about security and my responsibility as a squad leader. I took it all without an argument. In fact, I don't remember even saying, "Yes, sir," or No, Sir." Finally, I was dismissed.

As I walked back up to my squad in the Third platoon, I realized the big change that had come over our company headquarters. There was hardly a man there that I knew. Now I realized how the average rifleman in the platoons regarded his headquarters section and the men that were in it.

The following day, my letter to Jean reflected my feeling towards the army after the above incident. I wrote on April 18, 1945:

"It is another beautiful spring day and everything is just fine here. But I am longing for you sweetheart, and the good old USA. I am so tired of the army and war. When I recall maneuvers with the First Army in Virginia and New York in '39 and '40, they bring memories of long rides, long hours and constant dust, heat and fatigue. Add to these hardships a real enemy, shooting live ammo and no knowledge of when it all will end, and you can get an idea of just how it is here in Germany.

"But it can't be long now, darling, until the finish. And I can see a postwar period of prosperity. Especially for toolmakers. Maybe I won't make the money I made before at Bendix, but we should be able to get a new home and a new car. Nothing can ever bring back our sweet, dear Janey, but we can have a new baby. Are we all agreed? If you can endure your waiting and longing and periods of anxiety and fear, I can be brave and continue on to fight this war to a final decisive victory."

My closing paragraph contained the usual hope and prayer: "Keep loving me, dear, and keep writing, and take good care of our Billy boy. I love you both and pray each day for our quick reunion."

CHAPTER XX
A Strange War

It was a queer war that we were fighting now. A couple of English soldiers came into town and announced that they were POWs on leave of absence from their Nazi captors.

They had to report back that evening. And they did! The next day they visited us again and gave us much information about the town they lived in. It seems that the Jerries were now so short of men they were forced to pull away most of the guards on the POWs and in some cases there were no guards at all, just checks in the morning and evening; hence, these fellows could take the day off and tour the countryside. They were even armed with pistols! They insisted on reporting back every evening so that they could spend the night with their German sweethearts.

Mike also made checks for us on the enemy positions by changing into civilian clothes, hopping a bicycle and taking a tour of the towns up ahead. Mike reported a lot of undefended trenches.

On this particular beautiful spring day, a fair fraulein peddled her bike into Brehna announcing to Max and the hungry lieutenant from Mike company that she had fled Halle to escape the fighting. The girl wasn't exactly a youngster. She looked as though she had been around and knew the ropes. She might very well have been a spy. She was rather beautiful and very intelligent. Her personality won her an immediate welcome to our big house. Max and a couple of the boys entertained her on the porch with flattering remarks, cigarettes, and chocolate. They got in plenty of lewd and wise remarks in English that were supposed to be beyond her understanding, but I wonder now if they were. Sitting with her legs crossed and her skirt above her knees, she flounced her foot up and down until Max and the Mike lieutenant were drooling on the edge of their chairs. They were building her up for a big after-dark offensive. And no doubt she was going to meet the attack with everything that she had.

Max almost reached the crying stage. He wanted to sleep with the fraulein that night but at the same time he wanted to be absolutely faithful to the girlfriend back in Nebraska. Max was fighting a battle within a battle all afternoon and evening. When someone stole the fraulein's bicycle from in front of the house, Max started hopping all over town to find her another one. Finally, he had to buy a bicycle from a farmer.

Another amusing incident was the surrender or capture of two supermen. Anyway, they were dressed like supermen or I should say like Wehrmacht soldaten. The uniforms were too big. They were the youngest soldiers that I had ever seen, fifteen years old, perhaps; surely not more than sixteen at the most. In fact, they looked younger than fifteen.

They held their hands over their heads in the usual prisoner stance. We questioned them. "Vie alt?" we all wanted to know. They claimed to be seventeen.

They also came in for the usual searching. One boy had a Mickey Mouse child's type watch on his wrist. We passed it up because we had the best. However, a couple of DPs that were standing nearby watching the proceedings asked for the watch and then reached over and took it from the boy's wrist.

"Bitte! Bitte!" the boy cried. " Mine fader gaben me das vatch. Do not take it!" He was choked with childish emotion and the big tears rolled unchecked down his smooth face. I wanted to help him. I wanted him to have his watch back. But I didn't intercede. All Germans must now suffer, even the children, the only ones that were innocent.

We moved to new positions that evening, right on the very edge of town. Mike company set up their heavy machine guns and we put out some outposts as though everybody really expected a counterattack. Perhaps our information was wrong. Maybe the Jerries were still strong enough to press an attack. Anyway, I planned our defense with great thoroughness and still with much thought for the comfort and convenience of the men in my squad. As usual I included myself in the outpost schedule.

The night passed without incident. The fraulein from Halle got less sleep than we did. She cried like a virgin, so I was told. And she was even ashamed to come out of her room (or whosoever room she slept in) into the light of the new day. When she did emerge she took off again for Halle without even waiting for breakfast. I guess her appetite had been well satisfied.

I didn't write again to Jean while I was in Brehna. We were too busy. A raiding party was organized and some time near the middle of the day we swept out of town on M-10's. I am not sure of the official designation of the vehicles but they were mounted on multiple big rubber tired wheels. The armament consisted of a .37 mm gun and a fifty and some thirty caliber machine guns. My Third squad rode on the outside of the vehicles just the same as we had been doing with the tanks and TDs.

Our sweep through the villages was made without bloodshed. The infantry cautiously entered the towns first and then the armor pulled into the squares.

My squad made a circle around the left side of one village and then we worked our way toward the center. The burgermeister was there on hand to greet us, standing in front of the local bier hof. As I recall, he had a sort of experienced air about him. It seemed as though he had been through the routine before.

I gave him the usual spiel, "Alles foto apparod, glasses and waffens verboten."

Without hesitation, the robust mayor opened his coat front and reached into one of his vest pockets. Pulling out a small piece of white paper he handed it to me. This was a new routine.

I opened the paper and read, " Sorry, I've been here before you. T.S." Signed "GI Joe."

Well, that was a good one on us. Some rear echelon guy was working ahead of us. He had plenty of guts and quite a sense of humor. We all laughed including the burgermeister. I interrupted his fun when I spied a big silver watch chain stretched across his broad front. Reaching out and relieving the burgermeister of his big watch and chain, I remarked, "Here's one thing, GI Joe missed." Oddly, the burgermeister made no objections.

Inside the beer hof it was a different story. We ordered up a round of drinks and to our surprise the man and woman behind the bar demanded gelt (money). We honestly didn't understand at first but when we realized what they were talking about we could hardly believe it was true. We were both amused and at the same time angry. It is a good thing that we were amused, otherwise, we might have shot up the place a little. Here was another sign that the war was nearing the finish. We just couldn't adjust ourselves so suddenly to doing things the normal way. It had been a long time since we had traded with gelt. The war hadn't quite ended yet, so we didn't do any trading. We drank up and shoved off. The three towns were flushed without any shooting.

On April 19, we left Brehna by truck and moved to Petersrode in preparation for an attack on Bitterfeld from the southeast. As usual, the Third platoon was on the edge of town. We had some nice houses for quarters. Allan Wilson met a woman from his hometown in one of the houses in our section. In fact, they knew each other from back in the States. The woman had married a German; hence, her reason for living in Petersrode.

We naturally were able to converse easily with this American-German, and we naturally asked a lot of questions. We wanted to get different answers than what we had been getting from the native Germans. But the answers were still the same. We were pretty mad when this American-born woman said there were no slave workers in Germany. Within three hundred yards of her home was a factory with a barbed wire enclosure right beside it. Inside the enclosure were wooden huts where the slave workers slept. Of course, they were empty now. But it was just like putting two and two together. I didn't bother to ask the lady for anymore facts or information.

Bitterfield was a fairly large city. We didn't know that it was our last objective. We didn't know that there was going to be some shooting and some dying. We just went ahead and planned our attack like veteran troops. We were scared to death, but we knew we would win.

To really set the record straight—we didn't even know there was a city called Bitterfield. In fact, we didn't even know the name of the town we occupied. We just went ahead as usual. I established an outpost and ran wires out. At the same time we had secured a ten-in-one ration and we had a nice German woman preparing supper for us.

The table was set and everything was just about ready to be served when we got an order from company headquarters to get ready to move out in five minutes. Naturally, Max was running around like a chicken with its head cut off. He wanted everybody out in the street in two minutes. There was never a more angry or hungry platoon of riflemen in the ETO that day. But the worst was yet to come.

It was dusk as we marched down the cobbled country road. We were minus one of our Yugoslavian recruits. He was last seen in company of a pretty German fraulein. However, we still had Mike.

It was dark when we reached the next small village. There was plenty of confusion. It was very hard to find a place to sleep. That problem was soon solved. Battalion headquarters had a nice "line of departure" for us to secure.

But first we got orders to form a patrol from the Third platoon and go up and measure the trees in the woods up ahead. Headquarters wanted the diameter of the tree trunks. If we were mad when we lost our supper, we were really mad now. Everybody was bitching and crying, even Max. Our general argument was that we wanted the whole platoon to move up and not just a small patrol.

Our griping must have reached headquarters because the order was changed. The whole platoon was to move forward and secure the line of departure. There was no further mention of measuring tree trunks. As it turned out, it was a good thing that this part of the order was rescinded.

It was a very dark night. In fact, when we reached the railroad embankment that was supposed to be the jumping off place the next morning, two of our riflemen got down into a foxhole within five feet of another hole occupied by two Jerries. Imagine their surprise the next morning.

Zurcher, one of the few remaining old-timers in company headquarters, accompanied us with his 300 radio so that we could keep in touch with battalion headquarters.

The area where we halted was flat and open on one side of the double track railroad embankment which varied in height. On the other side of the tracks, bushes and some small trees offered concealment. We didn't know which direction the attack would take, but there were other troops moving on our right and we knew that the area to our rear was taken. That left the area to our front and also to our left open to suspicion. As it turned out, the attack moved to our left front toward a large wooded section that contained a considerable force of the remaining Wehrmacht.

The railroad ran perpendicular to our front and it was crossed by a road just at the point where we halted. Max set the platoon up along the right bank of the double tracks which gave us open land to watch. Two squads put a listening post on the other side of the tracks to intercept any Jerries that might come from the cover on that side. I put two men in the signal tower at the point where the road crossed the railroad.

The Jerries were quite obliging that night. They dug nice two-men foxholes along the embankment and then moved out when we came up. Our small force couldn't have scared them. It must have been the big unit that was moving on our right. Despite the darkness, I was able to see one bunch of GIs by the light of a distant burning house. It looked like at least two hundred men. Perhaps the Jerries saw these men and decided to move back. They all left except the two that had fallen asleep. They all decided to try to come back again.

The big outfit on our right moved off to the right front. Perhaps the Jerries didn't see our little force drop into their positions.

We got everything set up without any trouble or interruption. We even put one man out in the open to our right, or I guess I should say to the right of the railroad tracks. The railroad pointed to our front, but actually we were set up facing to the left.

Most of the platoon occupied a ditch along the railroad embankment. Max and Zurcher were back with the Third squad so they occupied a big hole with me. Of course, we didn't bother to get in the holes until the shooting started.

The Jerries didn't come out of the cover on the left side of the tracks, they came right up the middle, crawling on their stomachs. They were trying to get between our listening posts and the main body. It was a very brave maneuver, but naturally, it wouldn't work very well against experienced combat troops. It was real close fighting. One man at the first listening post had an M-1 shot out of his hands. It was shattered at the receiver. The Jerries made several attempts, but each one failed.

Nevertheless, we were plenty scared. So Max had Zurcher call back to battalion for 81 mm mortar fire. Battalion relayed the message to Mike company. After we got the message through we were more scared than we were before. It looked now as if we would have to duck our own mortar fire, as well as the small arms fire of the Jerries.

I couldn't for the life of me figure out how the Mike men would know where to lay their eggs with the little bit of information that we gave them. We told them we were on the right side of the tracks. That was all. We wanted them to hit the area immediately across from our positions and a little forward. That is where we figured the Germans were located.

As soon as Zurcher got the message through, I started to pray. We all got down as deep as possible in the foxhole. It was a tight fit for all three of us and the radio. We all were expressing the same fears. When they said "On the way," I knew the first round would soon whistle in. There was a rush of air, a muffled thud as the big hell hit the soft earth and then a big explosion right at the exact spot we wanted it!

It couldn't happen again. The second laying-in round was soon "on the way." I shivered and waited. I prayed some more. It was like lighting striking twice. They hit the same spot. Surely my guardian angel was still with me. It took an angel to guide those mortar shells, twisting and tumbling, rising and falling through the air, seemingly to always find the wrong target.

"Fire for effect!" Zurcher ordered. It was like a miracle. Our voices went invisibly through the night skies to our comrades far away. Our cry for help was answered quickly and with precision and power. The dark earth erupted all up and down the far side of the railroad. It took more than luck. It took more that skill. We knew the answer. We were thankful that our prayers had been answered.

The mortar fire quieted the Jerries for a while. But just before daylight, they tried a new approached. I was standing in the foxhole with Max and Zurcher when Max pointed out the head and shoulders of a man out in the open field on the same side of the tracks that we were on.

"Fire at him," Max ordered.

"I'm not going to shoot at him," I told Max. "He may be the man we put out there.

"That's not him. Go ahead and shoot," Max ordered. I refused again. I was almost sure it was our man. Max seemed confused. He was the platoon leader but he didn't seem to know whether or not we still had a listening post in the field.

I wouldn't change my mind, so Max crawled down the ditch to a point where he was just about opposite the figure out in the grass. The range was about one hundred twenty-five yards, perhaps less. Max fired and the form fell. The man was dead. Max luckily, was right. The man was German, as we found out later, and he was setting up a machine gun.

Almost at the same time another form came toward us through the grass. This German was well to the left of the machine gunner. He was pulling a panzerfaust as he crawled along.

Our great combat fighter from Boston, Murray Susskind, leader of the First squad, jumped up out of the ditch and walked directly at the crawling German. Mike was pouring a steady stream of lead from his grease gun as he calmly walked toward his enemy. The Jerry fired back with a P-38 pistol and hit Mike in the foot. But Mike kept moving in and finally ended the fight with a flurry of .45 caliber slugs.

The scene that followed was perhaps the funniest that anyone ever witnessed on the battlefield. Mike grabbed up the P-38 from his dead adversary and stuffed it in his belt as a souvenir. Then with a big smile on his face and a hearty, happy laugh for all, he started at the front of the platoon and shook hands with every single man.. He wished us all the best of luck and we called back our best regards along with plenty of shouts and remarks about being lucky. Mike hobbled away toward the rear, his fighting days over.

After Mike paraded down the line the way he did, we assumed everything was quiet again, so we got up out of our foxholes and the other men stood up along the ditch. In a matter of minutes we were joined by the rest of the platoons and we proceeded up along the right-hand side of the railroad to an underpass.

We passed under the railroad and then fanned out in a skirmish line. Practically the whole company moved abreast in a long line of riflemen. We had about four hundred yards to go to reach the big woods to our left front. The ground we were crossing was open but there were deep depressions from strip mining operations.

We hadn't moved one hundred yards when our supporting units started to pour a steady stream of shells and bullets into the woods in front of us. We didn't bother to shoot, mainly because we were not being shot at. The overhead fire was so terrific it would have been a waste of ammunition for us riflemen to start popping away, too.

After more than six months in combat we were at last seeing the ultimate in support fire. And it was accurate and sustained fire, too. And even the mortars were throwing their stuff right where we wanted it.

Glancing over my right shoulder, I saw Mike company machine gunners set up on top of the railroad embankment. Over my left shoulder a couple of Sherman tanks were firing their 50 caliber machine guns and also booming shells into the trees with their 75's. It was an inspiring sight. I thought it would make a wonderful color photo, so I tried to get my Kodak 35 mm camera into position for a shot of tanks shooting.

It took a lot of tugging and twisting to get the camera up into position, and then just as I had halted and turned around to snap the picture, Max started shouting and waving his arms, ordering us to step on it and get into the woods. I didn't get the picture.

We entered the woods and the overhead fire stopped. We went several hundred yards through the woods and still there was no opposition. The line stopped and we rested awhile. I kept searching through the small trees up ahead, looking for some movement or sign of the enemy.

We moved out again. The ground was sloping up and we hit some open spaces in the woods. We caught sight of some forms just leaving one of these clearings. Some of the men on the left side of the line fired through the trees.

I guess the other platoon leaders or perhaps the company commander, if he was with the outfit, knew the direction to take and also our objectives.

The Third platoon had not been briefed. We just kept in contact with the rest of the line and kept moving.

Near the crest of the high ground we came out into the open. There was high grass and bushes, which offered plenty of cover. We moved over the crest and stopped and hit the deck. We watched the scene out in front and below us. It was another beautiful, bright spring day. In the distance were several small towns. Immediately to our right front was a big, long, red brick building with a lot of glass windows. One of the platoons sent a patrol down to see what the building contained. We fired a few shots into the upper part of the structure.

In less than ten minutes we were on the move again. The Third platoon moved ahead and a little to the left. Below us was a very steep grade with a road at the bottom. Before we left the top of the hill, I caught sight of a tank, that appeared to be ours, parked beside a building at the edge of the nearest small village. It must have been American or we certainly would have been under fire.

There were some small trees again on the steep slope. On my right the boys got up a couple of Jerries that immediately surrendered. They threw their pistols down the slope and we spent about ten minutes trying to find them. We made the prisoners direct the search, but we had no luck.

At the bottom we turned left and moved about seventy-five yards to some brick buildings. They looked like small power stations or perhaps they housed electric transformers of some kind. I didn't enter the buildings. I noticed a road block made of trees, stones, and rubble. It connected with one of the buildings on our side of the road.

It had defenders. A couple of more Nazis surrendered in back of the buildings. Down the tree-lined road toward the area that should be our rear, I spied several foxholes. I moved toward the nearest one, about twenty-five yards in front of the road block. Looking down into the tunneled-out hole, I saw just the one shoulder of a Jerry rifleman.

"Kommen raus!" I ordered, pointing my '03 at the German's head. He jumped out of the hole, put his hands over his head and moved toward the other men standing near the two buildings.

There were other foxholes along the bank of the road. They were spaced about ten yards apart in front of the road block, on only one side of the road. I approached each one at the ready position and each superman meekly surrendered and joined the other prisoners.

Patton, myself, and a couple of others collected the Jerry rifles and some 8 mm ammunition and started to blast the glass insulators on the electric wires just to see how the German rifles worked. It was just a short time before or after this shooting that the company received a directive forbidding all troops from firing at glass insulators or any other communication equipment. It was very obvious at this late stage of the game that telephone communications weren't going to help the Nazis' cause very much, but at the same time it would mean a lot of work for our communications' men if things were destroyed wholesale and without good cause.

We fooled around with the German rifles for about five minutes and then we got organized with a couple of squads from the First platoon and we formed a skirmish line and pushed back again into the woods. The first line of trees were about fifty yards away from the road at this point and the ground was level. We started in just about where the roadblock reached across the road.

Some First platooners soon uncovered a bunker in the side of a hill on our left flank. It contained a number of wounded German soldiers. They had been wounded during the shelling and strafing of Bitterfeld. The men that we had seen running through the trees earlier were headed for the bunker.

When we checked and found all wounded Germans, we pushed on into the woods where we understood there were many Jerries set up in a defensive position.

We moved forward in a skirmish line with about three to five paces between each man. There weren't more than two full squads.

We hadn't gone more than seventy-five yards when the Jerry riflemen opened up on us. The bullets zipped through the trees but the fire was light. They had machine guns, too, but none fired. Without command and with no hesitation, our men kept moving forward and we opened fire as soon as we were fired on, even though we couldn't see the defenders.

I didn't move another five yards before I saw the mounds of earth which indicated the defensive positions. They were only ten yards away. They had been cleverly dug and camouflaged, that is why we had to get in so close before we could see them. The defenders were at the bottom of the holes, ready to call it quits.

Just in back of the holes ran a high wire fence topped with barbed wire. I fired a couple of shots at the mounds of earth as I moved in, halting each time to aim and shoot. Suddenly two German soldiers appeared right in front of me, but on the other side of the wire fence. They were running to my left, perpendicular to the direction we were moving and apparently, they wanted to get into some of the empty holes on our side of the fence.

"Hands up," I shouted bringing my '03 up to my shoulder. The Germans were surprised and frightened. They dropped their rifles, which they had grasped at the balance, like hot potatoes. I directed them toward the gate in the wire as the rest of the boys were rounding up another thirty or forty Supermen from their holes in the ground.

In back of the wire fence was a barracks-like building. We had run into a small, well camouflaged camp. Altogether we must have taken more than one hundred prisoners that morning. We lined up a big platoon at the camp and marched them out to the road.

Except for the prisoner guards, the remainder of Love company straggled back cross-country to the town where we started the night before. It was a rather primitive country German village. We were able to wash up and sit and rest in the sunlight. We were tired but victorious soldiers. We had sustained no casualties while cleaning out dangerous, well-hidden forces of enemy riflemen.

Soon after dinner we were on the move again. First, there was a movement by truck and then a road march into another small village. We set up a defense and planned to spend the night. Just about supper time, the enemy lobbed in some mortar shells and a couple of men in the kitchen section were killed.

My squad had a comfortable setup in a farm home near the edge of town. Some of the boys were trying to make time with a teenaged deaf and dumb girl. She was sure cute but the sign language had us all stopped. I believe we would have all taken up lip reading if we would have stayed there twenty-four hours.

We left early the next morning, headed for our last attack, our last job. Of course, we didn't know it at the time. We were still sweating out the finish and if we had known that this was the last attack, we would have all died of fright.

Our village must have been a suburb of Bitterfeld because we were in the city in short order. The Third platoon struck off through some back yards. We ran into plenty of trouble in the form of fences and a small canal or waterway. It wasn't very wide but it appeared to be very deep. Luckily, we were not under fire. There was absolutely no resistance.

We made our way along this canal for several hundred yards. On the left were houses, on the right the canal and open fields. We must have been moving along one edge of Bitterfeld. We were not briefed so we didn't know where Max was trying to take us. I don't know whether or not he knew his destination. As I recall, we were supposed to go to the center of town. Reaching a bridge, we crossed and started to move down what looked like a main road leading out of town.

We moved along the road with most of the platoon in a skirmish line stretched out in the open fields to the right side of the road. I was out in the field with my squad, on the right hand end of the line.

For some reason or other I expected to run into enemy soldiers. I suspected every object and fold in the ground to sprout a Jerry rifleman or machine gun.

Observing quite far ahead I noticed a turn in the road, a sharp turn to the left. At this point, I was almost sure I saw a foxhole or some sort of defensive position. I opened up with my Springfield and quite a few other riflemen in the line started to use marching fire against some of the houses, trees and other likely hiding places in front of us.

The men up on the road crossed a concrete bridge that crossed a gully. Just about at this point Max halted the column. At our end of the line we had a small bank to lie down behind.

There was a consultation. I told Max that we were getting farther and farther out into the country and that it would be better if we turned around, recross the two bridges and head back toward the houses we had just left. We decided to go back.

The Jerries spurred us on. They opened up on our line with rifles and machine guns. The machine gun fire was coming from a very big house in back of or in the middle of a large group of trees and bushes. It was located about four hundred yards to our left front which put us in a very good position to cover the second bridge.

It was disappointing to hear practically no return fire from our line of riflemen. In fact, I think nearly everyone started running to the rear. That was okay, too, but the men up the road ran across the bridge in bunches. That is two or three at a time. The others didn't bother to fire to cover the running men.

I started shouting my head off for the other men along the line and up on both sides of the bridge to give some covering fire, but they didn't hear me or at least acted as though they didn't hear me. I did get several shots off, aiming at the upper windows.

We got out of range without suffering any casualties. On the way back I sent Sergeant Rowe and another man around to the far side of a big fence that surrounded a large building and some trees and open ground. In the meantime, we stopped and waited at the main gate.

After ten or fifteen minutes, I started to get worried about the two men that were circling the wire. I figured they should have been able to get around the place in less than ten minutes if they didn't run into any trouble.

I stood there debating with the other men in my squad what to do, when someone shouted to us from the building, which was about fifty yards inside the fence.

Naturally, we shouted back, ordering everyone to come out of the building or we would fire. After some difficulty, a couple of men came up out of the basement from a side entrance. They were followed by several hundred men and four women. They were all prisoners of the Germans. Perhaps the captors were still in the building on the upper floors. We didn't have time to investigate. Rowe and the other man showed up just as we were being cheered as liberators. The hundreds of men were French. That is, all except four. The four men accompanying the four women (who were Parisiens) were English. But at this point the women decided they had had enough of the English and they took off with us toward a beer hof on the other side of the canal bridge. But we knew that several hundred Frenchmen couldn't be wrong, so we gave the dames the brush-off.

Near the beer hof was a huge barricade across the street. After halting for about five minutes we filed past the barricade and took off up what looked like a city street.

It didn't take long to reach the center of town. We moved along in two columns, one on each side of the street. Most of the time we stayed close to the buildings. It must have been a public building that we entered near the city center. It was vacant. We went in one side and out the other and then we found ourselves at the rear of the company column.

One block away we entered a public park with a pool or reservoir in the center. The column halted at the upper end which meant that we stopped about the middle of the park.

In a few minutes some German women came from a house nearby and offered us some soup. It was getting to be a cinch now. Besides no resistance, the enemy population was offering, of its own free will, to feed us. We were hungry, so we didn't hesitate to accept the offering. And it was very good soup.

But our free lunch was soon interrupted by a long burst of German machine gun fire. Two men in the First platoon were killed.

Strangely enough, nobody took over. I did see a machine gun squad run over and take position in back of a concrete culvert. They dueled with the German gun. We sat down and finished our soup. Even the German women stayed outside. This was a queer war now. With hot lead flying about less than a city square away, the remainder of Love company stood or sat along the street eating, smoking, and relaxing.

In a few minutes, word was passed down the line to send up a tank destroyer. In another few minutes, a tank destroyer raced up the street to quiet the German fire. The TDs got into position and proceeded to punch big holes into the apartment house where the Jerries were holed up. That was just about the final resistance that Love company faced in Bitterfeld.

The remainder of the small city was cleared with little trouble. The Third platoon took its own route and we must have headed for the north end of town. We ran into some of our tanks and also the battalion commander who seemed to be lost. The weather was cloudy and a slight drizzle made it imperative to find some good shelter.

In the hallway of an apartment house we sought directions from the battalion commander. He had a big map, but perhaps he would have been better off without it.

"According to this map," the CO said, "We should be well out of the city, but we still haven't reached the edge of the town."

An enlisted man soon found our trouble. Down in the right-hand corner of the map was the date—1923.

In cooperation with the tanks we moved a few more blocks and, of course, we finally ran into open fields again. Moving in single file we went up along one side of a beautifully modern apartment building. On our left were victory gardens and beyond, open fields.

In the distance was a small bridge, about six hundred yards away. Near the left end of the bridge was a small red building. Suddenly, two men in long overcoats started across the bridge toward the house. The Third platoon acted as one rifleman. There was a tremendous burst of rifle fire. I was right next to a street lamp post so I leaned against the pole in order to steady my shots.

One man dropped wounded, the other one made it to the house. It was impossible to tell who made the hit. Every man in the platoon must have fired three or four times. Many army men would have said we were a trigger happy bunch. And I will agree—but not along the same line of thought. We weren't the best soldiers in the world yet. If we were, we would have automatically given each other covering fire when we withdrew from our position on the other side of town. But we were seasoned veterans, especially when it came to offensive tactics. As long as we were "trigger happy," if you want to call it that, we dominated the enemy. When they were throwing most of the lead, we were the ones that were being dominated. It all boils down to the same old story. You must have fire power to win wars. Fire power and numbers to furnish that fire power.

CHAPTER XXI
The War Will Soon Be Over

As I write this, the war in Korea is many weeks old. The outcome is uncertain. But the side that can get the most men with the most fire power into position in the shortest time will be the winner. I think our high officers realize this now, but it may be too late.

For the last couple of years they have been advancing the idea that we could defend ourselves successfully by having a small army with superior weapons. This theory is wrong as it was proven during the last war. Germany had superior weapons but they didn't have the numbers. It would be the same setup if we ever went to war with Russia.

But the really sad part about our position is that the generals were saying we had this superior equipment or were implying that we had it or could produce it quickly, when, in fact, it was only on paper. In the meantime Russia had not only built more tanks but better tanks than we have.

Further proof of the decadent outlook of our top military brass is the way the North Koreans overwhelmed the South Koreans. The North was trained by the Reds. The South Korean army was trained by U.S. officers. The Red Army men were probably teaching the Northern boys how to shoot and how to use their weapons, tanks, etc. They no doubt taught them plenty of tactics. At the same time, I would bet my right arm that the U.S. Army officers were teaching the South Koreans military courtesy, map reading, physical training, ju-jit-su, aircraft identification and a host of other unimportant subjects. They probably had those Southern boys on so many road marches and standing so many inspections and marching in so many parades they thought they were tin soldiers instead of fighting men.

The sooner we get the old tradition out of our ranks, the sooner America will be safe. This change must take place, or else, because today the Red Army could overwhelm us even though we might use the atomic bomb.

After this shooting episode, we took up positions in the block-long apartment buildings. My Third squad housed up in an end apartment and I stationed an observer at a big window on the second floor landing.

We lost no time in getting acquainted with the apartment dwellers. They were all in the cellar and they had all their valuables down there with them.

We became very friendly with a woman in one of the first floor apartments. She made tea for us and also cookies. Looking around the place I soon found a lot of 35 mm transparencies. With some difficulty, due to the different languages, I finally understood the woman to say that the camera that took the pictures belonged to a neighbor. Well, I thought this was a stall so I called in Mike, the Yugoslavian. Mike would say things to the Germans that made them tremble all over. I made Mike understand that I wanted the camera that took the 35 mm pictures and he immediately went to work on our hostess. The woman stuck to her story, so I told Mike to tell everyone in our section of the apartment that alles foto apparel was verboton.

A few minutes later I walked over into the apartment just across the hall. There I met Frau Dorly Liborius. We were to become very good friends. Frau Liborius was a meek, mild, German housewife. Big tears were streaming down her round cheeks. They dropped on a Leica camera, held reverently in her two hands as though in prayer.

Here at last after traveling across more than half of Germany I finally saw the prize I wanted most. "Alles foto apparel verboten," I said as I reached out and took the Leica.

"Bitte, bitte," Dorly cried. "It ist mine heren!" Later she explained to me in English that the camera was to her, just like her husband because it was his and he prized it so much.

It was with relief that we moved around the block to another house late that afternoon. Every time I saw Dorly she was crying. When she mentioned one time that the camera cost four hundred fifty marks, I offered to give her six hundred marks, but Dorly didn't want money, she wanted the Leica.

We moved again the next day, another three or four blocks toward the Mulde River where we set up defensive positions. This line of foxholes along the river bank was maintained at all times, but we lived in a nice row of modern homes. During the day we had only a few men on the river. At nighttime about one-half or one-third of the company moved down to the river.

The first few days we were opposed by the remnants of the great or once great German Wehrmacht. They threw some mortar fire and they did some long-range sniping. Our last two casualties were hit by snipers, accurate shots through the neck. The men of course were killed.

It was now that I found time, again to write to Jean. My letter on April 23, 1945 was routine:

The Letters of a Combat Rifleman

"I have several letters from you which I must answer. The one you wrote March 30 was long and dear, just as usual. Then I have two from April 11. You said you are ill. I am so sorry, and I wish I were home to care for you. I know I could help some.

"Billy was a good boy to drink all his cocoa. He is some big boy, too, to be able to make it himself."

It looked as though the war was nearing a close, but we still thought it would go on and on. I wrote to Jean:

"The war news does look good. I am hoping for the end soon. But, of course, no one can tell how long these Nazis will keep fighting. And as long as they fight it means that someone must get hurt and that is why we are sweating out the finish."

I wrote five or six more paragraphs. There was nothing important to tell. The shooting war was over for us but of course we didn't know that. In fact the tone of the letter seemed to indicate that I thought there was still fighting days ahead.

On the last page I said, "I am a sad and lonely husband, too, dear, and I will hurry home because I want to be with you, no one else in all the wide world.

"I did not receive your night letter but I am receiving your other letters. Do not worry, sweetheart.

"Give my Billy boy a big hug and kiss. I love him and I know he is a good boy and will take good care of his mother. Keep praying and keep writing. As ever, Your loving husband, Charles."

Three days later I wrote a much more pleasant letter, starting, "Darling Wife, I have several most recent and most loving letters from you. Everything is going okay with me and I am looking forward to the end of the war. How soon it will be I do not know, but I am hoping and praying that I will be home with you by summertime.

"Do not worry about the mail anymore because we are getting some every day now.

"I am glad Billy saw his daddy in the newsreel. He must have gotten quite a kick out of that. I have a Leica camera now and I am taking quite a few color pictures. If they turn out, there should be some real good ones. By now you should have my photos from Paris; if not, you had better write to the studio."

Here was the first indication that we expected the war to end soon. This letter also indicated that we were no longer sweating it out in the sense that we were afraid we would get hit at the last minute. The shooting had stopped entirely. We were waiting for a flare signal from the Russians now.

I took two full thirty-six exposures with the Leica before I found that you were supposed to pull out the lens before taking a picture. Many wonderful shots were lost and I was plenty angry with myself.

One paragraph in this letter described our reaction to President Roosevelt's death: "We were all very surprised to hear about the President's death, but over here it seemed that just another good soldier had been lost. It must have been a great shock to everyone in America."

Another paragraph reassured Jean of my love: "You seemed so worried about my love in your last letter. Honest, darling, I live only to come back to you. There is no one else in the whole wide world that could ever take me away from you. I am much older and much wiser than I was eighteen months ago. There are no blondes that can ever change my mind. Redheads, too, and also brunettes. I love you. I am proud of you. I want to work for you and our children. I want to get you another new and beautiful home and I want to try to make you happy. Arid I'm looking forward to teaching you how to drive! Time out for some love!"

A weather report took me to page three: "The weather here is clear and cold. I will be glad when it warms up again. You can tell by the radio news about the army I am in and just about what I am doing at the present. The end should not be far off.

"Keep writing, sweetheart, and keep praying, and I will be home soon. I love you—all of you. As ever, Your loving husband, Charles."

We were living an easy life now, except for the duty every night up on the river. We had two very good hot meals everyday, and in between we made coffee and snacks in the German homes where we lived. Some of the squads were eating venison. Patton killed a small deer in front of our positions. It made good eating.

The German civilians weren't forced to move except in a very few cases. It was better to have them around—for several reasons. They did all the housework. We weren't yet bothering to wash Our clothes. The weather was still rather cold so we didn't mind wearing the same clothes for a long time. In fact, we were still sleeping most of the time in our complete uniform. It was going to take a couple of months yet to get used to putting on a clean pair of socks every day and clean under clothes several times a week.

Living with the German civilians had other advantages. We were learning to speak their language and we were learning about their customs and habits. We learned that the German woman is a clean and affectionate person, agreeable and easy to get along with most of the time.

The German woman, we found, did not occupy the driver's seat in the German home. And apparently, they were satisfied with their position. When I helped dry the dishes one day in a German home, the women were amused and seemed delighted. But actually, I think they looked down on me. I guess they just could not imagine a real, good fighting soldier drying dishes.

Hitler may have advocated free love. However, we found the German women to be the one-man type. Of course, I am speaking of average cases. At this time in history, love was the only commodity that was cheap. In America, England, Italy, Germany, and many other countries many women wanted to do their part with everything they had—and for free.

In France, it was a different story. France was on both sides. Or maybe one should say they were playing both ends against the middle. Anyway, the French girls made everybody pay. In Paris, they charged twenty dollars per night for their lovemaking. There were lesser charges, according to the time consumed.

We had plenty of time to write home, now, and of course, we were getting our mail regularly. On April 28, I wrote to Jean:

"Yesterday I was a lucky man to receive two dear letters from you. The kiss at the top impressed me and made me long for one, a real one, from your beautiful lips.

"Your love letter paper is very sweet and as far as I'm concerned, you could have picked none more beautiful.

"I still have a cold. Of course, if you were caring for me I know I would be better now. The weather here has been cold and wet and sleeping on the ground does not help. And the officers, most of them, running this army still have little conception of how to handle men or fight effectively. They think they are fooling us when they say discipline is the most important thing and they constantly talk of that and of military courtesy instead of weapons training and tactics. Very few understand the principle of keeping a force compact and together. They do not understand that to deploy means to lose power and control. But what can you expect of three-year men who should be back at their jobs as clerks or auto mechanics. Don't mind my bitching, honey. I just have to let off steam once in a while. I should be back making tools for dear old Bendix."

I couldn't help writing the above diatribe. I had no doubt contacted my cold from sleeping or trying to sleep, in the foxholes down near the river. However, as a squad leader, I didn't have much of an opportunity to relax while we were on duty. The positions were spaced about one hundred yards apart and I spent most of the time walking from one end of my squad positions to the other end. There was a machine gun squad in our line, too. One hole had a field phone that went back to company headquarters. Walking was better than sitting or lying down because it helped to keep me warm.

The distance from our thin line near the river, back to the company headquarters near the edge of suburban Bitterfeld was about one thousand yards. If the enemy hit the right spots, they could have moved right through us and we never would have known they had passed until we heard the shooting in Bitterfeld. Also, it seemed to me that they still didn't know how to deploy machine guns property. Machine guns on the embankment that we occupied would have had excellent fields of fire and this would have been fine during the daylight hours when they could open up while the enemy was still a thousand yards away. But at night, we never would have known the enemy was moving in until they got right on top of us or until they started shooting in Bitterfeld. The setup was a fine example of how not to deploy.

But it just seemed that the officers could not stand to see enlisted men comfortable. Some trip flares or a roving patrol was all that was needed. The rest of the men could have been back in the shelter of the houses.

I wrote a lot more to Jean—four full pages. But there was nothing important. I asked about the Bendix gang at Broad and Allegheny Avenue in Philly, and about Jean's sister, Helen. I commented on my Happy Chappy boy and how he would rather have soup than ice cream. I also mentioned my Bronze Star award and the pictures that Jean wanted me to send. My last paragraph closed with the usual manifestations of my love and desire to be home with my darlings.

Two days later I wrote again. It was April 30, 1945. The war was to last only ten more days.

"Hello, Darling," I wrote. " Well, I'm still sweating out the end and I'm dreaming and longing for our oh, so happy reunion. I am doing okay but next to getting back to the States, the thing that would make me the happiest man in the world would be to get that piece of paper we all want—our discharge from this army."

I said I was still sweating out the end but it seemed that I wasn't worried anymore about getting hit. "When would I get my discharge papers?" seemed to be the big question now. But that was getting a little ahead of things because the war was still on, plus some occupation duty, plus a long trip to France, plus an ocean voyage.

It was a short letter. On page 2, I ended with:

"Darling, keep writing. Don't give up hope. Just now the radio says there will be big news soon, and I hope it is good.

"Give Happy Chappy a big hug and kiss. He is a lucky boy to have a most loving and helping mother. Hope I can join you both soon."

We never did contact the Russians at Bitterfeld. It must have been April 29 when we moved by truck to Gallen, a very small German village. It was a great deal different than our setup in Bitterfeld.

We didn't like to leave the nice homes and the friends we made in Bitterfeld. The German people in that small city would not soon forget the Timberwolves.

The Seventh armored division took over where we left off. But I don't think they maintained our river positions. There was really no need for that. The German army had disappeared and as yet the Russians weren't in sight.

Some POWs were arriving in Bitterfeld. They were mostly Americans. The last day I went down town. Standing on a street corner I was approached by some American POWs. They were in pretty bad shape, and they wanted to know where they could get something to eat.

We talked for a while. They told me about their hardships and hunger. It seems that they were caught between the Russians driving toward the West and the Americans and British driving toward the East. Depending on which front was moving faster, their German captors moved them in the corresponding direction, East or West.

One of the POWs suddenly pointed down the street and started to swear. I turned and saw a rather beautiful German woman approaching us. She was still a block away but the POW recognized her.

Before that woman reached our little group, I had a pretty good picture of her immediate past. It seems that she was a mistress of the commander of their POW column and that she goaded him into more severe and brutal treatment for the POWs.

She certainly was brazen—and smart. She walked right up to me and asked where the military governor's office was located. After the way those POWs talked about her, I don't know how they restrained themselves from giving her a little pushing around. More than likely, they were too weak even for the four of them to grab the woman and hold her.

She was a big woman—and not bad to look at, either. But my trained eye caught only one object. She was wearing an expensive ladies' wristwatch. I ignored her question and told her to give me her watch. She refused and so I grabbed her wrist.

"I'd love to get a watch for my wife for a souvenir," one of the POWs remarked.

"Well, you can have this one," I told him.

I tried to unfasten the strap but couldn't manage it so I ordered the woman to remove it herself while I held her arm in a tight grip.

She complained bitterly. I told her to beat it and go tell her story to the military governor. Those POWs were enjoying themselves more than they had for many months. As the German woman backed away, I handed her watch to the POW who wanted it as a gift for his wife.

It wasn't a very long trip to Gallen. The sun was shining brilliantly and the weather was getting warmer. We stayed overnight in the small village and the next day we found time to clean up a little and to write home.

I wrote to Jean and Billy: "There has been no mail now for a few days. I am not worried, darling. When I write I like to have one of your letters to answer but that is not an absolute requirement. I'll always write, letters or no letters.

"It is a beautiful spring morning but rather cold. (It warmed up during the day and most of my squad washed out their combat jackets.) Most of our homes have warmth and are clean. There are exceptions, like the one here. It is plenty dirty. I never remember seeing a German home so filthy. I hope we don't stay long.

"The most striking thing about Germany," my letter continued, "is the people's ignorance (pretended, no doubt) of the crimes committed by the army and the party—and these two groups encompass about seventy-five percent of the population. They are very convincing, too, and even have me feeling sorry for them because of their hunger and uncertain future. Compared to the US they do eat very little, but they have more than any other European country. They will not believe this. They continually speak of their poverty and of the wealth of America. They flatter us by saying they want to live in America. I believe in being firm with them. They must be punished for all their crimes. We must not let them talk us out of it."

On the second and last page I wrote " Rumors really are flying thick and fast now. The best one I heard was that the war was over. When I hear the real news it will be hard to believe. Anyway, it should end soon and then I may get home."

The reference to, "I may get home," must have referred to my doubts about getting home anywhere in the near future. There were rumors of the Germans fighting on in the mountains. And, of course there was still the Japanese war to finish. We weren't worrying about occupation duty.

On May 3, I wrote again to Jean from our new location. We were in Bennewitz to guard the Mulde River at this point.

"Dearest, life for me here just seems to drag on with all the distasteful and weary hours and days mounting into weeks and months and still no real good news.

"To brighten my life, three very beautiful letters arrived yesterday. They were from a beautiful American woman. In fact, this gorgeous creature enclosed a very recent and interesting photograph to make me feel even better. When I receive mail like that I am happy and proud and once again I have a written reassurance of a steadfast love."

In the next paragraph I brought up the subject of the Japanese war. "You mentioned the Pacific in your last letter. I do not know the answer to that one and I couldn't say if I did. We can both hope and pray for the best—when the time comes. No one knows when this will end over here and I won't be safe until the last shot is fired.

"I was glad to hear about Madeleine McGrath and her husband. The McGrath's certainly have done their share in this war." The McGrath's had been our neighbors in Upper Darby. The husband had received his discharge after many years of service.

"Billy sure is a remarkable boy, making ceramics. Beginning at such an early age he should turn out to be one of the world's best manufacturers of ceramics. Tell Bill I am a very proud daddy, having such a talented son.

"I have just heard some astounding news over the radio—," my letter continued, "Hitler is dead!" We finally got the radio to work and at last got BBC and just in time to hear this terrific news. I am living in a Nazi lieutenant-general's home and as usual, the Frau said 'everything is kaput.' Now that we have evacuated her and her sixteen-year-old daughter, we are getting things to work. Alles ist nicht kaput. The girl said her father was captured about four weeks ago by the Americans or English. He certainly had some neat uniforms."

The "Hitler is dead" news was to start a controversy that would probably never end. The German people we spoke to after hearing the announcement

The Letters of a Combat Rifleman

that Hitler had committed suicide, were divided. Some said Hitler was still alive, others said he was kaput—everything is kaput. The German nation had just about reached its lowest ebb.

"Generallietant GRAFF v. ORIOLA" was the way the house owner's calling card was printed. I still have a picture of the general standing in the snow on what appears t be the Russian front. He was a small man, just about my size. His snazzy Nazi dress uniforms fit me perfectly. When it was my turn to stand on the outpost between our house and the river, I wore one of the generals great coats. It was lined with fur.

The general's young daughter kicked up some trouble with my squad. That is why we asked the two women to leave. I was so mad about the whole affair that I would have thrown them out bodily if Max had not ordered them out.

The generals frau went to Max complaining that two of my men were molesting her young daughter. Max never bothered to hear our side of the story. He started to give me hell.

"What's wrong with you, Max?" I asked. "Are you going to take that damn Nazi's word against mine?" I knew the two accused boys were innocent. They hadn't even touched the girl.

Realizing that the women were trouble makers, I demanded that Max give me permission to throw them out. He finally agreed after a lot of arguing. Max, the combat soldier, had started to change. As the weeks went by Max got more and more chicken. As a garrison soldier he was a washout. He worried too much. And he never sided with his men. The trouble with the two women marked the beginning of Max's decline in popularity with his men. While he was fighting, Max was happy and carefree. He thought of his men first, last and always. Now it was going to be different. I was determined not to let the garrison type life change me or my relationship with my men.

Jean enclosed a picture of herself in one of the three letters I received May 3. It was a good one and made me very happy—and anxious. I wrote, "The picture was swell. Don't tell Helen but I think you look better than your ten-year younger sister. Years of rationing has beautified many deutsch fraus and frauleins but I didn't know points were so hard to get in America.

"I am anxious to hear that you received my gifts and pictures from Paris. They should have arrived long ago. If you don't like my pictures, I'll have to have some brighter ones taken. However, I may look a little older and a little grimmer than I did a year ago. I hope you are not too disappointed. From your picture, I think I will be overwhelmed—by so much loveliness."

The next day I wrote a short letter, using the generalleutant's engraved stationary. It contained important, happy news.

"The war news is all good. I just heard on the radio that northwest Germany, Holland and Denmark had surrendered to Montgomery. I sure hope that in a few weeks I will be on a big boat—headed for America and you. The end is in sight. Yesterday we heard the war had ended and we had a "dry run," so to speak, which wasn't so dry. We were happy for a while.

"Darling, I love you. You are my dream girl, my American beauty. It is so nice to have such a good and beautiful woman to go home to. And that is my only desire."

We spent about a week on the Mulde River near Bennewitz. It was a very happy period of my life despite my extreme longing for my family. I had survived many months of terrible danger and hardship. I was in perfect health. My guardian angel had watched over me carefully. Now I was safe. And in a reasonable time I should be back in America reunited with my loved ones.

In the meantime we didn't have to work hard. We maintained a guard on the partially-destroyed railroad bridge that connected with Wurzen and we posted a guard every night along the riverbank.

There was plenty of sleeping rooms in the general's big house and everyone had a bed. Some even had individual bedrooms. I had a small private room on the third floor.

The food was good but a little short. We were feeding a lot of POWs that were crossing the river daily.

We had two young girls come in every morning and clean up the place. Every night the men made quite a mess in the kitchen.

As yet, we had no training program. That was to come later. Every morning I took the squad out in the yard and gave them a half hour of calisthenics.

There wasn't much to drink but the company did ration out some kind of wine. My squad saved its ration for the celebration we planned when it was announced that the war was over.

It was on May 3 that we got the news that the war was over. This later proved false, but we celebrated before we found out the truth. We let this celebration stand, as any further celebration would have been anticlimactic. It was the "dry run" celebration that I mentioned to Jean.

It was a beautiful afternoon. We shouted, laughed and shook hands. There was a couple of English soldiers (POWs) staying with us at the time, and they joined us.

We put the metal chairs and tables together out on the side verandah of the house and we set out the bottles of wine and the best of the general's glassware. There were about ten of us seated at the tables. We drank one toast after another. And then when the wine was exhausted, we got out our weapons and started the fireworks. BAR's, grease guns, rifles and bazookas were all blasting at once. The rifle fire was aimed across the river. The Russians had not yet entered Wurzen. We fired rifle grenades and bazooka shells at the big stone wall that surrounded the general's home. We were lucky. Nobody in my squad was killed or wounded. We had done our last shooting of the war.

On Sontag, Mai 6, 1945, 1 wrote to Jean: "I want to write to say I love you, dear. My Sunday morning musical of the AEF program is on the air and the only things missing are the Sunday paper and most important of all, my beloved family. Darling, please wait and pray and I will be there with you some Sunday soon.

"They are now broadcasting a church service from the Little Church in the Hills in Texas. The pastor is also captain of the Texas Rangers."

I was enjoying health and happiness, but every day I was thinking more and more of Jean and Billy.

There were several more paragraphs. The Russians had finally reached the river and I spoke about them for the first time:

"I have had the opportunity to take a picture of a Russian chief of staff. He was a very clean and fine looking soldier and appeared to be about twenty years old. If it turns out, I will send you a print."

There was still no way to spend money so I sent it home. I mentioned each pay so that Jean would know how we stood financially.

" Yesterday, I was paid for April and it came to sixty-eight dollars and seventy-six cents, so I asked for another fifty dollar money order which I'll send as soon as possible.

My letter continued, "It must be four days since I received a letter from you. The mail service runs hot and cold.

"This is some of the generalleutenant's writing paper. I had to cut the address off. I'll enclose one of his calling cards for a souvenir.

"How is my Happy Chappy boy? I'll bet he likes the school he is going to. Tell Billy I am just about finished spanking Germans and that I may be home this summer to go swimming with him."

On May 8, I wrote: "Darling, Jean, and my Happy Chappy boy, tonight I sit in mein home in Germany and the light is turned on and I can look out the window and see the lights of the next town! There is no more blackout! The war in Europe is over!

"Yes, darling, the Lord was good to me. He answered all my prayers and has brought me many kilometers through Germany without even a scratch! Pray God, I will soon be on my way back to you, my beloved wife and my charming boy. It has (the end of the war) all come about very gradually here and we are just carrying on as usual. There are no big celebrations. We must now sweat out the war in the Pacific and it looks to me like I'll be helping the boys down there before it is over.

"I received three letters in the last two days. I'm so glad you liked your gifts from Paris. I liked giving them more than you did receiving them because you were so pleased. Glad to hear you received my other souvenirs.

"You did not mention the powder set I sent from Paris. I hope you get that, too. And also the pictures. Have you been able to read Billy's book yet? I guess it was a 'little German boy who drawed in his book.' The toy I sent from Paris was about the best they had.

"Maybe my letter of April 9 did sound a little discouraged. It must have been about the time we were trying to cut up the Ruhr pocket and everything was pretty rough for a while. You perhaps read every day about armored spearheads gaining many miles. That was true. But us doughboys were sitting on the outside of that armor or else going ahead of it when the going got real tough."

I had written at that time " But if I am still called to join our Janey, I know you will be well taken care of. Billy will have a loving and good mother, and you, darling, will have a good brave son to help and protect you and take care of you." It was a one-page letter.

CHAPTER XXII
We Meet the Russians

My first letter to Jean after the war was long and interesting. Our mail was still being censored, but we had more freedom in writing than we had before. The name of the town was not on the letterhead, but we were now stationed in Kothen, a large town in the same general vicinity. There were VI 0 maps available so we did not know the location of the various towns and cities that we had occupied, but we did know that we had never moved very far.

"Dearest," I wrote, "This evening I received two dear letters from you and one only six days old. I am glad You liked the powder set from Cologne. I picked it especially for you.

"Everything is fine here. The weather is very hot. The last two days I have been taking sunbathes. We didn't even have any training today. A couple barrels of beer instead. The chow is excellent again. I had a hot bath and have been parading around in a pair of Heinie sandals.

"It all sounds as if I am perfectly content and happy. But I'm not. There is one thing missing and the beautiful German frauleins could not come close to giving me that one thing that spells happiness for me. That is (I won't hold you in suspense any longer) you, darling.

"I don't know when I'll get home and if I did I probably couldn't tell you anyway. Let's hope and pray that it will be just a few weeks.

"The Lord was good to me and perhaps it was for Janey's sake. I know our dear Jane helped me through many weeks and months of hardship and terror. I always looked forward to joining her and it comforted me more than anything else possibly could. Yes, the Lord has been good and I trust Jane is with Him.

"It sounds as if you have found some nice friends in the Marletters. I'd sure like to see the picture of Billy working in the victory garden. Your letter sounds as though you had quite a time visiting them. As for us living there, it hardly makes much difference anymore where I live. I'm so used to seeing new homes, new faces, moving at all times of the day and night, sometimes across the street, sometime fifty miles. Even Germany would suit me. There are no Nazis in Germany. At least I never met one! But like every nation, Germany has it's faults and its good points. It is more like America than any other country I have been in, including England. In general, the people are very clean and very industrious. The children seem to have had an excellent education."

In further reply to Jean's letter I wrote, "I met some of the Russians but never saw any Russian Wacs. There are very, very few in the combat units. Everybody in Europe seems to hate and fear the Russians. They are very secretive about their weapons, etc., regardless of the pictures you may have seen. However, I don't think they are as sadistic or cruel as the Germans. One time I put a German civilian up against a wall because he said he had no beer in his gasthaus, and I said to the Russian soldier with me, 'Shall I shoot him?' The Russian acted quite natural. He became excited and rushed over to stop me. Of course, I wasn't going to shoot the German. I just wanted to see how the Russian would react. He told me how the Germans burned the Russian cities, but he said the Russians were not burning the German homes. As far as I know, he was right. But the Russians have raped quite a few German women. Three young German girls begged me to let them cross the river one morning. They stood there with heavy packs on their backs, tears streaming down their cheeks. One girl turned her head as the other two told how she was raped the night before by the Russians.

"The Russians are great drinkers. They slug vodka down like we do water and they can hold their drink."

Jean was to question me later about the Russians and about the girls on the bridge. My contacts with the Russians were limited. When they reached the river they put a guard near the railroad bridge, too. But our men controlled the traffic and said who would cross and who wouldn't. The Russians missed the boat on this deal because they could have and probably would have made it a better racket than we did. Jewelry, money, and girls opened the way for many fleeing German families. We allowed all nationals to pass back and forth but Germans were forbidden to cross the river in either direction. It gave us an opportunity to become rich but we weren't interested. Some of my men did get some nice wristwatches but that was mainly the limit of the bribes accepted.

One morning when my squad was on the bridge I gave the two little girls who cleaned our house, permission to cross the bridge in order that they might visit some of their friends Wurzen. They were sisters, one seventeen years and the other only fourteen. They were blondes and pretty as a picture.

The Letters of a Combat Rifleman

Their home was right on the river, in the same house that platoon headquarters occupied.

At first I refused their request. It wasn't that I didn't want them to cross the river. I was afraid the Russians would grab them. There was one story around that the Russians had hanged two teenage boys in a tree immediately after arriving in Wurzen. This story may or may not have been true. I didn't see the youths.

The girls understood the danger and so did their parents. But they still insisted that they wanted to cross over for a few hours. It was after two or three days that I finally agreed. I told them the hour to come down to the bridge. My squad was on duty and I had two men posted on the bridge. I waited with the two guards for the girls to appear.

They showed up on time, dressed in their best clothes. That made it worse because, I reasoned, that the Russians would be more likely to notice them that way.

They started off into Wurzen looking very young, beautiful, and happy. I told them to be back within two hours because my squad would no longer be on duty after that. They promised they would be back in time.

The two hours went by quickly enough. There was always something happening at the bridge. We were told there was a dead man in the canal that led off from the river on the Russian side. I went over and saw the body floating face down. A tremendously big, ferocious-looking dog tried to intercept me near the canal bank. I almost was tempted to kill him. Once I had to fire my rifle into the ground in front of me to keep the big beast from jumping on top of me. The dead man in the canal was perhaps his master and he wanted to protect him.

French and other nationals crossed the bridge into the American zone at almost a hundred per hour rate. German nationals were continually trying to get across, too. They flashed wallets filled with German marks. It was worth money to get across that bridge. French POWs tried to get their German sweethearts across with them. Incoming American and British POWs told of hardships and hunger. There were extremes of sadness and pleasure. There were new human interest stories almost every minute. There were stories that sounded unbelievable and unbelievable stories that sounded true. There were people dressed in rags and were some dressed in riches. Some were disguised as soldiers (we accepted German soldiers as prisoners) and some soldiers were disguised as civilians. Some lied and some told the truth. They were all excellent actors because their very existence, perhaps, depended on it.

The two hours were up and the girls did not appear. But I didn't give up hope yet. It was seldom, if ever, according to the stories, that the Russians ever attacked women during the daylight hours. It was after dark that they went to the homes of the girls they had spotted during the day.

My guards were relieved by the new detail but I stayed on at the bridge to see that the girls were allowed to return. And finally they did reappear, safe and in good health and spirits. They had visited their friends without any trouble whatsoever. If any Russians had followed them, the girls did not know it.

My experience with the Russians were very limited. We were issued a booklet or pocket guide before the Russians reached the river. I can remember only one thing about this guide. It stressed the severe discipline in the Russian army. But like most intelligence data or information obtained by our army, I found just the opposite to be true.

When the Russians entered Wurzen, they came in all manner of sizes, shapes and forms. Some walked, some rode in jeeps, and some were on horseback. There were big groups and little groups. Some were riding motorcycles and some were driving horse and wagons.

But the payoff took place a few days later. I was standing on the road leading out of Wurzen toward the south. A young Russian soldier was with me. He was my companion for the evening, having promised to get me a drink of vodka. He was showing me his tommy gun and he even had let me fire one burst at the side of a big German farmhouse. Hearing a motorcycle in the distance, the Russian said, "It is my company commander."

"Should we salute him?" I asked.

"No, we only salute officers from battalion commander on up," he replied.

But that answer didn't agree with our pocket guide. According to the guide, the Russian GI even had to salute the noncommissioned officers.

Well, the motorcycle soon appeared around a turn and it sped on past as we stood almost in the middle of the narrow road, watching. We didn't salute and it didn't make any difference apparently to the officer riding the motorcycle. He kept right on going. I thought about the pocket guide and I laughed to myself.

In regards to the Russians' ability to drink, we found some truth to this rumor. Our battalion officers first invited the Russian high officers in Wurzen to attend a dinner on our side of the river. They came early in the evening. That is when I got the picture of the Russian chief of staff that I told Jean about in my letter of May 6.

They left late but they were still steady and sober.

Our battalion officers were, in turn, invited to a feast in Wurzen. They, too, returned late at night. They were so drunk they crawled across the railroad bridge on their hands and knees, afraid that they would fall off into the water.

I finished my letter from Kothen on May 12 as follows:

"The Red Cross girls are outside with their smiles, doughnuts, coffee, and music. In Bitterfeld, they visited us and there was one girl from Upper Darby. It was too far to walk so I did not see her. I'd go down now and take some color pictures but it is too hot. And besides, I want to finish writing to you.

The Letters of a Combat Rifleman

"Billy sure must like the book I sent him from Germany. Has he been able to read it with Granny's glasses?

"Well, darling, I think that answers your letters. And also your doubts. I love you, dear, and I think I'll be seeing you soon. ('vielleicht' (maybe))."

We were one of the first divisions to return to the States. Of course, we sweated out a couple of months of occupation and travel. In the meantime, I wrote almost daily to Jean. Our letters were no longer censored so I could say just what I wanted.

Our last weeks were spent in Hohenthurm. I mentioned it to Jean in my letter of May 26, "The setup here is really nice. It is just a small town and we generally don't like that, but practically everything is owned by a count and he really has the stuff."

The Third platoon lived in the administrator's house. There were frozen food lockers in the basement. There were about one hundred good dairy cattle in the barn. We had an unlimited supply of potatoes. Almost every night before going to bed we had steak or eggs with french fried potatoes and coffee with cream. And for dessert we had fresh cherries and strawberries out of the garden.

We ate well and we exercised hard. On May 23 I wrote to Jean " How are my two darlings today? I am still rejoicing over the news that the 104th is going to return to the States. However, the next few weeks will probably drag along like three years. We have a training schedule here and tonight we even had a night problem!"

And almost every day we played softball or soccer. And for a while I had the pleasure of riding some of the count's horses. I wrote to Jean saying, "I have been riding horseback every evening. They have horses that are worth four hundred fifty thousand marks. They have taken many first prizes in Berlin, Paris, Dresden, Koln, etc." The count complained to our Texan company commander and he ordered me to stop riding.

I described our house to Jean as follows: I am living in an old but very beautifully- decorated farmhouse. There is a modern tile bathroom, hot and cold running water in every room, a big modern kitchen, inlaid hardwood floors, central plant heat, etc. The chinaware and glassware are just marvelous. I understand the place is owned by a general. They claim he once saved Churchill's life."

On June 1, I wrote to Jean: "I received three very recent letters from you today, all mailed May 26. They made me very happy, needless to say, as all your letters do. You never fail to keep telling me how much you want me and I want and need you in just the same degree and in all the exact same ways."

And now that it was definite that I was coming home, Jean had started to make plans. And for the first time in about two years, Jean was shopping to buy some new clothes.

My letter continued: "I am still in the same situation here in Germany. Rumors are still as prevalent as usual. We may make a tour of the States as a show team. It's strictly a rumor. We may leave in a week. That is another. Anyway, I do hope and pray I'll be home with you soon. You are the one and only girl for me in all the world I wanted (and got) for my beloved wife. There is none other and never will be. Darling, please be good to me and I will be good to you, and always try to please and satisfy you and we will be happy.

"I liked it when I read you were going shopping. I know you are happy and it must make you feel like a bride. And I'm sure our second, first night together is going to be even better than the first, first night.

"Don't be afraid of America or Americans hurting me, darling." My letter continued, "I know how America was and I don't think it has changed anymore than us GIs have changed. We combat men all laugh at these jokers who say we must be rehabilitated. They think up all kinds of stories about how to treat us when we get back, but we don't want any list of do's or don'ts for you to check off. We just want you to act toward us like we were just ordinary everyday Americans, which is all we are. Combat has not effected or changed me one bit except perhaps to give me more confidence in myself. I always thought I would be able to carry on under fire and now I know I can. Until a man is actually tried in a real fire fight he never really knows. Noises or explosions on the streets will not bother me. Perhaps some returning GIs have said in print that noises will bother them. They are the men who have been sent home for "combat fatigue." They could not take it. I don't mean to criticize these men. Their emotional makeup is just against them. I am glad to say their number is very few. The number of good, brave men whom I have seen far out number the battle fatigue cases. Many of these good and brave men will not come back but some will. Of course, the great majority did nothing outstanding but just tagged along and they get just as much credit and just as many points. It's just like being an average American.

"Well, sweetheart darling, that's about all for tonight. It's getting time for my snack of fried eggs and potatoes and then it's off to bed—only to be awakened about 3 A.M. for a night problem! Silly world, isn't it? Silly army, that's sure!"

On June 4 I wrote, "I got quite a kick out of your interest in the three girls who wanted to cross the bridge to escape the Russians. I don't know why, but I did not let them cross. We Americans are so softhearted and careless with such things that the Germans undoubtedly take advantage of us at times. And especially the women. You know how an American falls for a woman's line. They were pretty—since you asked, but honest, honey, I turned them down flat. It was my duty as the noncommissioned officer in charge. I am surprised that you ask if I have raped any girls or that I even wanted to. In the first place, it is hardly necessary to rape anyone. And since I've waited this long, I know I can wait another few weeks. I must be truthful and say that it has not been easy. But I have found out that men can hold back, too, and I am glad it is so. You are the one and only woman in the world for me, darling, and I am proud and glad to say so. And I will admit that I have known some of the best women that Germany has to offer. I know your blood is beginning to boil and here I go putting my foot in again. But I'm prepared to fight you and demand that you love me because I love you and I want you and I must have you. And I'm saving all for you regardless of what I say about Heinie women. I know I'm just as dumb as the next American when it comes to women, but just the same, that doesn't mean that one of these blonde Nazis can pull the wool over my eyes.

"But the more I talk the more I'll get in trouble with you and that is the last thing I want to happen sweetheart, darling. You look for teeth marks on my shoulders when I get home and you will know the sixty-four dollar question as we call it. I don't know why but they tell me they bite.

"Who is it that ribs you so much about the French and German girls? And how do they know what goes on over here?

"I have your picture sitting on the desk in front of me. You are very pretty and very, very alluring. On the other side to match your beauty I have a red-colored carnation. If only you were real and alive like that carnation!"

And it wasn't many weeks until I realized my dream. I took my "real and alive" wife in my arms and it was like a second honeymoon. We were very, very happy in those days. The world was at our feet. We were conquering warriors home from the battles, welcomed by the flower of womanhood of America. We were serenaded in New York harbor and the name "Timberwolf" was in the newspaper headlines.

The enemy had come close to killing me. But my guardian angel was always near. And now I found what I wanted most. I was loved, and I returned that love. Jean and I proved that the experts could be wrong. We were both in love to stay.

940.54   82061
DAV   DAVIS, CHARLES

       THE LETTERS OF A COMBAT RIFLEMAN

SOUTHERN LEHIGH
HIGH SCHOOL LIBRARY